MARITIME HISTORY OF
FALMOUTH

THE PORT, ITS SHIPPING AND PILOTAGE SERVICE

D. G. WILSON

HALSGROVE

First published in Great Britain in 2014
Copyright © David Gordon Wilson 2014

A CIP record for this title is available from the British Library

ISBN 978 0 85704 223 1

HALSGROVE
Halsgrove House,
Ryelands Business Park,
Bagley Road, Wellington, Somerset TA21 9PZ
Tel: 01823 653777   Fax: 01823 216796
email: sales@halsgrove.com

Part of the Halsgrove group of companies.
Information on all Halsgrove titles is available at: www.halsgrove.com

Printed in China by Everbest Printing Co Ltd

CONTENTS

ACKNOWLEDGMENTS

My grateful thanks to the following who in various ways have helped towards the compilation of this work, especially with the provision of photographs: David Barnicoat, Sandra Gibson, Brian Kennell, Tim Knight, Margaret Miles, Tony Pawlyn, Luke Powell, Ann Ringrose, Lynne Vosper, Tom Welch. Also Amanda Martin, curator of the Isles of Scilly Museum, Janet Spargo, curator of Helston Museum; the staff of the Cornish Studies Library at the Cornwall Centre, Redruth; the staff of the County Record Office, Truro (CRO); Michael Bradley and members of the Royal Cornwall Polytechnic Society local history group in Falmouth (RCPS); the curatorial staff of the National Maritime Museum Cornwall, and my fellow volunteers at that Museum's Bartlett Library. Special thanks go to Denise Davey and my wife Roma for their invaluable word processing skills in transferring my scribblings into readable text.

PROLOGUE

Carrick-roads, the castles of St Mawes and Pendennis, guarding the entrance, with the Black-rock and its pole in the centre, and the signal station at St Anne's (St Anthony) Head to the eastward, every time that my view was turned in that direction I was gratified by the sight of ships and smaller craft in every variety of position. Sometimes as many as ten frigates and several smaller vessels of war would be in the outer roads at once, with a crowded fleet of merchant ships wind-bound, and waiting for a change, to sail under convoy to the East or West Indies, North or South America, or the Mediterranean: while the inner harbour would be crowded with the handsome packets in their gayest trim, each distinguished by a special signal, and constantly exercising their crews in bending and unbending sails, reefing, sending up or down top-gallant yards, striking lower yards and topmasts, hoisting in boats, water, or provisions, and on a calm day the shrill whistle of the boatswain was distinctly heard, as well as the cheering cry of "All's well," at the relieving of the watch, and the morning and evening gun at sunrise and sunset.

A description of Falmouth Harbour, circa 1820, from the Autobiography of
James Silk Buckingham, published in 1855.

INTRODUCTION

DURING THE EIGHTEENTH century new inventions and technological development in agriculture, science and engineering, plus a relatively stable financial system, had put Britain well on the way to being one of the most advanced nations on earth. Explorations in distant lands brought opportunities for trade: manufactured goods were sent out in exchange for raw materials such as cotton and timber, and luxuries of spices, fruit and wines. In the face of competition from European neighbours, Britain's merchant fleet, sometimes with the assistance of the Royal Navy, endeavoured to maintain and advance the nation's share of world trade.

As the century progressed, and in spite of frequent dissension with one European country or another, as well as the American States, an increasingly affluent society generated an insatiable demand for commodities from abroad. Enormous profits were made by the exchange of goods across continents, often controlled by such trading organizations as the East India Company. Unfortunately a large percentage of those profits was made in the trade in people between Africa and the Caribbean. Friendlier contact with other indigenous peoples led to the establishment of coastal trading posts in the Far East, India, Africa and the Americas. Lands were annexed, trading posts became colonies, fought for against European rivals, to the eventual, almost accidental, establishment of the vast British Empire. This small offshore island of Britain, inhabited by people sharing a gene pool derived from a mixture of prehistoric hunter-gatherers, celtic farmers, Iberian fishermen and North European seafarers, for a time became the most powerful nation on earth.

Britain's success was only possible through the expertise of British ship-builders and the fortitude of her mariners. Throughout the eighteenth and first half of the nineteenth centuries, her merchant fleet grew apace to cope with the movement of materials feeding the Industrial Revolution. Other nations, seeing the benefits brought by industrialisation, also increased their fleets to compete with Britain, in friendly and not so friendly ways.

Most of British and Northern European shipping, at least those vessels moving to and from the Mediterranean, Africa and the East, or on trans-Atlantic routes, had to pass, as today, along the English Channel via the Western Approaches, that is: between Ushant, off the Breton coast, and Cornwall. In the days of sail, when vessels were at the mercy of wind strength and direction, good navigation depended on the skills of the Master of the ship, using basic instruments and charts, and his knowledge of the sea, to work out his position. The English Channel is comparatively narrow, and bounded by unforgiving rocky shores on either side. This knowledge of position was a matter of life and death for ship and crew, apart from the potential loss of a valuable cargo.

Vessels heading to London or European ports, having not come to grief on the Isles of Scilly or the Land's End of Cornwall, would hope to make a landfall at the looming bulk of Lizard Point, where they would know that they were on the right course along the Channel. Under ideal conditions, with all shipshape on board, the crew would thankfully greet the first sight of land. Otherwise, in heavy weather, perhaps at night and in an unsound ship, the rocks of Cornwall might strike fear in their hearts. The coastline certainly impressed one seasoned traveller, the renowned Daniel Defoe, even from the landward side, as he passed through on his 'Tour' in the early years of the eighteenth century: '... the Lizard is the general guide, ... and is therefore the land which ships choose to make first, for then they are sure that they are past Scilly, and all the dangers of that part of the island.'

He goes on to describe the fearsome rocks of Scilly and West Cornwall as acting as defences against the might of the Atlantic Ocean:

'The whole terra firma, or body of the land, which makes this isle of Britain, seems to be one solid rock, as if it was formed by Nature to resist the otherwise irresistible power of the Ocean; and indeed if one was to observe with what fury the sea comes on sometimes against the shore here, especially at Lizard Point, where there are few, if any, out-works (as I call them) to resist it. How high the waves come rolling forward, storming on the neck of one another, particularly when the wind blows off the sea, one would wonder that even the strongest rocks should be able to resist ...'

From Falmouth's Pendennis Point the eastern edge of the Lizard peninsula can be seen as a high plateau on the far side of Falmouth Bay. It falls into the sea in a series of windswept headlands composed of hard metamorphic rocks originating from deep within the earth's mantle. Here below these high cliffs or on unseen outlying reefs so many ships were wrecked and countless lives lost. Over the centuries the people of the small coastal villages, the most southerly in Britain, spent their lives halfway between land and sea: when not farming or quarrying they were fishing, salvaging or smuggling. During the nineteenth century there were Coastguards employed among them to try to curb their illicit pastimes, but with the establishment of cliff rescue units and a volunteer lifeboat service, all came together to attempt to save lives when ships foundered on this treacherous shore. One of the grandest headlands on this coast is the 60 metre-high Bass Point; originally known as Beast Point, a fitting description of its looming presence to mariners on a dark and stormy night. It lies a little to the east of Lizard Point and its lighthouse, and is of higher elevation. With an uninterrupted view across the Western Approaches it was aptly chosen as the site of Lloyds Signal Station, which from 1872 to 1951 passed on the news of the safe arrival of shipping from all over the world into British waters.

These ships were met offshore by a hardy company of men, the Falmouth pilots. They lived a few miles to the east of the Lizard, on the shores of the estuary, or ria, of the River Fal, which forms a great natural harbour, one of the largest in the world. Its entrance is gained through a one mile wide gap in the defensive rock wall of the Cornish coast, although the main deep-water channel is very much narrower. It opens up into a four-mile long sea-lake, defended from strong winds by low hills along its shores, and from enemy attack from the sea by the Tudor forts of Pendennis and St. Mawes on either side of the entrance. It has been renowned for centuries as a haven for shipping; a place to lay up and refit after voyaging to distant lands; for cargoes to be discharged or taken on board, or for fleets of merchantmen or ships of war to gather before sailing out in convoy.

From the Middle Ages trade on the Fal was carried on from the two estuarine ports of Truro and Penryn. Much of their business was taken over in the seventeenth century by the establishment of quays and a Custom House at the new town of Falmouth, sited in the shelter of the Pendennis Headland close to the harbour entrance. Falmouth's dominance was reinforced in 1689 when it was chosen as a base of the Post Office packet service: for over 150 years small sailing vessels arrived and departed, carrying vital mail, bullion, cargoes and passengers to and from Spain, Portugal, the Mediterranean, Caribbean, and the Americas. During the Industrial Revolution, at the height of the British Empire, Falmouth was known internationally as the port where merchant ships from around the world, on their arrival in British waters, called for orders from shipping agents regarding the destinations for delivery of their cargoes. The harbour also became vital as a base for the building, repair and victualling of ships. Port services were developed to cater for all the needs of the mariner. The port's Trinity House pilots were a group of men who served their apprenticeships sailing in seas on a coastline which at times could be the most dangerous in the world.

The Falmouth pilotage service is still vital to the success of the port and to the safety of the ships entering and leaving the District. In the nineteenth century the pilots cruised in all weathers in small, but sturdy sailing boats, for up to 40 miles from port, to board and take control of ships to bring them into Falmouth. Apart from the London District, the Trinity House outport of Falmouth was the busiest in the United Kingdom. In the year 1872, at the century's peak of maritime trade, Falmouth's pilots took charge of nearly 4000 arrivals. This is the story of that service, of the pilots, and of the small fleet of sailing cutters they owned and cared for. These boats had the perfect hull form and versatility of sail management to cope with ever-changing sea conditions, although unlike fragile racing yachts, their strong weighty construction didn't necessarily allow for easy movement in 'light airs'.

This story is set against a background of world social and economic changes, in which Falmouth played a valuable part in Britain's prosperity, gained through its maritime trade. It can be traced through the pages of the contemporary local newspapers: in ship arrival lists, and reports on harbour matters, trade, ship repairing at the docks and smaller yards, and the exploits of pilots. A number of nineteenth century reports of Lizard shipwrecks are included in the story. They demonstrate the vulnerability of ships, their cargoes, passengers and crews, at a time before the advent of sophisticated navigation aides and weather reporting; when, if not by ignorance or carelessness alone, they might be overwhelmed by the majestic but terrible power of the sea. The newspaper reports, apart from those containing bare statistics, obviously must sometimes be treated with the proverbial pinch of sea salt. The reporter can only work with the information he sees at a particular time, or with what he has been told by a participant or bystander; and there's the editor who accepts or rejects the text. However, a

Victorian newspaperman in a port would be expected to write a knowledgeable and basically true account of any particular dramatic maritime incident, but can be forgiven for elaborating a story to make it interesting for the general reader.

In this work, apart from where news items are quoted verbatim, the writer has sometimes put his own interpretation, and where available, added further background information to particular incidents; any unintentional inaccuracies are therefore entirely the responsibility of the author. In most cases the news reports have been chosen to illustrate aspects of the work of the pilots. With regard to references: the original news items may be found in the appropriate local paper around the dates in question. All these newspapers are on microfilm at the Cornish Studies Library in The Cornwall Centre, Redruth. Other sources are Lloyd's Registers, Mercantile Navy Lists, and the Minutes of the Falmouth Sub Commissioners of Pilotage and Falmouth District Pilot Boat Association, all within the archives of the Bartlett Library, National Maritime Museum, Cornwall.

The Land's End.

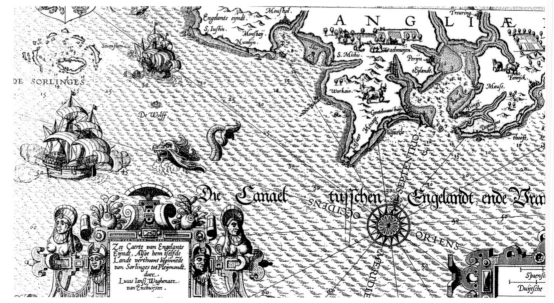

The Cornish Coast from Scilly ('De Sorlinges') to Dodman Point, published by Dutchman Lucas Janz Waghenaer in 1584. The Lizard and Fal estuary feature prominently to emphasise their navigational and strategic importance.

CHAPTER 1
EARLY FALMOUTH

THE PIECE OF LAND, known from early times as Arwenack, and on which the town of Falmouth was to be built, was owned by the Killigrew family. They had acquired the manor possibly as early as the thirteenth century, building a house fronting the little bay in the lee of the isthmus of the Pendennis Headland. This high promontory, which is likely to have once been occupied by an Iron Age fort, provides some natural protection for shipping in the great natural harbour which became known as the Port of Falmouth. In the 1540s Sir John Killigrew leased the promontory to the Crown for the construction of Pendennis Castle, which with St. Mawes fort a mile away on the opposite shore of the estuary, protected the harbour from enemy incursion. The Arwenack manor house was rebuilt on a lavish scale at about this time. Sir John and several of his successors were to be governors of the castle.

Some Killigrews were Members of Parliament, sometimes in favour at Court, sometimes not; their fortunes similarly fluctuated. Cornwall was a long way from London and the King's Law: in common with many of the local inhabitants, of all classes, the Killigrews earned considerable

Detail from the 'Burleigh' map of the Fal, c.1585, viewed from the north, with the defended manor house in the centre. It covers much of the Arwenack estate, with the boundary wall or pale along the Gyllyngvase shoreline and culminating at Smithick cove, bottom right of the picture.

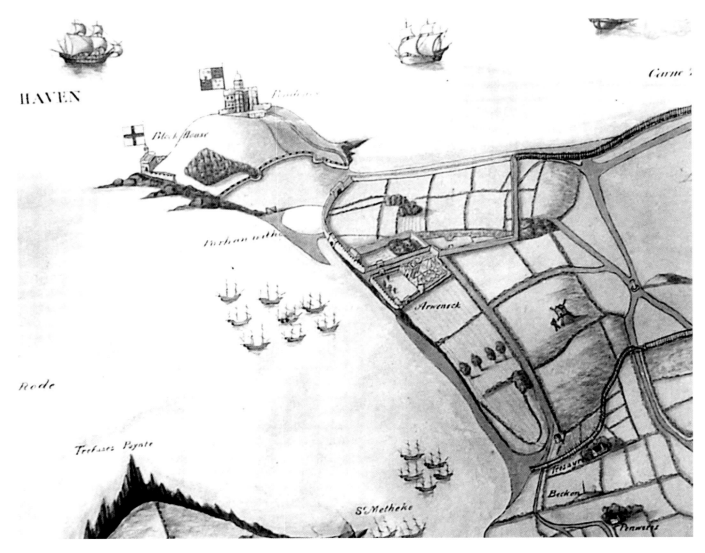

A view of Arwenack
House, believed to
date to before the
Civil War. (RCPS)

income from smuggling and even piracy. However, they weren't averse to promoting legitimate projects: in 1619 the fourth Sir John eventually obtained permission from the Lord High Admiral to have a light tower built at Lizard Point, where many ships had come to grief. The light was probably coal-fired, and therefore not very effective, even so the locals took a poor view of the project which they thought might deprive them of their wrecking proceeds. Unfortunately for him, Sir John had not thought the project through properly: contributions towards the cost of the light were to be obtained from shipping, at first on a voluntary basis, and later a toll per ton of cargo was to be charged on passing ships. Unsurprisingly the collection of such tolls proved nigh impossible; the scheme, for the moment, was soon abandoned.

Fortunately Sir John had other business ideas up his copious sleeves: it was possible that income could be obtained virtually on the doorstep of his manor house at Arwenack. Most of the merchant ships that entered the great estuary of the Fal passed straight through to the up-river ports of Truro or Penryn; why not capture this passing trade by providing facilities here? In 1613 Sir John had received permission from King James I for the construction of a small settlement of houses and four inns on the rocky edge of the harbour a short distance away in a northerly direction from the manor house. The place chosen was a cove containing a few fishermen's cottages at the base of a small combe dropping down to the sea. It was then said to be known as Smithick or Pennycome-quick. The project quickly went ahead: contained in the State Papers is a query from Sir John about four years later, asking if he should appoint the keepers of the four victualing houses for the relief of seafaring men, erected on his lands at Smithick, *near Falmouth*, on his engaging himself for their good behaviour.

Neither of those two names, Pennycomequick or Smithick, was noted when the title of Falmouth, as a place, appeared on an official document two centuries earlier. By the mid-fifteenth century at least, the natural harbour was already well-known to English and foreign mariners as Falmouth. During the Hundred Years War the English Chancery Courts sometimes dealt with complaints such as from Breton ship owners and merchants that their ships and goods had been illegally seized by the English. One particular petition concerned the capture of a ship and its cargo of wine off the French coast in June 1417, by a fleet commanded by the Cornish knight, Sir John Arundell. The text, translated from the French, states that the ship and its cargo were brought to Falmouth and the latter 'was discharged at the inn of David Urban, Lieutenant of Sir John, in the presence of the good people of the town who could testify to it.' Commissioners of Penryn *by Falmouth* were appointed to investigate the case. Other petitions mention ships of war based at Falmouth, their captains living there.

During these years hundreds of devout English pilgrims were journeying by land and sea to the shrine of Saint James at Santiago de Compostela, in Northern Spain. A number of Southwest ships were involved in this lucrative, but sometimes hazardous, passenger trade across the Bay of Biscay. Ship owners required special licenses issued by the Crown for this, which were recorded in Treaty Rolls (*Calendar of French Rolls,* P.R.O). Most of the ships came from the Tamar and Fowey, but two operated from Falmouth: The *Mary* carried 40 pilgrims in 1428 and the same number in 1445. The *Trinity* carried 24 in 1432, 40 in 1434, and 50 in 1445. The merchant vessel *Trinity of Falmouth* was also noted in 1450. Many such vessels were impressed into the service of the King at this time: Halliday, in *A History of Cornwall,* states that over a five year period

Penzance and Marazion supplied six; Saltash six; Landulph, on the Tamar, five; Looe five; Mevagissey one. Fowey was able to supply an impressive 19 vessels. On the Fal estuary, Truro, Penryn and Falmouth sent two each; from this it again appears that Falmouth was already officially recognised as a place in its own right. But where was it; was there an official controller of ships there, a place where they could be refitted and victualled? Perhaps it was the anglicised name for the Smithick/Pennycomequick cove, names possibly derived from the original Cornish language, then still used by many of the local population.

With respect to the name Smithick, Susan Gay, in her classic book, *Old Falmouth*, prefers the derivation current in her time, that of the more prosaic 'Smith's Creek'. That latter curious name, Pennycomequick, mentioned in the first Falmouth charter of 1661, and given various derivations by nineteenth century historians, was most likely the nickname of one small inn, perhaps even that of the earlier David Urban mentioned above. The name would be appropriate if the place was once the base for privateers or pirates. However, none of the early maps give the cove either title; the Burleigh map of c.1580 leaves it unnamed, but does have 'S Metheke' marked offshore, but nearer to the later Flushing village side of the harbour than to the Falmouth side. There is no known ancient monastic site dedicated to a Saint Metheke on either shore. On his meticulously drawn chart of 1597, Baptista Boazio has 'St. Mithicks Roads' (roadstead), marked in the channel towards Green Bank, again, some distance from the cove. Was this from local enquiry or was he copying the Burleigh map? On the other hand, he gives the cove the title of 'Lymekill Baie', with 'Porengassis Baie' close by. An early lime kiln must have been situated here. Porhan or Poren is thought to have been the Cornish name for port, and the likely name of the hillside on which much of the town was to be built.

A map of 1615, possibly drawn to delineate the boundaries between the Killigrew and adjoin-

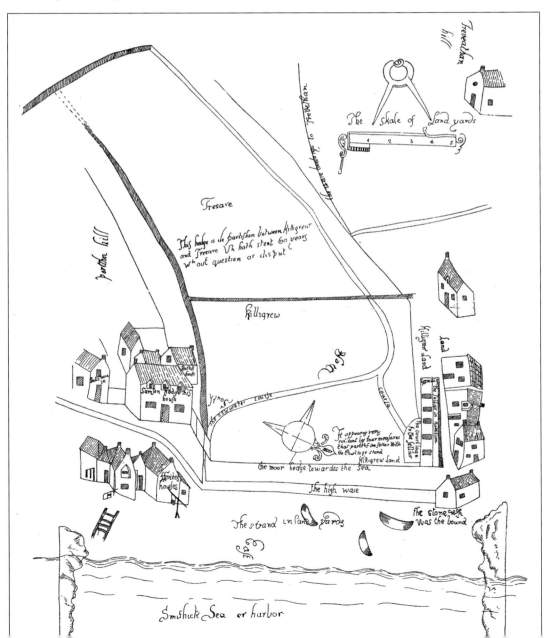

Detailed Killigrew boundary dispute map c.1615, depicting Smithick cove. It features a watercourse and boundary bank across the later Moor area. At the bottom boats are on the foreshore or Strand. Buildings include pilchard cellars and possible inns.
(*Journal of the Royal Institution of Cornwall*, 1886, pp147-59).

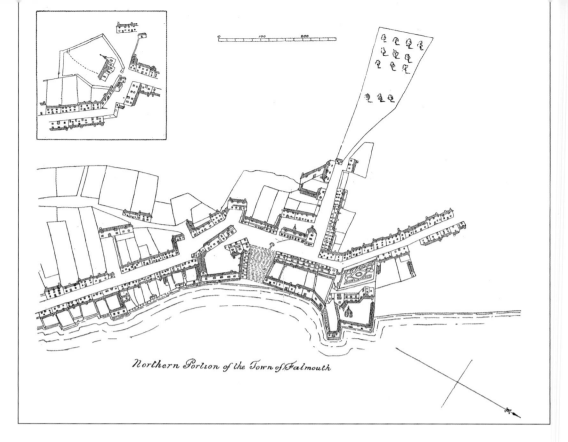

A map of 1691, showing the early development of Market Street and High Street on either side of Smithick cove, plus an inset of the new parish church area. Buildings now surround the strand, leaving a paved, sloping hard for vessels to rest. To its left the upside-down building probably represents an inn which was later to become the King's Arms Hotel. (*Journal of the Royal Institution of Cornwall*, 1886. pp147-59).

Northern Portion of the Town of Falmouth

ing Tresare and Trevethan lands, depicts pilchard cellars and a dozen houses or inns around the cove. Boats are drawn up on the 'Strand' or foreshore; below this is written 'Smithick Sea or harbor'; passing across the Strand is 'the high waie'. By the time of George Withiels' map of 1691, depicting the northern portion of the new town, the present Market Strand, Market Street and High Street appear to be well developed, the streets being lined with houses or shops. There was already a highway from the town of Penryn to Arwenack: this followed the edge of the Penryn River, skirted the side of Beacon Hill, past the Green Bank area, down to the Smithick cove, and from thence above the harbour foreshore to Arwenack. The Killigrews no doubt would have made many improvements to this road during their centuries of occupation; other minor roads existed on the surrounding higher ground.

These were not the best of times to establish a new town on the south coast of Cornwall: *The Calendar of State Papers* reveal that the population was suffering great hardship. In 1608 the Justices of Cornwall appealed to the Mayor of Southampton for a supply of corn 'for the Western Parts, which are in great distress'; other appeals to Hampshire followed. The Crown, through a warrant to Sir Francis Godolphin, Receiver General of the Duchy of Cornwall, purchased large quantities of tin 'for the relief of the tinners of Devon and Cornwall". A later order to the Officers of Customs put restrictions on the export of tin; 16,000 pounds weight of tin was to be delivered to the King's pewterers annually.

The construction of Pendennis and St. Mawes castles had at least brought some protection to the shipping and any new settlement close to the entrance of Falmouth haven. In 1609 Sir John

Pendennis Castle, by Lowry, 1786. Later stages in the construction of outer defences include artillery platforms at the base of the cliffs and the Civil War hornworks on the landward side.

Killigrew (the fourth in the line with that Christian name) was paid over £230 compensation for damages and expenses of his late father in the building of Pendennis castle. Two years later the then captain of the castle, Sir John Parker, received nearly £300 for repairs to the fortifications. At this time all coastal defences were being put under alert because of a threatened new religious war with Spain and raids by fleets of pirate ships from cities such as Algiers on the Barbary Coast of North Africa. In 1620 subscriptions were being raised in coastal towns to fit out warships to try to combat this latter threat. Unfortunately the English vessels were not often successful when trying to pursue the Mediterranean galleys which, being rowed as well as sailed, were more manoeuvrable and faster, particularly upwind. Fleets could comprise a formidable force of between 20 and 30 sail.

Pendennis Castle from the west in 1823, by H. Gastineau. This fine view of the outer defences has since been obscured by tree growth.

The pirates, generally known as Turks, were not only interested in capturing ships and cargo, but to also take their crews back to the slave markets of North Africa. The Cornish fishing fleets were particularly vulnerable to the marauders; in 1625 the Newfoundland fleet, laden with dried or salted cod, was attacked on its return into the English Channel. The town of Looe was badly hit that August: it was reported that in ten days 27 ships, probably mainly fishing boats, and 80 mariners were taken at sea. Two hundred people were also captured when the town itself was raided. It was estimated that in one year alone on the South Coast 1,000 people were taken into slavery. However, with the current disorganisation under the new King Charles there was not the will, nor the finances, to make a concerted effort against England's foes. In spite of the supposed refurbishment of a few years earlier, in November 1626 it was reported that Pendennis Castle was defenceless: not a gun was mounted, there was no ammunition, and the garrison of 50 men had not been paid for three years.

From 1642 to 1646 the country was embroiled in civil war. Much of Cornwall remained loyal to King Charles; the Pendennis defences were strengthened and the castle became a base for imported royalist arms and supplies. A Cornish army was raised, and for a time had some successes against the Parliamentarians, in 1643 advancing into Somerset. However, due to poor leadership it received huge losses at the siege of Bristol and thereafter would play a less active role. Eventually the Royalist cause began to falter; at the beginning of 1646 the King's army was pushed back into Cornwall and on 12 March surrendered to Thomas Fairfax at Tresillian Bridge, just to the east of Truro. However, Sir John Arundell, in charge of a large force within Pendennis Castle, stubbornly dug in; setting fire to Arwenack Manor House so that it was useless to the Roundheads. No doubt the garrison took in as many supplies as possible from the surrounding area. There is no hint of what happened to the local population. On 19 March it was reported that two of Cromwell's regiments were quartered 'in the village of Pennicomquicke', having prevented the defenders from burning it. The reporter, apparently a Roundhead officer, stated that the village and Penryn could accommodate 2,000 troops while besieging Pendennis. This was a time of great hardship in Cornwall: mines were flooded through lack of manpower, and the countryside stripped of crops and livestock to feed the troops of both sides. The Pendennis garrison, starving and diseased, held out bravely until 17 August, when it was granted an honourable surrender by Cromwell's officers.

Following the war, and in spite of a small local anti-Parliament rebellion in 1648, development of the new town continued. Sir Peter Killigrew, who like most of the Cornish gentry had assisted the King's cause during the war, in 1650 managed to have the important collection of Customs removed from the ancient port of Penryn to Smithick. Two years later he was granted the right to hold a market and two annual fairs. With the restoration of the monarchy in 1660, Sir Peter, who had helped with negotiations to bring back Charles the Second to England from the Continent, was thanked the following year by being granted his request for his new town, now to be called Falmouth, to receive its charter of incorporation. The presence of other Killigrews at Court also helped: Henry Killigrew was a favourite, and Elizabeth Killigrew was to bear one of Charles' many children. In spite of the recent troubles the town's population was said to have already reached about 700. In 1664 the parish of Falmouth was established out of Budock parish; the town church, dedicated to King Charles the Martyr, being built on high ground above the extending streets.

Sir Peter Killigrew died in 1667, being succeeded by another Peter. He in turn was granted permission to build a quay on the waterfront, at his own expense, the present Town Quay, thereby enabling large trading vessels to tie up in the heart of the town; the quay was completed by 1676.

It is easy to see why King Charles sanctioned the Killigrew ambitions for the new town. There were practically constant hostilities among European neighbours, England being frequently at loggerheads with one country or another. As well as the commercial possibilities, and although there was already a naval base at Plymouth, the development of Falmouth harbour would provide shelter, supplies and refitting facilities for the English fleet, at no cost to the Crown.

In 1676 parliamentary commissioners were allotted the task of defining the bounds of the new port of Falmouth. Starting eastwards from Boyer's Cellars (the ancient pilchard works adjacent to the modern Falmouth Marina), the port area was to encompass the whole of the natural harbour, including the Carrick Roads, Percuil River, Restronguet Creek, and the River Fal as far as Tregony. Seawards the area extended eastwards along the coast to the Deadman's (Dodman) Headland, and from there in a direct line westwards to the Lizard Point, including Helford River. This was where the nineteenth century Falmouth pilots would earn their fees for bringing vessels safely into port, although many were boarded much further out to sea. The port pilotage area is still the same, except that the western limit is now Black Head, six miles short of Lizard Point.

Above left: A view of Penryn in 1816, by T. Ashwin. Vessels lie at Exchequer Quay, with quays and warehouses to the left and right. By this time schooners and smacks had begun taking locally quarried granite to London and elsewhere, returning down-Channel with many necessary commodities.

Above right: The Truro/Falmouth harbour boundary stone at Penarrow Point, made of finely dressed granite. It stands at a midway position on Carrick Roads and opposite to two others on the rocks of Messack Point, St. Just.

The ports of Penryn and Truro were understandably upset about the transfer of their ancient rights over the estuary to the usurper. Trade was brisk, their contemporary port books record the movement of merchant vessels such as the *John*, *Maudlyn*, *Dolphin* and *Emanuel*, all with the suffix 'of Falmouth'. They were arriving with cargoes such as coal from South Wales; salt, wines, iron and dried fruits from France, and general goods from London. Exports were mainly tin and pilchards. If wharves, repair yards and other facilities were established near the harbour entrance this up-river trade would decline. Following petitions to Parliament Customs powers were given back to Penryn, and Truro harbour's official boundary was brought seawards to take in half of Carrick Roads, the four-mile-long natural harbour, to a line between Penarrow Point, Mylor, and Messack Point, St Just in Roseland.

Trade into Falmouth was increasing; there were now ship-building and repair yards and victualling houses. In 1689 the harbour was thought to have sufficient facilities to be chosen as the base for the Post Office packet ships, initially sailing on routes to Spain and Portugal. The anchorage for these was to be the King's Road, the new name for the old 'Smithick Sea or harbor' on the map of 1615; in other words, the present Inner Harbour. Previously, in around 1660 on the opposite shore to Smithick, landowner Francis Trefusis had employed engineers from the Netherlands to construct a sea wall in front of the hamlet of Nankersey. From this the small village Flushing developed, apparently named after the place where the Dutchmen originated. With no restrictions on growth through local politics and the like, Trefusis built quays, warehouses, and provided plots on which living accommodation was to be rented out. This was to prove ideal for the officers and crews of the packet ships, which at the height of the service numbered over 40. During the later war against Napoleon two squadrons of frigates were also based in the harbour; a number of naval officers also took up residence, bringing their families to live in attractive houses that were being built in Flushing or across the water in the Green Bank area of Falmouth. A busy social scene developed, to the satisfaction of the providers of domestic and catering facilities and purveyors of wines and spirits. Income was also generated by the building and refitting of the packet ships in Falmouth or at the Little Falmouth shipyard close to Flushing.

Top left: The village of Flushing on the north side of Falmouth's Inner Harbour, drawn by Joseph Farington R.A., c.1810.

Bottom left: Farington's view of the Falmouth waterfront, c.1810.

Below: The old Town Hall at the top of the High Street. It was built as a congregational chapel, but in 1725 presented to the town by Martin Killigrew.

Bottom: The Killigrew monument, photographed in the 1960s before land reclaimation and development obliterated this view of the Inner Harbour and docks. (RCPS)

Peter Killigrew died in 1705, his only son George having pre-deceased him when killed in a duel in Penryn. The estate was to be inherited by the Wodehouse family, via Peter's eldest daughter Francis and the Erisey and Barkeley families. Meanwhile Peter's younger daughter Ann had married a Martin Lister, who took the name of Killigrew. He seems to have done his best to manage the Falmouth enterprises, which at one time had been threatened by a corrupt estate bailiff. The borough officials now mainly consisted of merchants who had settled in the new town, and who sought to eradicate the influence of the Killigrews. However, the estate still controlled the majority of the rented properties in the borough, and Martin Killigrew was said to have treated his tenants fairly. In 1725 he gave to the Corporation its first Town Hall, which began life as a Congregational chapel, situated on a plot at the upper end of the developing High Street. In 1737 Martin also financed the construction of a 40-foot-high granite pyramid as a monument to the achievements of the Killigrews. This was first erected in the grounds of Arwenack House, but a century later moved southwards to higher ground on the Pendennis isthmus. However, it proved to be in the way of the construction of the railway or property development, and by 1871 had arrived at its present position in a small fenced garden in front of the restored Arwenack House. The area was once a green space close to the harbour's edge, but land reclamation now finds it surrounded by a town car park and modern development.

The new town rose on an area of the Arwenack Manor estate, part of which was possibly once a deer park, enclosed by a fence or bank which seems to be depicted on the early Burleigh map. It encompassed an area from Gyllyngvase, on the shore of Falmouth Bay, to the Smithick cove. Much of the estate must have been agricultural land, but the steep hillside on which the town was to be built was probably little more than rough grazing. From the Arwenack surveyor's point of view, as he laid out the rectangular plots along the proposed streets, either down to the shore or up the opposite hillside, it was a most awkward site. However, its sole purpose was to accommodate a population concerned with the ships, English and foreign, mercantile and naval, which came into the port in increasing numbers as the years progressed. Merchants, shipwrights, sailmakers, chandlers, vintners, clothiers, shopkeepers, innkeepers and boarding house proprietors: all needed to be close to the shore to catch the business as boats were rowed onto the beach from ships anchored in the harbour.

Before any substantial buildings could be erected along the southern road from Smithick towards Arwenack, the ground had to be cut out and levelled along an area between the steeply sloping hillside and the drop of between five and ten metres to the foreshore. The ground consists of Devonian rock, part of the Mylor Slate formation, best seen in section in the Quarry car park on the north side of the town. On the landward side of the new streets the hillside in places had to be cut away to accommodate the buildings. Steep alleyways or steps still lead to the higher backyards and gardens, and to higher streets. The quarried stone was used to build up the foundations of buildings rising from the bedrock exposed on the shoreline. These foundations still support shops and offices today. The stone for the construction of early buildings was of course handily on site; timber for the same was no doubt being shipped into the port during general trading from Scandinavia.

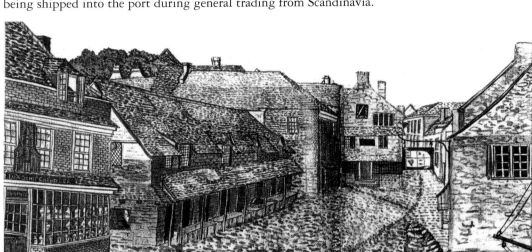

Right: A view from the King's Arms Hotel in 1778, by Jan Brandes, looking up the cobbled High Street, which is partly obscured by the hanging sign of the Royal Standard inn. The early market house is on the left; the bowsprit depicted on the right indicates that a small vessel is drawn up on the slipway.

Below: An early photograph of the Strand slipway, bordered with quay walls and buildings. The rear of the King's Arms Hotel is on the right. In 1871 the slipway was filled in to form the Market Strand pier. (RCPS)

The development of the town would have been overseen by the Arwenack estate officials who set the property boundaries and fixed the rents. By the 1660s the swampy ground of the Smithick cove had been raised and consolidated, apart from a wide central slipway (The Strand). Sea walls were extending in both directions along the shoreline. Buildings included fish cellars, inns, Custom and market houses. Close by in prominent positions were the large houses of merchants, who perhaps had moved from London and elsewhere. This area is still known as Market Strand. The first planned street would have been the present Market Street, extending southwards from the Strand. This was the most desirable area, being close to the centre of trade on the Strand (and later quay that was built over it). The present main shop frontages must reflect the seventeenth century boundaries. Modern large-scale maps show that those on the seaward side, although not of exact equal widths to each other, are comparatively wider, and the strip down to high tide level longer than the rest of the town. Shop property boundaries on the other side of the street are generally narrower: large development was restricted here by the slope of the hill, although the maps indicate a plethora of ancillary buildings on several levels to the rear of the main properties. One can imagine that in the early days the shopkeepers or artisans who rented the properties, having perhaps built them themselves, would have lived behind or 'above the shop'. Naturally there have been major architectural changes to all the streets since the seventeenth century.

Although there has been a massive infilling of the original valley and cove, the contours can still be observed at Market Strand and The Moor behind it. Market Street rises quite considerably from the Strand, and follows the curving line of the foreshore as far as Fish Strand. As the name suggests, in the days when Falmouth had a substantial fishing fleet the catch was landed and sold here. A long quay was later built over the open beach. At an adjacent site from 1819 a large platform was built out into the harbour; this held the town gas works, an essential but ugly feature of the waterfront

Market Strand c.1920. The tiered buildings of the High Street lie beyond. The columns and balcony on the right mark the entrance to the former King's Hotel this replaced the previous King's Arms Hotel in 1903. The Market Strand/Prince of Wales pier is to the right behind the boys.

Left: Advertisement from Warne's Falmouth guide of 1864. The new Globe Hotel was situated on the Town Quay.

Far left: Looking down the ope to Fish Strand Quay. (RCPS)

Below: A rather grandiose but informative advertisement for the Royal Hotel, published in Philp's *Panorama of Falmouth*, 1827. Some recognisable elements of this building still remain at the junction of Market Street, Church Street, and Fish Strand Ope.

Old properties on the west side of Church Street before demolition in 1905. The walls of killas rubble and narrow frontages may date them to the earliest development of the town. (RCPS)

The premises of the Arwenack Shipping Supply Company, one of many chandlers in the town, stand opposite to the Custom House. By 1930, the approximate date of the photograph, fewer chandlers were needed; now townspeople could expect an abundance of fruit from home and abroad and confectionary made from sugar from the West Indies. The building still remains relatively unaltered. (RCPS).

until 1950. An equally inappropriate waterside car park now occupies the site. The thoroughfare bends slightly to become Church Street; in contrast to Market Street this is perfectly straight, possibly showing a later and more organised stage in town planning. The map shows that the straight property boundaries on either side are generally wider to seaward than the hill side, although much rebuilding has swept away or hidden the original buildings. Church Street culminates in a sharp dogleg in the road alignment. Originally this was to sidestep around a small inlet known as Harvey's Dock, which was a gap in the otherwise fairly continuous stone sea wall that supported and protected the warehouses and workshops above. The inlet was filled in during the mid-nineteenth century, but the kink remains. Above this an outcrop of rock forms a buttress on the hillside, providing a convenient base at a higher level than the street for the building of the parish church from 1662. This first structure went through many alterations until a major rebuilding around 1896. The ancient church graveyards on the slope above eventually became hemmed in by streets of small terraced houses. The graveyards and many of these houses were swept away during the clearances in the 1960s.

The road continues as the perfectly straight Arwenack Street, with planned property boundaries at 90 degrees on either side. The frontages are generally narrower here than others towards Market Strand, reflecting the size of the shops or homes that were first built here. Warne's Directory of 1864 lists over 50 retail and other businesses in the street, a number being involved with harbour shipping, including 5 chandlers and 8 outfitters. (The total number of provision outlets then operating throughout the town seems extraordinary today: 17 butchers, 21 bakers, 52 grocers, 9 greengrocers. Other businesses listed included 10 chandlers, 24 tailors and outfitters, and 44 lodging houses). Past the Town Quay, the imposing façade of the Custom House, and the Victorian bonded stores (now a department store), the road opens out onto The Bank. This was once the harbour foreshore, the road being protected by a sea wall. The sea was pushed back in the 1920s and in later decades, as the beach was used as a dump for material from various Falmouth dock excavations. The area has since become a car park, with added leisure and commercial development. The south side of The Bank road, at least, is lined with buildings with a more gracious aspect: a number of three storied red-brick and stuccoed houses, built in the eighteenth century, which would have impressed mariners with the apparent wealth of the port as they approached the Town Quay.

Near the quay stands a town house leased in 1771 by merchant George Croker Fox, which he used as offices and accommodation. In the same year he leased part of the grounds of the nearby Arwenack House for the construction of his family home Grove Hill House. Another property on The Bank is the imposing Bank House, believed to have been built for Robert Were Fox in 1788. Close by is the terrace of 1-3 Bank Place: the central property was once used as the Customs Office, that having been moved from its first location close to Market Strand. It was later moved to the Town Quay: according to a Killigrew estate lease of 1792 H. M. Customs had converted an existing Lords warehouse on the present site, utilising the cellar below as a tobacco store. A kiln was erected at one corner for burning contraband tobacco; the brick structure survives as 'the King's Pipe'. (*CRO, BRA2231/20*). The Sailors Home once occupied part of Bank Place, being just one example of the changes to the properties over many years. The same applies to the adjacent Grove Terrace, which matches its neighbours in height and elegance. Presumably first built as family homes, the properties later became hotels, public houses and commercial offices. The final property on The Bank, the sixteenth century Arwenack Manor, had remained semi-derelict following its damage in the Civil War. It had since been used for a variety of purposes until attractively refashioned as three adjoining houses in Tudor style in the 1960's. Across the road stands Martin Killigrew's pyramided monument to his adopted family. Before the modern car parks and numerous buildings infilled the original shoreline this area was Arwenack Green. The high tide came right up to Grove Place; on the flooding tide vessels were brought up to lay on the beach for repairs. The whole area to the right towards the present docks was a tidal creek known as The Bar. There were tide mills and shipyards here, dating from the seventeenth century. It was probably from here that the first large Falmouth-built ship, the '*Falmouth Frigatt*', was launched in 1668.

Returning to Arwenack Street, halfway along, the road is crossed by the continuous Quay Hill and Quay Street, falling steeply down from the higher part of the town onto the Town, or Custom House, Quay. Generations of pilots and other local mariners tramped this lane, to and from their boats at the quay and their homes in the terraced cottages above the parish church. The tidal basin, small by most standards, was built to the instructions of Peter Killigrew from 1674; It was originally called Charles or New Quay. There is one small ship entrance but otherwise it is enclosed by massive stone piers. These were widened during general improvements to the waterfront in 1903. Running back along the town waterfront is North Quay, fronting warehouses or workshops. It was once busy with cargoes, particularly coal, being landed from coastal vessels tied up alongside.

Above left: A view of the Inner Harbour and Carrick Roads from streets above the parish church. (Cornwall Centre)

Above right: The pretentious doric columns of the Custom House. This grand street façade contrasts markedly with the plainer walls fronting the Town Quay. A number of mariners, perhaps some pilots, plus schoolboys, pose for the photograph. The building ceased to function as a Custom House in March 2012. (Cornwall Centre)

Top: The Royal Coat of Arms on the frieze above the entrance to the Custom House.

Above: A full-beamed topsail schooner on Grove Place Beach awaiting hull maintenance when the tide ebbs. Beyond, from the left, are Grove Place, Bank House and Bank Place, followed by the end of Arwenack Street. The nineteenth century bonded store warehouse is to the right. (RCPS)

Right: Quay Street, leading down to Town and North quays. The area was occupied at various times by the Seaman's Bethel, Sailor's Refreshment Rooms, and liquor establishments such as the Pilot Boat Hotel, Marine Hotel, Navy Hotel, and Commercial Inn.

Moving back to Market Strand, the northerly road towards Penryn passes up the narrow High Street, named more for its steepness rather than its prominence as a shopping centre. The early highway on which it was built runs along the edge of an almost cliff-like drop to the rocky waterfront. Even so, being close to Market Strand the commercial possibilities were such that it soon became lined with houses or business properties. Because of the terrain the boundaries of these are somewhat closer together than elsewhere. However, behind the street on the seaward side there were several levels of timber or stone built premises down to high tide levels. They included several shipyards and large warehouses. Also crammed into the area were small courts of humble housing, thrown up in a hurry during the early expansion of the town. During the nineteenth century such places gained an unenviable reputation because of the frequency of visits by sailors when the fleet was in the harbour. These small courts were swept away during housing improvements in the 1930s, the residents being moved to the huge new council estate on the approaches to Falmouth. The waterfront areas have since been redeveloped, with blocks of attractive apart-

JOHN TRIGGS,
STEAM COAL MERCHANT,
Grove Place, near the Custom House,
FALMOUTH.

Coal Contractor to the Board of Ordnance.
Steam Coal Contractor to the Lords
of the Admiralty.

STEAMERS SUPPLIED
With Welsh and Newcastle Steam Coals. Depot of 600 Tons
always kept afloat in deep water, ready to deliver alongside at the
shortest notice, and at all times of Tide.

Stocks also at the Market Strand Wharf, of Cardiff,
Newport & Newcastle

BEST HOUSE COALS.

Top: The Town Quay, c.1920; towards high water. The Custom House and Harbour Master's office are on the left of the Globe Hotel. The ketch *Regina* appears to have been unloading stone, probably brought from the Lizard quarries. (RCPS)

Middle: The inner wall of the Town Quay at low water, illustrating the clever construction of the town's seventeenth century sea walls: interlocking vertical slabs of local stone were built upon the underlying rock and back-filled with rubble. The seaweed line marks average high tide levels.

Bottom: North Quay warehouses, c.1960. They date from at least the mid-nineteenth century but could be much older. Occupants included sailmakers, ship owners, chandlers and coal merchants. (Cornwall Centre)

Inset: Advertisement from *Warne's Directory* of 1864.

Below: Old salts cast a critical eye over this trading ketch laid alongside North Quay, c.1930. (RCPS)

ments with views over to Flushing. From the beginning access to the various levels and the shore throughout the town was accomplished via steep narrow alleyways, sometimes with flights of steps, known locally as opes.

The main area for early residential housing seems to have developed as stone-built terraces on the high ground behind and in parallel with the main commercial streets. These were based around the early upper road from Market Strand to Arwenack. Richard Thomas on his town map of 1827 gives it the old name of Porhan Lane. By now the hillside had been infilled by housing around Porhan Street and New Street. The 1880 Ordnance Survey Map shows that Porhan Lane had been renamed as Smithick Hill From Market Strand, becoming Glyllyng Street on the high ground past the church. In the twentieth century there was realignment to some roads, including clearance of the early poor quality housing. The Thomas map shows that rows of good quality terraced villas had sprung up along the hillside towards Green Bank, and up the valley beyond The Moor, where some municipal buildings now stood.

The approach to Falmouth from the north at Green Bank. Packet vessels lie at their Inner Harbour moorings. Aquatint by W. Daniell, c.1825.

Advertisement from Philp's *Panorama of Falmouth* of 1827. The hotel is said to date from 1785 but there may have been earlier inns on the site. Note the sketch of a 'modern' steam packet at the bottom.

Further along the waterfront towards the narrowing estuary of the Penryn River lies Green Bank, probably named as such because of its once rural situation. By at least the early nineteenth century a quay, building yard, and other properties including the Green Bank Hotel, had been established here. The hotel gathered its custom from the Flushing ferry trade, and from the crews and passengers arriving and departing on the packet ships. The adjacent area of land between the steep rocky foreshore and the rising slopes of Beacon Hill behind it was some distance away from the cramped overcrowded streets and smoking chimneys of the town. It afforded fine views over the 'King's Road' or Inner Harbour, and was soon to be blanketed by rows of terraced houses and the larger villas and gardens of ship owners and the like.

From 1689 to 1850 the town's business community prospered from the fleet of Post Office packet ships based in the harbour. Shipwrights, rope and sail makers and chandlers profited from maintenance of the vessels; victuallers supplied food and drink for crews and passengers. Whether proceeding to or from the Mediterranean or crossing the Atlantic, most travellers had to pass through Falmouth. Outgoing, they may have travelled across country for several days on a lumbering horse-drawn coach; or inbound, endured a long sea voyage in a packet ship's tiny cramped cabin. Therefore travellers saw Falmouth as no more than a staging post between two uncomfortable but necessary modes of transport to achieve their destination, and were usually anxious to depart the place as soon as possible. In March 1787, 27 year-old William Beckford, heir to vast sugar estates in Jamaica, was in Falmouth intending to voyage to the West Indies, presumably on a packet ship. Whilst here he wrote to his mother: 'We are waiting in this most detestable town for a wind to carry us into a still more detestable situation, — the very sight of the waves gently heaving vessels in the harbour makes me sick, — so I leave you to judge what will be my sensations when we board,....' (Matthew Parker, *The Sugar Barons*, 2011).

Seven years later the wealthy cosmopolitan traveller James Forbes made a tour through the West Country, resting his coach horses at Falmouth. He took a walk around the town and was

Packet ships off the town in 1827, a view drawn on stone and published by J. Philp, whose premises were at the landing place, Fish Strand, to the right of the steamer. (Cornwall Centre)

Below: A *Falmouth Packet* newspaper report of 4 August 1840. These weekly lists gave names of vessels and masters, departures, destinations, and estimated return to Falmouth.

not displeased with 'the richest and best trading town in Cornwall', although it differed little from other seaports he knew. He rested awhile in an upper room of an inn on Market Strand, indubitably the same inn, the Kings Arms, from which in 1778 Dutch traveller Jan Brandes drew his sketch of the rough stone buildings of Market Strand and the High Street, complete with the intruding bowsprit of a ship on the fore-shore below his room. Forbes writes –

'As to the best inn at Falmouth if you should ever travel this road I must say that Blundstone's Hotel is the capital house but, as I am fond of variety, I cannot help adding at the same time that the room from whence I write my hasty itinerary is so situated that its bow window looks over all the humors of a populous and plentiful market-place, immediately under it; and at the same time is so close to the harbor that the boltsprit (bowsprit) of a tolerable large vessel projects beyond the window, and of course I overlook its decks and the harbor beyond it.' (*Tour into Cornwall and the Land's End, etc.* Journal of the Royal Institution of Cornwall, Vo.9, part 2, 2nd series, 1983).

The keepers and employees of the town's inns and boarding houses were there to cater for, and profit from, the needs of the weary traveller, although it appears that some didn't have much sleep whilst there. The poet Robert Southey must have passed through the port on several occasions on his journeys to and from Portugal. In 1807 he describes the goings on at a Falmouth inn, (was it also the King's Arms?) within his book *Letters from England*, writing under the pseudonym of a Spaniard Don Manuel Alvarez Espriella. After complaining about local wartime Customs regulations, poor food, beer and wine, he continues –

'The perpetual stir and bustle in this inn is as surprising as it is wearisome. Doors opening and shutting, bells ringing, voices calling to the waiter from every quarter, while he cries 'coming', to one room, and hurries away to another. Everybody is in a hurry here; either they are going off in the packets, and are hastening their preparations to embark; or they have just arrived, and are impatient to be on the road homeward. Every now and then a carriage rattles up to the door with a rapidity which makes the very house shake. The man who cleans the boots is running in one direction, the barber with his powder-bag in another; — and the hall is full of porters and sailors bringing in luggage, or bearing it away; — now you hear a horn blow because the post is coming in, and in the middle of the night you are awakened by another because it is going out. Nothing is done in England without noise, and yet noise is the only thing they forget on the bill'.

FALMOUTH PACKET LIST.

☞ *The Packets having no dates against them are reported to take the next Mails under their respective heads.*

SPAIN, PORTUGAL, GIBRALTAR. - By steamer, every Monday for *Vigo, Oporto, Lisbon, Cadiz,* and *Gibraltar*; taking mails for *Malta, Greece,* and the *Ionian Islands* every fortnight; and for *Egypt* and the *East Indies* every month. The mails for MALTA, GREECE, and the IONIAN ISLANDS are forwarded from Gibraltar every fortnight; and the letters for EGYPT and INDIA, from *Malta* once a month, by steam-packets after the arrival of the mails from England.

Packet	Commander	Sailed	Due	Returned
Adelaide ..	Baffy	June 22	July 13	July 11
Braganza	Lewis	July 6	July 27	July 25
Tagus	McLeod	July 13	Aug 3	———
Royal Tar.	Brooks	July 20	Aug 10	———
Iberia	Cooper	July 27	Aug 17	———

LEEWARD ISLANDS and JAMAICA—12 weeks: sails 3rd and 17th of every month, unless the 1st and 15th fall on a Sunday, when the packets sail on the 4th and 18th.— ROUTE- To *Barbadoes, Tobago, Trinidad,* (remain five days ;) *Grenada,* (receive the return mails from *Demerara* &c. ;) *St. Kitts,* (receive the return mails from the Windward and Leeward Islands ;) *Tortola, St. Thomas s,* (receive the La Gusyra mail ;) *St. Juan (Porto Rico,) Cape Henri,* (meet the Jamaica packet,) *Falmouth.* Passengers for Jamaica and the other Islands, to be forwarded from Barbadoes as usual by steam and mail boats.

Reindeer ..	Dicken	May 17	Aug. 9	———
Mutine	Pawle	June 3	Aug. 26	———
Swift	Welch	June 17	Sept 9	———
Ranger	Turner	July 3	Sept. 23	———
Hope	Creser	July 17	Oct. 7	———
Pandora ..	Innes			
Linnet.....	Forrester			
Peterel	Crooke			
Lyra	Collier			

MEXICO and HAYTI—18 weeks. sails 17th of every Month unless the 15th falls on a Sunday, when the Packet sails on the 18th.— ROUTE - To *Crooked Island, Havannah, Belize,* VERA CRUZ, *Tampico,* Vera Cruz, *Havannah,* and *Falmouth*

Tyrian	Crocker....	April 17	Aug. 21	———
Seagull	Parsons....	May 17	Sept. 20	———
Penguin ..	Luce	June 18	Oct 21	———
Skylark....	Ladd	July 17	Oct. 20	———
Crane......	Hill			
Star	Smith			

MADEIRA, BRAZILS. and BUENOS AYRES—20 weeks: sails Friday after 1st Tuesday every Month —ROUTE—August to January inclusive : *to Madeira Santa Cruz, Pernamburo, Bahia, Rio de Janeiro,* and *Falmouth.* — February to July inclusive. *to Madeira Santa Cruz, Rio de Janeiro, Bahia, Pernambuco* and *Falmouth —*(This packet takes out the mails to Monte Video and Buenos Ayres, which are forwarded from Rio de Janeiro by branch packets.)

Pigeon	T. James	Mar. 6	July 24	———
Spry	R. B. James	April 10	Aug. 25	———
Sheldrake..	Passingham	May 8	Sept. 25	———
Delight....	Lory	June 5	Oct. 23	———
Alert	Jennings ..	July 10	Nov. 27	———
Magnet....	Griffiths....			
Lapwing ..	Coghlan ..			

During the 1830s there was growing concern in the port that the Post Office intended to remove its packet ship base away from Falmouth, possibly to Southampton. Changes were occurring in the types of vessel using some routes in the search for greater efficiency. Marine steam engines were becoming more efficient and reliable; as long as space below decks was given over to large coal bunkers and cargo kept to a minimum, small steam vessels, initially paddle driven, were now capable of reaching the Mediterranean and even crossing the Atlantic. The Post Office began to award contracts for the carriage of mails to a variety of concerns such as the new steamship companies P & O and Cunard. The number of sailing packet ships in Falmouth began to decline. The service had begun by using privately owned vessels, but latterly Royal Navy vessels and crews had been used. A variety of design changes had been made over the years to improve the speed of these small armed brigs, however one design was anything but an improvement, earning the class the unenviable title of coffin ships.

Over several years meetings were held in the county to engender opposition to the proposed move. To show the town's willingness to improve facilities for the packets, in 1835 a detailed survey of the bed of the Inner Harbour and the packet ship moorings was carried out. The surveyor recommended that dredging was required over the nine acre area of the moorings, between Flushing and the town, plus an approach channel towards Trefusis Point. This would accommodate any future deeper draughted vessels. At this time only nine vessels, moored to long heavy ground chains, could be kept there. Although packet numbers had been reduced, there were still 26 using Falmouth, including several steamers. Because of the high cost of purchasing a steam dredger, a tug and hopper barges, plus running costs, it seems that at that time the work was never carried out.

In spite of appeals to Parliament, including a deputation of local businessmen and gentry lobbying the Prime Minister, in 1850 Falmouth ceased to be a packet station. In any case sailing packet ships were to become redundant: overseas communications were to improve via the new telegraph system; the mail and valuable cargoes such as specie and bullion could be sent more quickly and safely in the new steam powered packet ships and larger merchant and passenger steamships. With the loss of the packet fleet there was major concern about the future prospects for employment and business interests in the town. But the world was rapidly changing: within little more than a decade the industrial age would come to Falmouth. The same gentlemen who had tried hard to retain the packet service now lobbied successfully to bring investment for the construction of commercial docks across the pristine maritime approaches to the town. Work began in 1860; within three years facilities had been provided for handling cargoes at the wharfs and two graving docks were busy with ship repairs. In 1863 the Falmouth branch of the Cornwall Railway was completed, connecting the docks and town with the rest of the country's railway network.

During the eighteenth century there was rapid population growth leading to a chronic housing shortage. According to statistics compiled by Dr. James Whetter and others, in 1801 the town had

The packet vessel *Crane*, drawn by J. Condy in 1851. It is said to commemorate the last packet voyage from Falmouth on 6 September 1850, presumably to South America or the West Indies. Most packets were brigs, however the artist has drawn her as a schooner–brig or brigantine. (RCPS)

Early wharves and
warehouses on the
undercliff below the
High Street, including a
possible packet ware-
house. A sketch by
J.O.B. Dixon, RWS.

a population of nearly 5,000, living in 578 houses. That gives a figure of about eight people, perhaps two families, per house. In 1785 a Richard Davis gave his heartless view of the situation: '... these houses are for the most part low and ill-built, but perhaps are more convenient for the inhabitants than modern buildings would be, although of this sort some few have lately been erected...' The French traveller Louis Simond was not impressed with the town on his arrival in 1809, although he may have mistaken some waterside workshops and warehouses for houses: 'The houses in a confused heap, crowded on the water; the tide washes their foundations; a black wall, built of rough stones that stand on end to facilitate the draining of water; and steps, overgrown with sea-weeds, to ascend to the doors'. On visiting some of the more respectable citizens he found them living '...in very small, old habitations, of which the apartments resemble the cabins of vessels'.

The previous year the Reverend Richard Warner had published his book *A Tour through Cornwall* in which he enthused over the beauties of the Fal estuary and Carrig Water (Carrick Roads) and King's Road (then the name of the Inner Harbour between the town and Flushing), but:-

'It must be confessed, however, that the charms of Falmouth are *external*; and lie without its immediate limits. Irregular in form, with houses of no elegance; streets that follow the capricious risings and declivities of the unequal ground on which they are built, and paved with the execrable pointed pebbles from the shore; it has no claim to attention, except the activity of its trade, the bustle of its quay, and the great variety which it exhibits of human countenances, whose commercial concerns bring them from all parts of Europe, in the packets which sail on stated days in the week and month to the various parts of the West Indies and the Continent. It is, however, a place of great population, wealth and respectability; and from the unequalled convenience of its harbour, deserves a much larger portion of the attention and encouragement of the government than it has been honoured with. Unhappily, to use a proverbial expression, it has no friend at Court; in other words, it does not return any members to the British senate; though its dirty little opposite neighbour, St. Mawes, a mean village, with no house of God in it, and few houses fit for the residence of man, enjoys the privilege of being represented in Parliament.'

The town's population continued to grow rapidly during the first half of the nineteenth century. In 1811 there were an estimated 740 houses with about 6,000 occupants and by 1821 this had increased to 850 houses with 7,000 occupants; therefore the cramped living conditions showed little chance of improvement. However, the town continued to expand over the previously culti-vated hillsides; during the middle of the century the population stabilised for several decades at

Falmouth Town and
Inner Harbour, 1900,
published by Lake.

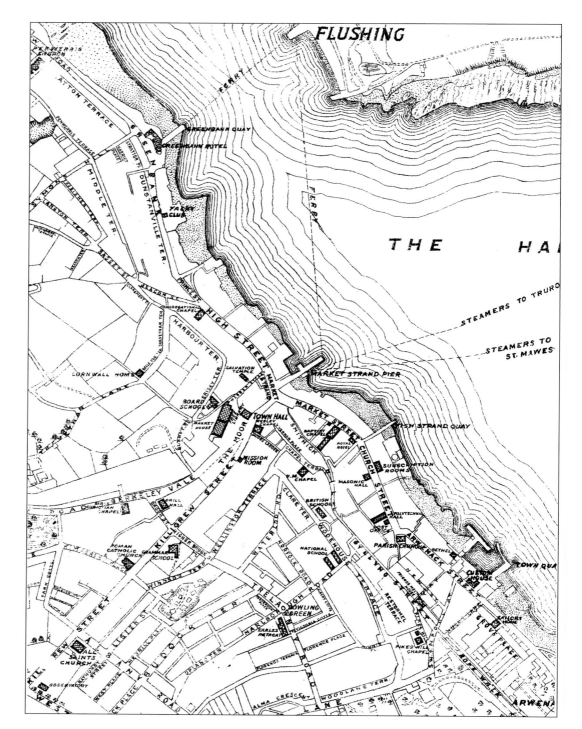

Detailed section of the
harbour walls at North
Quay from the rock base
to paved top.

around 7,500, before climbing again. Better health care, housing, and working conditions, and improvements in education brought higher standards of living. Better off workers could now afford to rent one of the terraced houses on new streets, some of which were named after the local families; Berkeley, Killigrew, Kimberley and Wodehouse; or with names familiar to every Englishman, such as Wellington and Waterloo, which dates those particular developments.

Although the waterfront was to keep its necessarily workmanlike appearance, the wealth generated by the harbour brought the construction of some grand houses and elegant terraces on the hilly outskirts of the town, some to be occupied by merchants, ship owners and captains. A Cornwall trades directory of 1856 lists the public buildings as the Custom House, Post Office, Polytechnic Hall, Savings Bank, Dispensary; the Subscription News, Reading and Billiard Rooms; also the Athenaeum, Mechanics' Institute and Library. There were places of worship for Baptists, Independents, Wesleyans, Quakers, Roman Catholics and Jews. The Classical and Mathematical School was opened in 1824, becoming the Grammar School in 1856. In 1833 the young Anna Maria Fox, of the wealthy Quaker family, was inspired to set up the Falmouth Polytechnic Society, which only two years later became The Royal Cornwall Polytechnic Society.

CHAPTER 2
A HARBOUR FOR
THE WORLD'S SHIPPING

FOR THOUSANDS of years Man has felt the need to sail the seas and great rivers of the world, to discover and explore new lands as conqueror or peaceful settler, or to trade, carrying surplus commodities to where they could be exchanged for things otherwise unobtainable in his own country. Ancient Egyptians used the artery of the Nile to transport building materials and agricultural produce and had sea-borne trade with other nations. In their turn, Minoan, Greek and Roman fleets transported olive oil, pottery, stone and cereals throughout the Mediterranean. Likewise, the coasts and rivers of India and China were busy with different kinds of ships, but carrying similar cargoes. In the West, the Roman naval ships, which helped to subdue Britain, were soon followed by robust merchant vessels, built by native Celtic shipwrights and crewed by mariners used to the unpredictable English Channel.

By the early Middle Ages, the merchants of the developing nations of Northern Europe were investing in increasingly larger transport vessels such as the cog. This was a square-sailed and deep-hulled ship, capable of carrying a heavy cargo and stable enough to weather the stormy North Sea. Ships such as these required considerable investment in construction and operation, in days long before there was such a thing as insurance cover. It is natural that owners and captains of ships throughout the world would have been grateful for any assistance in bringing a cargo safely into an unknown port. From early times, local experts would have helped visiting vessels and obviously would have taken a fee for the work. Anyone offering to help piloting such a vessel would take on a very serious commitment and responsibility for the safety of the crew and the value of ship and cargo, especially if they had been paid for the service. One can imagine the recriminations if things went wrong, and fear for the safety of the pilot!

For centuries, sailors traversing the open oceans had great difficulty in trying to work out their east/west, or longitude position, particularly in this case, on their approach to Southwest Britain. This problem was not solved until the invention of reliable timepieces in the late eighteenth century. Up until then, mariners from overseas attempting to reach ports in the English Channel from the Western Approaches might only have a vague idea of their estimated position. The task was compounded if contrary easterly winds made tacking necessary, or the ship was driven miles off course by gale force winds, hence the hundreds of wrecks on Scilly and the coasts of Cornwall. During the nineteenth century, affordable chronometers, accurate charts and other aids made navigation easier, but not an exact science. A dark stormy night, rain or fog, when trying to make a landfall on a strange coast might send a navigator into a blind panic, especially if a lookout shouted that there were breakers ahead. There would be relief throughout the ship on the sight of a small sailing vessel or rowing boat, pilot flag aloft, appearing out of the murk, and the call of, 'Do you want a pilot?'

In 1840 Captain J. N. Tayler R.N.C.B. published a book of charts and navigation notes, which includes advice to seafarers on entering and proceeding through the English Channel. He stressed the importance of taking soundings, i.e.comparing the number of fathoms (one fathom = six feet) read on the lead line to the depths given on the chart (one league = approximately three miles).

'Having entered the Channel, it is not safe to keep near the French shore. You will easily know when you are to the southward by the coarse ground, and the overwhelming of the tide, which whirls round in several places with breakers. Keep upon the English coast from five to seven leagues distant, till you are as high as Portland.

'After you are past Scilly, continue running Eastward for ten or eleven leagues, coming no nearer the English shore than fifty-three or fifty-four fathoms, or further to the southward than sixty, after you have run this distance, the Lizard will bear N.E. or N.E. by N. about eight leagues, and you will have from fifty-three to fifty-five or fifty-six fathoms with sandy bottom.

'Ships, when coming from the southward into the English channel, in thick weather and light winds, frequently get much to the northward of account, and fall into the Bristol Channel, (which may be owing to the tides running nine hours to the northward, and only three to the southward), or to the N.W. of Scilly. This unequal stream of tide begins about fourteen leagues west from Scilly. It first runs N.N.W., and continues to alter until it comes to the E.N.E. the flood-tide then ceases to run. The flood runs here on the full and change days, until forty minutes after seven o'clock, at which time it is nearly half-ebb at the Scilly Islands. The flowing of the tide is rather uncertain. About seven leagues W.S.W. of Scilly, it is known to flow till 25 minutes after four o'clock; and in St. Mary's Sound, Scilly, till forty minutes after four.

'When coming into the channel in the night, or in thick weather, you should not at any time come nearer to Scilly than sixty fathoms, nor to the Lizard than forty-six fathoms.'

When describing the northerly stream of tide past Scilly Captain Tayler was probably referring to what is known as Rennel's Current. This is an unpredictable tidal stream, which runs in conjunction with the normal tidal ebb and flow along the English Channel. The stream originates in the Bay of Biscay and sweeps northwards past Ushant and Scilly. It can move vessels up to ten miles to the north of their intended course in a day if not taken into consideration by the navigator; it was probably a contributing factor to the cause of some notable Scilly wrecks.

Sailing for Falmouth from the west, and after correctly identifying the Isles of Scilly, a mariner must steer due east for almost 40 miles before hopefully seeing the great bulk of the Lizard peninsula off to port. Falmouth Bay lies beyond these notorious rocky headlands, and under sail, and perhaps in bad weather, mariners would pray for assistance to reach the safety of the harbour. It is highly likely that long before there was documentary evidence to the fact, enterprising local boatmen and fishermen, familiar with tides, reefs and shoals around the haven, took

Above: Southwest Cornwall and the Isles of Scilly, Henry Boswell, 1749.

Right: The Cornish coast from Plymouth to Falmouth, by Henry Boswell, 1749. (Note the possible depiction of a tin smelter or 'blowing house' attached to the cartouche.)

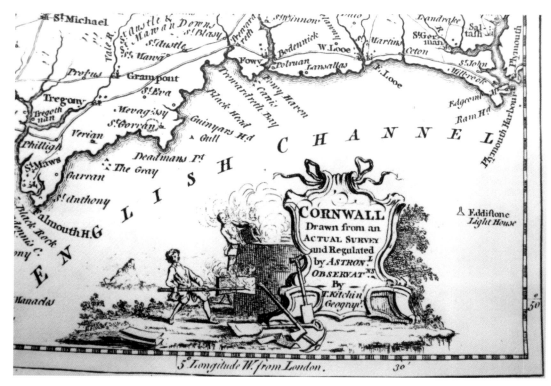

An 1804 etching of a view of Lizard Point from the dramatic Kynance Cove.

on the task of piloting the ships of strangers to a safe anchorage within the harbour, or up the tidal rivers to the ports of Penryn or Truro, for the appropriate fee, of course.

In Europe, at least, as merchant ships became bigger and therefore more costly to replace if lost, shipping concerns in major ports such as London, developed guilds, on a par with the merchant guilds, to organize the previously independent or loose associations of local pilots into professional pilotage services. From the sixteenth century, the River Thames and the approaches to the Port of London became controlled by the Corporation of the Brethren of Trinity House; this body eventually became responsible for most aspects of navigation around the coast. Pilotage was included in later legislation introduced to improve the safety of shipping; pilots were to be required to serve apprenticeships and to pass examinations before receiving licences allowing them to work

The Lizard peninsula and Fal estuary surveyed by John Norden in 1597 and republished by William Pearson in 1728. The outline of the Fal estuary between St. Just and Moze (St. Mawes) Castle differs from most charts in that the shallows off St. Mawes are drawn as dry land, perhaps emphasising their danger to mariners.

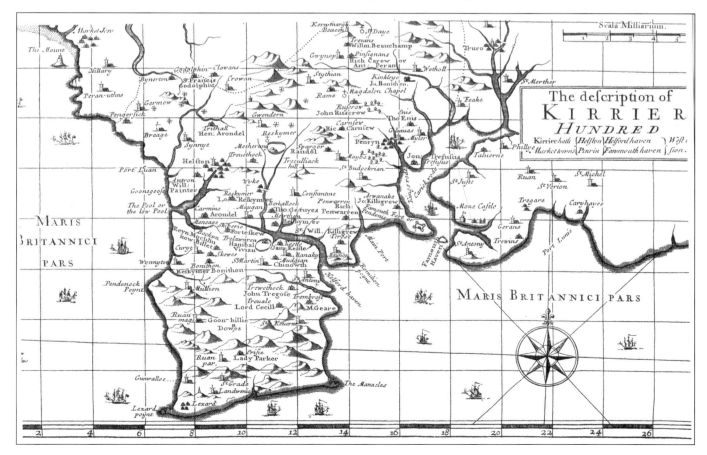

A 1779 reprint of the 1691 chart of the Fal estuary by Greenvile Collins. Additions to the earlier well-known chart include layouts of the streets of Falmouth, Penryn, Flushing and St. Mawes, additional fortifications on Pendennis, and the dual naming of Black, or Parsons Rock. Depths are marked in fathoms.

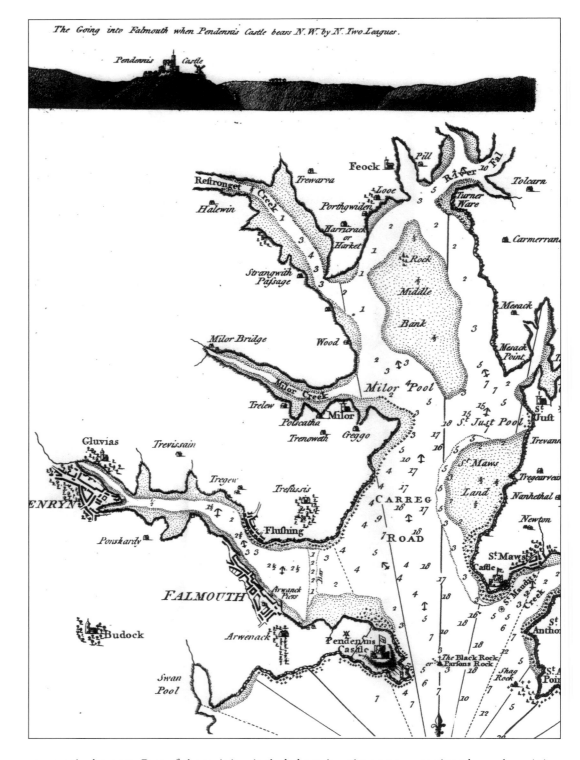

The Going into Falmouth when Pendennis Castle bears N.W. by N. Two Leagues.

at a particular port. Part of the training included serving time on square-rigged vessels, gaining knowledge of navigation, and the capabilities of vessels when bringing them to anchor. There were severe penalties for later incompetence, breaking maritime laws and demanding excessive pilotage fees.

The Trinity House control of local pilotage was extended around the coast by the Pilotage Act of 1808. Pilotage districts were set up, each containing a principle outport, perhaps with the inclusion of a number of smaller harbours along the coast close to it. Local Sub Commissioners, usually officials within the port, were appointed by Trinity House for general discipline and administration. Initially, a request was made to port officials, usually the principle officers of Customs, for a list of recognised pilots already in business in the port. The following notice appeared in the *Royal Cornwall Gazette* on 1 April 1809. Ten of the surnames on the list are those of families, residing either in Falmouth or St. Mawes, who produced generations of pilots throughout the nineteenth century.

PILOTAGE OFFICE
Falmouth, March 1809.

Pursuant to the directions of an Act passed in the 48th year of the reign of His present Majesty, 'for the better regulation of Pilots, &c.' the Corporation of Trinity House, of Deptford Strond, have appointed and licenced Pilots at Falmouth and Penzance, for the harbours and coasts within those districts; and do cause notice to be hereby given of such appointments as per lists annexed: and further, that from and after the 24th April 1809, all ships and vessels sailing, navigating, or passing into and out of the said ports, or navigating by pilots upon the coasts thereof, are to be conducted and piloted by such pilots only as have been so licensed as aforesaid, and by no other pilots, nor by any other person assuming to act as pilot. But, in relation to British ships and vessels now absent on foreign voyages, the corporation do appoint further time beyond the said 24th day of april next, for compliance by the masters or commanders of such ships and vessels with the provisions of the said act, namely, the time of return of each such ship or vessel into port from their present voyages respectively.

For Falmouth
First Class

Henry Vincent	Bennett Lowry
Samuel Lowry	Isaac Lower
James Pascoe	Matthew Jenkin
Richard Trewavas	William Dash
Richard Tonkin	

Second Class

Samuel Lowry, jun	John Barker (1)
Francis Lowry	John Barker (2)
Nicholas Jenkins	Joseph Sanders
Joseph Libby	James Barker
Richard Andrew	Nicholas Johns
William Collins	Henry Williams
William Fittock	William Warren
Henry James	William Bolitho

Licenced to take charge of ships and vessels in and out of Falmouth Harbour, St. Just, Carrick Road, and Helford Sound, along the coast from the Dodman to the Lizard and in and out of all ports and places within those limits.

Published by command of the said Corporation, signed by order of the Sub-Commissioners for this District,
H. Barnicoat, jun.
Secretary, Falmouth District.

The notice was published on behalf of Trinity House by H. Barnicoat Jnr., first secretary of the Sub Commissioners, Falmouth District. A list of pilots for Penzance was also included, the district being from Land's End to the Lizard and all places in Mount's Bay.

In 1812 an Act was passed "for the more effectual regulation of pilots, and of the pilotage of ships and vessels on the coast of England". At the same time Trinity House issued byelaws for the regulation of pilotage. Each district was described and the names of the current pilots listed. The Falmouth District was said to be from the Dodman to the Lizard and all ports and places within those limits. The District pilots were more or less the same as on the 1809 list, with the addition of Second Class pilots Joseph Levy, Philip Redman and Joseph Vincent, plus pilots Stephen Old and George Tonkin who were based at Porthoustock. The Act stipulated: when bound for places within the Falmouth district a ship master was obliged to take on a licensed pilot if approached by one at sea, and pay the appropriate rate, which depended on the draught of the ship. This varied from 24 shillings for a draught of 8 feet or under to 120 shillings (£6) for 22 feet draught. There was also an initial charge, varying from 10 shillings 6 pence to £3.3 shillings depending on the distance from port when the pilot boarded.

H. Mitchell's 1806
panoramic view of
Falmouth, depicting
St. Mawes Castle,
St. Anthony Head,
Pendennis, the Bar
shipbuilding area and
Town Quay, with
Flushing and Little
Falmouth (bottom right).

H. Mitchell's 1806 panoramic view of Falmouth, depicting St. Mawes Castle, St. Anthony Head, Pendennis, the Bar shipbuilding area and Town Quay, with Flushing and Little Falmouth (bottom right).

In 1724, the Swedish traveller, Henric Kalmeter, had described a little of the port's trade, this included vessels taking copper ore to Wales and returning with coal; others carrying ingots of tin to London, France and Spain; the packet ships taking mail and passengers to Lisbon and Corunna, and Norwegian vessels bringing in timber. The dues imposed on incoming ships included 'polage' for the maintenance of the warning beacon on Black Rock at the harbour entrance; a fee of six pence for foreign vessels discharging cargoes; four pence per ton was collected for the support of the second Eddystone lighthouse (light dues). Pilotage for bringing vessels into the port was five shillings.

The nineteenth century was one of massive change throughout the western world. Britain was at the forefront of the Industrial Revolution, which, together with its growing empire, was to bring about great prosperity to the nation, although earned at great cost to many at home and abroad. As an island nation, Britain's wealth, and sometimes even survival, was dependant on her merchant fleet, and the fighting ships to protect it. As the century progressed and trade increased, ships of other nations, as well as British, became familiar sights in the port of Falmouth, strategically situated at the entrance to the English Channel. This had been a ship-building, trading and fishing port for centuries, well-known for its fleet of Post Office packet ships and its large natural harbour, which provided a haven for shipping from storm and enemy alike. Borough officials and customs officers controlled the efficient running of the port. There were also a host of people earning their living around the harbour, such as shipwrights, merchants, ship agents, victuallers, wharfingers and pilots. All had a vested interest in the ships and sailors that came their way, not only for profit, but also a professional concern for all those that voyaged on the unpredictable sea.

The century had begun with turmoil throughout Europe. The French monarchy had been overthrown in 1792 and the new government wasted little time in proceeding to tear up treaties and declare war on Britain and most of its neighbours. In spite of opposition by allied forces, by the end of 1794, the French armies had overrun the Netherlands and adjacent United Provinces. Britain retaliated by using its navy to good effect, capturing French possessions in the Caribbean and blockading French ports to cut off trade. The undertaking was made more difficult in 1796 when, before it in turn was invaded, Spain joined the war on the French side. The British therefore had three navies to fight, French, Dutch and Spanish, (although the Dutch fleet was put out of action in October 1797 at the Battle of Camperdown). On land, the brilliant young general Napoleon Bonaparte had taken command of the French forces. However, his ambitions in Egypt, to control the Mediterranean, were to receive a severe setback when his fleet was decimated at the Battle of the Nile, encouraging Austria and Russia to support Britain. Russia later changed its mind and formed an alliance with Baltic States who resented British attempts to control their trans-Atlantic trade with the newly independent American states. This alliance fell apart in 1801 with Admiral Parker and Nelson's destruction of the Danish fleet at Copenhagen.

Apart from the spread of revolutionary ideas, much of British concern over Napoleon's expansionist ambitions was about trade routes and markets. Having centuries of maritime contacts throughout much of the known world, and a growing empire, Britain's merchants had at their disposal a huge fleet of trading vessels, carrying cargoes vital to the nation's survival. Any disruption of her jealously guarded shipping lanes by a dominant power across the Channel would be disastrous, and of course, there would be the possibility of invasion. In years of poor harvests, food

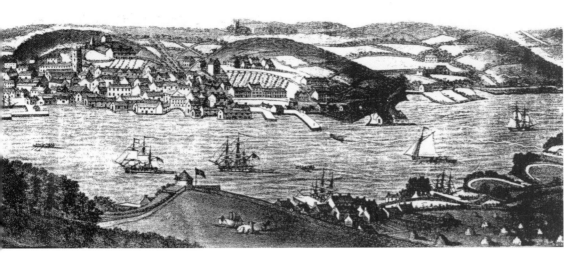

supplies had to be sought overseas and paid for by the sale of manufactured goods or raw materials. The war had, as always, brought profits to some British industrialists and ways were found to export goods, sometimes even to the enemy: bizarrely, Napoleon's troops were to have English-made greatcoats and marched in English boots.

Although many complained of the burden of taxes imposed to pay for the war, the economy of Britain was still growing. This was the age of coal, fuelling steam-power to drain mines and drive machines in new factories, with raw materials and manufactured goods being transported on hundreds of miles of newly-dug canals. Coal mines and foundries of the Midlands and South Wales blackened the countryside where miners' forebears once grazed cattle and sheep. Likewise, the tin and copper miners of Devon and Cornwall dug themselves into early graves for the enrichment of investors and landowners.

Carrick Roads from St. Mawes Castle. A lithograph published by Newman & Co., c. 1840. This is one of the first illustrations with features of the harbour drawn to a reasonably accurate scale.

Some mechanization and better management had brought more land into production to help feed the nation during the war. However, the major improvements of the Agricultural Revolution were some decades into the future. Import regulations and bad harvests led at times to near famine conditions, especially for those that could not afford the higher prices; the labouring classes lived at subsistence levels anyway. In 1801 there was rioting in many West Country towns, as bands of desperate women forced retailers to sell provisions at reduced prices, and in the mining districts armies of tinners threatened to hang farmers unless they dropped their corn prices. The fault also lay with the merchants who hoarded grain and the millers who made excessive charges to grind it into flour. Some also colluded with bakers in adulterating flour with large quantities of china clay, alum, etc. In April, the magistrates in Falmouth prevailed upon butchers and sellers of potatoes and other provisions to keep prices down; it would not have been good for morale to have to call out the newly-formed local volunteer militia to suppress disturbances.

The Falmouth victuallers, of which there were twelve in 1799, were also eager to obtain large quantities of provisions for the shipping in the harbour. They had regular contracts to supply the 40 or so armed Post Office packet vessels, which were based in Falmouth until 1850. They carried crews of about 30, plus passengers; provisions had to be sufficient to take them on voyages to the Mediterranean, or across the Atlantic, braving storms and enemy privateers. The packets were vital to British commercial interests overseas, carrying merchants' orders, letters, and sometimes returning with considerable amounts of specie and bullion in payment for exported goods. The war brought a constant movement of naval shipping into the harbour which needed supplying, an Admiralty victualling yard being built at Mylor, on the southern shore of Carrick Roads, in 1805. In September, the local newspaper commented:

'The pier about to be erected near the reservoir now forming at the entrance of Mylor Creek appears to be upon a much larger scale than is necessary for the purpose only of watering ships of war. Indeed, there is no doubt but a complete victualling office will shortly be erected upon the same spot. It is already in contemplation to take ground in building leases near the site of these works; and owners of lands, before they grant them, will be particularly cautious, it is hoped, in stipulating that no building be erected in a situation that may clash with the convenience and beauty of the future town.'

It is gratifying to know that in those difficult times someone at the newspaper was concerned about environmental matters. Fortunately, there was no room for the construction of a town on the site; however, 200 years later, environmental concerns received low priority when the old victualling yard and buildings became a pleasure yacht marina.

Trans-Atlantic trade still continued to flourish between Britain and South America, the West Indies, Canada and the new United States of America. Even though there was antagonism between British and American governments, the latter's ships, with cargoes of tobacco, coffee, sugar, hides, cotton and grain arrived in Falmouth and waited for orders; instructions from agents as to which port in England or Europe the cargo was required. However, unless it had paid duties in a British port, from 1807 any vessel trading to or from a port under French control could be taken as a prize by the Royal Navy. America, and also Canada, sent cargoes of wheat, barley and flour to Falmouth and other ports in England and Europe to relieve the famine conditions which existed because of the war and poor harvests. In spite of the threat of French privateers, lucrative cargoes of luxury goods for the well off also arrived in Falmouth, including oranges from St. Michaels in the Azores and fruits, wines and spirits from the Mediterranean, Spain and Portugal.

Some cargoes arrived due to the fortunes of war: hundreds of enemy merchant vessels, with their cargoes, were captured by English privateers and brought in and sold through advertisements in local newspapers, such as in 1803, when Samuel Pellew, Commissioner at Falmouth, advertised a 100-ton French lugger containing a massive cargo of 16,000 Newfoundland cod and hogsheads of train oil, duty free. The cod would have at least made a change from the perpetual Cornish diet of pilchards and potatoes. Occasionally the local Custom House might offer for sale a wide variety of goods captured from those members of Cornish society who sought to evade Customs duties altogether. The smuggling fraternity took full advantage of the opportunities offered by the imposition of high import and export taxes levied to pay for the war. Their fast luggers, bringing contraband cargoes from the smuggling network in France and the Channel Isles, were usually more than a match for most other vessels, including the revenue cutters. However, occasionally they were unlucky and vessel and contents might end up in the hands of the excise men. A Falmouth Custom House advertisement in April 1801 illustrated the kind of incredibly valuable cargo which was sometimes carried across the Channel. For sale was a lugger, but, as was usual with captured contraband vessels, cut into several pieces, and contents which perhaps did not benefit the starving but brought a smile to the faces of local vintners and provision merchants. In the hold there were over 6000 gallons of brandy, over 2000 gallons of Geneva (gin), 700 gallons of rum and 20,000 pounds weight of tobacco. There were lesser amounts of wine, coffee, sugar, chocolate and salt.

Prior to 1809 the Board of Customs generally fought a losing battle against smuggling, illustrated at a local level in October 1803 by a written appeal for help to his superiors by Isaac Head, Collector of Customs at the Port of Gweek. His jurisdiction covered the Helford River and the fishing coves westward to Lizard Point. He explained that the preventive officers of Coverack and Cadgwith had recently died (cause not given, but possibly at the hands of smugglers?). So far they had not been replaced. The four-oared Customs boat at Helford had become derelict since its officers and crew had been removed by the Service to Falmouth; therefore a boat, if available, had to be hired for a Tidesman, the inspector of cargoes, to reach ships arriving in the river. With considerable delays before inspection any contraband could be easily smuggled ashore. In the coves '....an illicit trade for Spirits Tea Tobacco Snuff Salt etc is carried on to the extent almost beyond conception to the great detriment of the Revenue.' *(CRO.DDT.2123).*

Smuggled luxuries were beyond the dreams of most of the population of Cornwall, over 7000 of which were men, women and children at that time employed in the mines. That number was to increase considerably later in the century. They worked for a pittance, raising valuable mineral ores from deep within the earth, and for much of the year existed on little more than barley bread,

Dolcoath mine, Camborne, by T. Allom, 1831. One of the first Cornish beam pumping engines, designed by Richard Trevithick to drain the mines, was erected here in 1816. Dolcoath became one of the most productive mines in Cornwall, at first for copper ore, shipped to South Wales via Portreath, and later for tin. Production of this peaked in 1906, when over a thousand workers were employed.

An etching by G. Townsend, c. 1860, possibly of Carn Brea mine. It produced copper and tin from at least 1845 to the First World War. The artist depicts the many engine houses dotting the landscape and tin dressing operations in the foreground. The whole mining area is now a 'World Heritage' site.

pilchards and potatoes. The steam engines designed by James Watt were powerful enough to pump mines dry to greater depths, allowing access to richer lodes of tin. In the early nineteenth century, further engine improvements were made by Cornish engineers, and iron foundries to make them were established at Hayle, Perranaworthal and elsewhere. Iron was the premier metal of the Industrial Revolution, but Cornwall had few deposits of iron ore, therefore the foundries had to use imported pig iron from sources such as South Wales and Portugal.

Although Cornwall lacked iron ore, it was rich in other metals vital to the modern industrial world. Until vast deposits were found elsewhere in the world, for much of the nineteenth century Cornwall was the main source of tin and copper. Combinations of the two, plus other metals such as zinc, formed the alloys of bronze and brass, manufactured into products from coinage to cannon. One important use of copper alloy at the time was in wooden shipbuilding. Massive copper bolts had replaced those of corroding iron to hold ships' keels and frames together, and copper or 'white metal', a copper/zinc alloy, sheathing on hulls prevented weed growth and damage by shipworm, especially in the tropics. It was introduced first onto naval vessels and later to merchantmen; hulls lasted much longer before requiring cleaning or renovation and were faster and therefore could often out-sail the enemy, until they too took up the technology.

The smelting of Cornish tin ores had always been carried out in the county; it was a comparatively simple process compared to that of copper, using fuel such as charcoal, culm and coal in the blowing houses and reverberatory furnaces. On the other hand, most copper was smelted in the Swansea area of South Wales, where expertise in refining a variety of ore types had been developed over several centuries. South Wales also had coal in abundance to burn in the hundreds of foundries, which at the height of the Industrial Revolution were belching their sulphurous fumes over the landscape. The copper companies of Cornwall had found that it was much cheaper to ship their ores to South Wales for processing where unlimited coal was available. Dozens of small sailing coasters were continually employed in the dirty and often dangerous trade of carrying up to 10,000 tons annually of copper ore to Wales and returning with coal for the mine steam engines, foundries and for other industrial purposes. Only the comparatively well off could afford coal for domestic use. The part played by these humble vessels and their crews in the success of Cornish mining has hardly been recognised by mining historians.

The mines of the Redruth and Camborne district were mainly served by the north coast harbour of Portreath, where facilities had been improved in the latter part of the eighteenth century and breakwaters, quays and a connecting railway were to be built in the nineteenth. The distance from Portreath to Swansea is about one hundred miles; with favourable winds and tides the passage could be made in a day or so. However, poor weather could lengthen the time considerably, forcing crews to stay wind-bound in harbour perhaps for days. The north coast of Cornwall is a dangerous place for engineless sailing vessels when strong westerly winds blow. Harbours of refuge are practically non-existent and many vessels were lost. The copper ore from the southerly Gwennap mining area was shipped to South Wales through small quays in the Fal estuary. The voyage around the Lands End to and from Swansea was nearly twice the distance than from Portreath, but Falmouth Harbour was safe and victualling and repair facilities available from suppliers, shipwrights and sailmakers. Copper ore was brought down from the mines by packhorse teams to small quays on the Upper Fal, which was administered by the port of Truro. As production increased in the early part of the nineteenth century, an inland tidal port was developed at Devoran and Daniel's Point on Restronguet Creek, where a railway brought ores to storage facilities close to vessels at the quays. Incoming cargoes such as timber and coal were then loaded onto wagons for transportation back to the mines.

In spite of the risk of attack by enemy privateers, traffic between Cornwall, Swansea, Bristol and other western ports as far as Liverpool, including Ireland, was carried on throughout the Napoleonic Wars. Trade also continued along the south coast of England, with vessels arriving in Falmouth from the Channel Islands, London, Southampton, Exeter, Plymouth and so on. The Falmouth and Truro shipping returns in the local newspapers listed the weekly arrival of up to several dozen coastal vessels, of which a dozen might be colliers, destined for quays at Falmouth, Penryn or the Upper Fal. At the height of the war, the coasters, being barquentines, brigs, ketches or schooners, went in convoy escorted by armed naval brigs, if the Admiralty could spare one from other duties.

For general oceanic trade, British navigation laws stipulated that most exports from the colonies must be carried on British ships and pass through English ports before being sent to their destination in Europe. Conversely, cargoes from Europe to the colonies were also to be sent via home ports. During the first decade of the nineteenth century the English parliament continued to upset the new United States of America by compelling all of their vessels heading for European ports under blockade to first call into English ports. American ships also suffered the indignity of being stopped and searched for British sailors who might have deserted from British ships. America sought closer ties with France and in 1812 declared war on England, threatening Canada and humiliating Royal Navy warships in a few sea battles. This Anglo-American war ended with a peace treaty in 1814. Until later competition by growing American and European merchant fleets, a large percentage of ships sailing the oceans were built by British and colonial craftsmen, manned by British seamen and operated by British merchants and agents. Organizations such as the East India Company received into their warehouses raw materials and exotic spices gathered from the remote regions of the world to be paid for with manufactured goods shipped back.

A vital necessity for the success of overseas trade was the ability of seafarers to find their way across the oceans to their intended destination. For generations navigators, particularly those on Royal Navy ships, had surveyed their routes and often compiled charts on newly discovered coastlines and safe harbours, noting hazardous reefs, tidal ranges and so on. Such charts could be copied and passed on to their contemporaries sailing the same routes. From the end of the Napoleonic Wars the Admiralty Hydrographic Service began to publish these and also sought to compile new ones. Survey ships were sent out to chart the coasts of Africa, South America, the Far East and, of course, the British Isles. Eventually copies of the resulting charts were sold commercially for the benefit of all sailors. Technology was also coming to the aid of navigators to find their longitude positions to fix them on their chart, for by this time accurate chronometers, the successors to Harrison's innovative timepieces, were being produced in large numbers and at prices within the reach of the Masters of merchantmen.

Throughout the century the bulk of trade with the colonies went by the consignment system: goods were consigned for sale through agents or banks at a commission. They were sold through commercial centres, sometimes by auction, at owners' risk. Colonial suppliers drew bills on their English correspondents on the amount they hoped the sale of goods would realise. Some exports to the colonies or foreign buyers were paid for with bullion or specie, sent back by ship, often on the Post Office packet ships, which always involved some risk of capture or shipwreck. Many cargoes, such as grain from the Baltic, wool from Australia, or cotton from the southern states of America, could be sold perhaps several times while the ship was on the high seas. The person who took final delivery and paid for the cargo and freight charges at the point of discharge could be entirely different from that of the original orderer. Therefore a system of ports of call were developed, where shipping agents of the final buyer could, by post, or later by telegraph or telephone, inform Masters of ships when they arrived at that port as to where the cargo had to be delivered. Falmouth, at the western end of the English Channel, was a major port for ships 'calling for orders'.

Falmouth's advantageous geographical position for sailing ships was explained by publisher William Penaluna in his *Historical Survey of Cornwall*, published in 1819:

'Many instances have occurred, in which vessels sailing hence, have entered the Atlantic and completed their voyage, while others from Portsmouth and Plymouth sailing at the same time, have been driven back through the Channel, and detained by contrary winds, until the former have returned. Outward bound ships from Liverpool, Bristol, Greenock, etc. rendezvous at this Channel. And as this is (in the west) the first port in England, the masters and supercargoes of both outward and homeward bound ships resort hither, to receive final instructions from their owners, by which they ascertain the state of the British and foreign markets, and regulate their future proceedings accordingly.'

Such communication was probably necessarily limited before the escalation in maritime trade following the Napoleonic Wars. One of the first printed local references to ships calling for orders at Falmouth appeared in a weekly shipping report in a Cornish newspaper in March 1801. During a time when, in spite of the war, the harbour was busy with coasting vessels, and our Royal Navy ships and privateers were shepherding in captured French luggers and such, trans-Atlantic visitors included the *America* from Philadelphia, calling for orders for the disposal of a cargo of sugar, coffee, hides and indigo. Another of what seems to be few examples at this time of ships calling for orders comes a few months before Waterloo, when shipping was beginning to move in relative safety. In January 1815, the Portuguese ship *Navio Linho* had been able to traverse the Atlantic with a cargo of cotton and arrived here for orders. Perhaps it was a communication problem which meant that she had an expensive delay here, not leaving for Liverpool, an obvious port of discharge for cotton,

Sail plans of nineteenth century merchantmen. From Paasch's *Illustrated Marine Dictionary*, published in Antwerp in 1885.

Top right: The notorious Black Rock, painted by Rachel E. Fox in 1833. The warning pole was maintained by a succession of parish rectors who received sixpence 'polage' from vessels entering the harbour. Trinity House were soon to replace the pole with the present granite beacon, taking over the polage dues. The incumbent rector was thereafter paid £20 compensation annually for the loss of this income. The arrangement ceased on the death of the Rev. W. Coope on the first of January 1870. (Falmouth Art Gallery).

Middle right: Trinity House commissioned local contractors Olver & Sons to erect this granite warning beacon on Black Rock. Due to structural problems and bad weather it was not completed until 1839. The two balls on the top of the post is the international maritime symbol for an isolated danger mark.

Inset: Notice published in the *Falmouth Packet* announcing the completion of St. Anthony Lighthouse.

Bottom right: St. Anthony Lighthouse, built for Trinity House by Olver & Sons. The purpose of the light was to mark the entrance of the harbour and assist mariners sailing from the west to stand clear of the Manacle rocks.

NOTICE TO MARINERS.

LIGHT FOR FALMOUTH HARBOUR.

Trinity-House, London, April 6, 1835.

NOTICE IS HEREBY GIVEN, that in pursuance of the intention expressed in the advertisement from this House, bearing date the 12th February last, *a Light on St. Anthony's Point, Falmouth Harbour*, will be exhibited on the Evening of Monday, the 20th instant, and thenceforth continued every Night from Sun Set to Sun Rise, for the guidance of Vessels entering or departing from that Harbour.

This Light will burn at an elevation of 65 Feet above the level of the Sea at High Water Spring Tides, and will be visible in all directions from S. 40° E. round Seaward, and up the Harbour of Falmouth. And in order to render it readily distinguishable from all other Lights in that vicinity, it will present a quick but regular succession of *Flashes* of Brilliant Light.

By Order,
J. HERBERT, Secretary.

351. St. Anthony's Light-house. W.M.H.

until a month later. Although the nineteenth century shipping reports show a practically endless stream of vessels in and out of Falmouth the suffix 'for orders' is rarely seen in the early decades, although this may just mean that many were not recorded as being here for that purpose.

When vessels anchored in Carrick Roads merely to wait for orders, the crews were generally kept on board during the visit: the Master and Mates knew that if sailors were let loose among the fleshpots of Falmouth they might have trouble rounding them up to continue the voyage. However, most crews were disinclined to 'jump ship'. They had signed on to complete the voyage to the port of discharge of cargo, and would not receive their wages until then. If vessels were in port for a considerable time, perhaps for repairs, sailors might be let ashore, perhaps with a few shillings in their pockets deducted from their final wage. All were welcome in the town, whether there to find solace in church or chapel, in one or more of the many public houses, or with feminine company. Over the years the consequences of the latter activities occasionally led to involvement of the local constables. One such incident occurred on a night in January 1839.

'The quay and its neighbourhood were seriously disturbed by the disorderly conduct of the crew of the *Twilight* of Philadelphia, now lying there under repair. It seems that the seamen had been paid their wages, and having got drunk, had come alongside with some prostitutes whom they wished to bring on board. The Mate objected to this, and called the Captain, who equally forbade it; and when he found the men determined to effect their purpose, he said he would fire upon them. The men drew off, but not before they had assailed their officers with a shower of stones.'

In a sometimes crowded harbour it was vital that ships were anchored in sufficient depth of water and space given between each vessel to avoid collision during varying wind and tidal direction. The local pilots with an intimate knowledge of rocks and shoals in the inner harbour and wider Carrick Roads, plus the relative tidal heights, brought ships to safe anchorages to the best of their abilities. Before ships had engines and the introduction of steam-engined tugs, if it was impossible to sail to an anchorage, harbour watermen in rowing boats might be hired to assist in towing. Other watermen were employed in ferrying passengers and crews or transporting stores and provisions between ship and shore. Before Falmouth Docks came into use from 1860, merchantmen too large to moor at the town quay to load or unload cargoes had to lay in deep water, requiring the employment of lighters, lightermen, porters and stevedores.

Many vessels came into the haven for repairs to storm damage, or because easterly winds prevented their passage towards London. Likewise, strong westerlies could prevent outward-bound vessels from escaping the confined waters of the English Channel out into the open Atlantic. During wartime the merchantmen often sailed in escorted convoy, leading to spectacular sights in Falmouth, such as in April 1801 when 130 sail of the Lisbon and Oporto fleet came in to anchor because of contrary winds. A few days earlier, in more favourable conditions, sentries patrolling on Pendennis headland would have observed 200 sail of the West Indies fleet reaching out towards the Atlantic. There were to be a number of scares along the English south coast regarding rumours of a French invasion, however, the people of Falmouth slept soundly in their beds knowing that the old Tudor castle on the Pendennis headland had recently been strengthened at several points with modern artillery and redoubts. The peace treaty between France and England, signed at Amiens in March 1802, was to last little more than a year. Napoleon invaded Switzerland and Prussia, where on the streets of Hanover the earlier Reign of Terror continued as French troops raped and pillaged. Troops and materials were also being gathered on the French coast for an intended invasion across the Channel. In May 1803 England understandably again declared war. There followed an uneasy stalemate; England could do little about Napoleon's advances across Europe, on the other hand her warships usually came out victorious in clashes with the French naval forces. All prospects of a French invasion were laid to rest by the annihilation of the combined French and Spanish fleets off Cape Trafalgar. Hostilities continued on land, especially from the winter of 1807 when French armies occupied Spain and Portugal. England's initial answer was to send a force under the command of Sir Arthur Wellesley (later, the Duke of Wellington) to the Peninsular in the following August.

After some successes in Spain, in January 1809 the English were driven back by superior forces; in Portugal, 14,000 troops, led by Sir John Moore, made a fighting withdrawal to Corunna. Transport ships eventually arrived to evacuate men, horses and baggage back to England. A fierce storm was encountered on the voyage home, a most unwelcome hazard for men who had survived harsh conditions in a foreign land. It seems that most of the fleet arrived home safely; the cavalry regiments and their horses disembarked at Falmouth and the infantry continued the voyage to Portsmouth. However, one transport never arrived in Falmouth. The *Dispatch* was driven onto the rocks and dashed to pieces at Coverack, on the Lizard. Of the ship's complement, only seven soldiers were saved, while three officers and 72 men of the 7th Light Dragoons and their horses perished. The men were to be buried at St. Keverne nearby. As a consequence of that particular storm, a number of vessels and many lives were lost off the Cornish coast that week. A trading vessel went down off Looe Island and another went to pieces on the rocks off Mullion, also two others on Scilly. An 18-gun naval brig, the *Primrose*, struck the Manacles, the notorious rocks on the edge of the Lizard peninsula just to the west of Falmouth. All the crew, apart from one little boy were lost. Six local fishermen were later rewarded for saving the boy and attempted rescue of others. The local press didn't expend too much newsprint covering such events: reports of loss of life on the rocks of Cornwall were frequent; the worst local wartime disaster of the period was the loss of the *Queen* transport in Falmouth harbour in 1814 when over 200 drowned.

St. Keverne churchyard, overlooking Falmouth Bay. The stone crosses were erected over the remains of the victims of the *Dispatch* and *Primrose* wrecks. The smaller memorial stone was contributed by one of the few survivors of the later *John* emigrant ship.

A 32 pound carronade salvaged from the wreck of HMS *Primrose* and displayed by the entrance porch of St. Keverne church.

Later in 1809, Cornwall saw further evidence of England's endeavours in the Peninsula. The local paper reported that the 16th Light Dragoons from Hampshire were to shortly march through Truro to Falmouth and there embark on 27 transports, supposedly for Southern Spain. In fact these must have been part of the army Wellesley took with him to Lisbon for another attempt to drive the French from Portugal. The war dragged on, with great loss of life on all sides, particularly during Napoleon's foolhardy 1812 campaign to Moscow. He didn't admit defeat until 1814 and abdicated in April. Elaborate victory celebrations were held in Falmouth in July; there were street parties, and town dignitaries and people of all classes marched in procession to the sound of the town band. Added attractions included shipbuilders J and R Symons' men hauling a highly decorated boat on wheels. The celebrations, however, were premature: Napoleon escaped from Elba, and it took the slaughter at Waterloo in June 1815 to finally put an end to French aspirations for European domination.

Throughout this time the growth of British industry was hampered by high taxation to pay for the war. Trade in Europe suffered because of enemy action and embargoes, although this was somewhat compensated by the East India Company's activities in the Far East. Trans-Atlantic shipping suffered during the American War from 1812 to 1814, otherwise trade to the West Indies and European colonies in South America increased, to the extent that at one time it was reported that there was a glut of British goods. At home there were taxes on a huge range of commodities, from luxuries to essential foodstuffs, leading to a colossal increase in smuggling. Imports of corn were restricted by duties placed upon them to keep up the price of grain sold by British farmers, which in years of poor harvests led to riots over shortages and prices the poor could not afford.

However, with a growing population Britain was sometimes forced to import considerable quantities of wheat, barley and oats, the latter primarily used for animal feed, especially for the huge number of working horses without which transportation overland was impossible.

Populations over much of Europe may have assumed that the end of the war would bring an improvement in the standard of living and more food to the table. In April 1815 few could have been aware that, thousands of miles away on a small island in the middle of the Indonesian archipelago, the volcano known as Tambora exploded. Apart from killing thousands over hundreds of miles, it sent a sulphurous cloud of ash and dust into the atmosphere, which for the next few years enveloped the northern hemisphere. The sun's power was reduced, leading to a fall in world temperatures. 1816 became known as the year without a summer: at that time the coldest on record. Crops failed in many areas across Europe, parts of Britain, and the corn-growing areas of North America. In southern Europe, many already weakened by starvation succumbed to a typhus epidemic. This is probably why the ship *Honduras*, sailing from Genoa with wheat in April 1817, was put under quarantine on reaching Falmouth. But life had to go on, and Britain still relied on its merchantmen for survival. Now that the war had ended, the danger at sea came mainly from the elements rather than enemy warships. Local shipyards were busy constructing schooners for the increasing coastal trade; ships continued to sail to far-off lands in the southern hemisphere, the dangers in this case being, perhaps, from tempest and piracy.

There was further depression in manufacturing industries into the 1820s, although advances in technological development and steam power were gradually being introduced to drive the new machines of mass production. However, such advances led to civil unrest as people that for generations had found employment in cottage industries were priced out of the markets and lost their livelihoods. Agricultural workers were also being forced from their land and cottages by the enclosure acts. Draconian powers were introduced to put down the Luddites and others calling for reform, leading to the massacre of Peterloo in 1819.

The population was growing; as people moved from the countryside to towns, the streets of back-to-back houses became seriously overcrowded, with open and overflowing cesspits and little access to unpolluted drinking water. Malnourished children, if they survived infancy could be sent to work a twelve hour day in the fields, mines or factories from the age of eight. The labouring classes, worn out by work, were lucky to survive beyond the age of forty, if not first struck down by smallpox, typhus or cholera. Various plagues broke out in Cornwall from time to time during the century, some being brought from overseas, therefore the inhabitants of ports were particularly vulnerable. In October 1820, during a period of stormy weather, St. Mawes pilots brought into harbour a large Swedish ship, which they had found abandoned by her crew. The salvage claimed by the pilots for the ship and its cargo of salt and other goods would have been considerable. On inspection by Customs officers of the ship's papers found on board it transpired that she was from Torrevieja in southern Spain. Apparently it was known that there was disease in that area, for the vessel was immediately put under quarantine. A total of 60 people, Customs and Excise officers, pilots and others in Falmouth and St. Mawes also found themselves quarantined. Fortunately no epidemic seems to have followed. Borough Boards of Health were established in 1831 to promote cleanliness amongst the population. In Falmouth, a seaport vulnerable to the prevalent infections of Asiatic cholera, inspectors had 'nuisances' removed from the lanes and alleyways, and the streets washed down daily. Such precautions were ignored along the coast at Newlyn. Many died there after the disease was brought in on a fishing boat from Ireland. In July 1832, a schooner from Liverpool arrived in Falmouth, the Master having died of cholera during the voyage. The vessel was immediately sent to the quarantine anchorage at St. Just Pool in Carrick Roads. The mate on board pleaded for the body to be taken ashore, but this was refused.

In early April 1829, there had appeared in the newspaper, the *Falmouth Packet*, one of the earliest of many reports that Falmouth pilots, when on duty at sea, were able to render assistance and possibly save the lives of other mariners. At about 7 o'clock on a Thursday morning, near the entrance to the Helford River in Falmouth Bay, a St. Mawes mackerel driver, a type of fishing lugger, was capsized by a sudden gust of wind. The crew of four were thrown into the sea. Three were picked up by the boat of a Mr. Chard, the other, the son of the owner of the lugger, was lost. There is little doubt that the rescuer was the pilot Chard (first name unfortunately not reported, but possibly John), one of the first of a long line of pilots of that surname that served into the twentieth century.

By 1832 the local newspapers were still reporting a general stagnation in trade; workers such as shipwrights were apparently finding it difficult to make ends meet. Perhaps prompted by

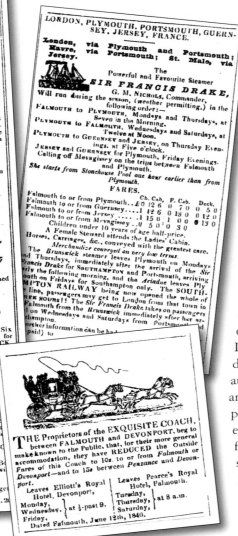

examples of other workers in the country, the Combination or Union of Shipwrights had requested a rise in their pay to 4 shillings and 6 pence per day, working a 6-day week. Their employers dismissed the claim, threatening that they were able to bring in men from elsewhere to repair vessels at £1 per week. The average pay for an agricultural labourer or mine surface worker at the time was a mere 10 shillings a week; others with special skills at about £1 per week.

The weekly newspaper reports of ship arrivals in Falmouth do not seem to reflect the other reports of a depression. The coastal trade continued as usual. Vessels on passage to or from London, the Channel Islands or South Coast ports called in en route to Bristol, Ireland or Liverpool, others brought in coal from South Wales and departed hence with copper ore. Small steamers were now to be seen, operated by several different companies. They carried goods and passengers on regular timetables along the South Coast between London, Plymouth, Falmouth and Ireland. Although during some weeks overseas traffic was relatively light, at other times up to two dozen large vessels might be at anchor in Carrick Roads. Merchantmen arrived from ports all over the world to pick up instructions for delivering cargoes or undertake repairs; others waited for a fair wind for departure to foreign shores. A random selection of countries and ports named in weekly lists included Sierra Leone, Honduras, Newfoundland, Lisbon, Rio de Janeiro, Havana, New York, Quebec, Boston, Leghorn, Rotterdam, Bremen and St. Petersburg. The town then had a truly cosmopolitan atmosphere as ships' officers of many nations consulted with

Above: Advertisement from the *Royal Cornwall Gazette*, 22 August 1828. At this early date in their development steam passenger vessels were calling at Falmouth on regular voyages between London and Dublin.

Top right: Notice from the *Falmouth Packet*, 13 July 1840, promoting the services of this steamer, which was a frequent visitor to Falmouth over a number of years.

Bottom right: Coach company advertisement in the *Falmouth Packet*, June 1840. The illusion of speed engendered by the galloping horses belies the true nature of coach travel, although new turnpike roads were making journeys slightly more comfortable.

agents, customs officials, shipwrights and provision merchants. A busy international port, although bringing a good standard of living to many in the area, could also bring unwelcomed visitations: in October 1833 the *Royal Cornwall Gazette* reported that there were 40 new cases of cholera in Falmouth the previous week, with 14 deaths. Fortunately this particular outbreak was over by Christmas.

In 1838 Falmouth had cause for celebration: all branches of trade in the country were said to be in a healthy and flourishing state, and in June there was the coronation of the young Victoria, head of a now vast British Empire. Falmouth spared no cost in organizing the celebrations: the streets and houses were lavishly decorated with banners, flowers and triumphal arches, and the packet ships in the harbour were dressed overall. One thousand poor people were fed dinner at ten tables in the street, followed at 5pm by two hundred ladies and gents sitting down to dinner, at which many toasts were given to Victoria. Eighty residents of the town poor house also received dinner, presided over by Messrs. Fox and Broad, both being merchants, shipping agents and Guardians of the Parish; Fox's offices being decorated with flags of the nations of his vice-consulships. Twenty-six porters who worked around the wharves and harbour were entertained to dinner by Mr. Earle, the quay master. Francis Symons, the shipwright, also provided a meal for his employees.

The annual regatta followed later in the year, being as successful as the previous two (see The Regattas chapter), apart from the fact that the pilots had not been invited to race their cutters. The reasons for this absence would have been discussed in the bars of Falmouth and St. Mawes long into the night. The following week a letter from 'Amacus' was published in the *Falmouth Packet*. It took the form of a tirade against the regatta committee and gives a contemporary view of the pilots' role and importance of the haven for shipping. Some of today's working boatmen will empathise with those pilots of nearly two hundred years ago as, perhaps for different reasons, similar situations can still occur.

'Sir – I cannot conceive how the committee of Falmouth Regatta could be so wilfully negligent or could be ignorant of the interests of this port, as to exclude the pilot boats from competing for a prize. The owners of the greater number of these vessels are spirited and deserving men, and have from time to time so improved their craft so as to be in possession of a class of vessels fitted for their purpose as any in the kingdom … they should receive all the encouragement that could be possibly afforded them, particularly from those parties who derive ten-fold more benefit from their labours than the pilots themselves – I mean the merchants and tradesmen of Falmouth.

First, then, Sir, I have only to call your attention to your shipping list during last winter, and you will at once see the great number of vessels, both homeward and outward bound, which were brought in by the pilot boats. Scarcely a day passed without there being some fresh arrival, and some new 'job', and at last the number of vessels was so great, and the repairs they required so extensive, that sufficient labourers and mechanics could scarcely be found to work on them. Their crews, in numberless instances were destitute of many comforts in the shape of wearing apparel, etc. , to supply which proved a source of no small profit to different shopkeepers. The provision merchants, likewise, came in for a share of the advantages; in fact, the whole of the inhabitants derived benefit in some way or other.

Now, it is very reasonable to suppose that if those pilots did not put to sea in the most tremendous weather, to the risk of both their property and lives, two-thirds of the disabled vessels which now arrive at this port during the south-west gales would either reach Plymouth or some other port further up channel. The same argument will hold good with respect to easterly winds. Vessels homeward bound very often come into harbour at the suggestion of pilots, when, if there were none in the way, they would probably weather the storm, or beat up as far as the Eddystone, where if the weather became violent, and compelled them at last to make harbour, they would probably find a Cawsand boat ready to take them into Plymouth …

But I have heard it whispered that the committee have been governed by this objection, viz:- that the major part of the pilot boats belong to St. Mawes, and that although these boats have carried away several prizes, no contribution towards the general subscription has been received from that place. How, in the name of common sense, could the committee ever suppose that the pilots could afford to make a donation: or, if they meant their argument to apply to the conduct of the more respectable inhabitants of St. Mawes, what kind of justice do they call it to punish a poor man for the mercenary conduct of his more wealthy neighbour? …' etc.

The arrival at Falmouth of the young Dona Maria II, Queen of Portugal, in September 1828. Her host was Lord Clinton of Trefusis, a reception being held at Fox's Bank House. Similar harbour ceremonies were held during visits by Queen Victoria and Prince Albert on the royal yacht in 1843 and 1846. (Falmouth Art Gallery)

It is enlightening to note the attitude of the time, insomuch that, even though Amacus was very concerned with the welfare of the pilots, he did not judge that they were 'respectable'. They raced again in the following year. Amacus might well have quoted an example from earlier in the year of hazardous work undertaken by pilots and their boats. During a period of stormy weather in late February 1838 reports were received in St. Ives, on the North Cornish coast, that vessels were in distress off Lands End. The St. Ives pilot boat *Caesar* was manned with extra hands and sailed out in tempestuous seas with a total of 17 on board. About 15 miles to the southwest they came across an abandoned French merchant brig, the *General Foy,* with sails in tatters and close to sinking. Hands from the pilot boat were able to pump out, set some sail, and eventually bring the brig into St. Ives. Six survivors were later found after days in an open boat and taken to a seamen's hospital. The *General Foy* had sailed from Guadeloupe, in the Leeward Islands, laden with a valuable cargo of coffee, rum and sugar. In May it was reported that the salvors were awarded the immense total of £1000 salvage money, to be divided equally amongst all those involved.

In November that year there occurred another example of the co-operation which could be generated amongst the coastal communities and professionals such as ship captains, pilots, shipping agents and the like, in the event of a vessel out at sea in distress. Fishermen, boatmen, and even the farming community were ready to answer the call to assist in a rescue. The motive was not always solely altruistic, for if there was a valuable ship and cargo to be saved from the rocks the agents were usually empowered to hand out substantial rewards to volunteers at a later date. If, on the other hand, through poor navigation or stress of weather, a ship was wrecked on the vicious rocks of the Cornish coast, the local fishermen were often the first to see it and attempt to rescue shipwrecked sailors. Local courts sometimes awarded sums for such actions. If cargo was later washed ashore, and if Coastguards or Excise men were around, goods might be taken to a bonded store, the finders possibly receiving rewards. If, however, there was no-one in authority present, goods, especially if they were drinkable, would conveniently 'disappear': that was usually the extent of so-called 'wrecking'.

An East Indiaman and pilot cutter (possibly from Cardiff?). Drawn by E. W. Cooke in 1828.

The incident alluded to above involved the *Larkins*. According to Lloyds' Register of that year, she was a ship of 700 tons, built, probably of teak, in Calcutta in 1808. The hull was sound, receiving a few years previously a sheathing of copper to prevent weed growth and damage by teredo worm. The vessel was London registered and owned by the Master, Captain Ingrams. The newspaper report of the incident refers to her as an East Indiaman, therefore she was likely to be under charter to that company. *Larkins* had been loaded with a valuable cargo at Calcutta and after a voyage lasting several months was approaching the English Channel on her way to the company's warehouses in the Port of London. As dawn broke on a foggy Sunday morning, Captain Ingrams had no way of knowing that the course the helmsman steered towards the English Channel had brought the ship about 20 miles to the north of the preferred safe position. Instead of being well south of Scilly, it was perilously close to the northern edge of the islands.

At this stage, Hicks, one of the family of highly-skilled Scilly pilots, found and boarded *Larkins* to warn Ingrams of approaching danger, but was too late to prevent the vessel from running onto the outlying rocks of the Seven Stones reef. When she slipped back into deep water she was leaking badly. The crew worked at the pumps but were unable to lower the water in the hold. After three hours without improvement, Ingrams took the mail and passengers aboard Hicks' cutter and they sailed to Penzance for assistance, a distance of about 40 miles. Winds were obviously light because although a pilot cutter was one of the fastest craft around at the time, it took them over ten hours. Once there, Ingrams raised about 50 hands to return towards the Seven Stones to assist the crew with pumping. The main pumps which would have been incorporated into a ship such as *Larkins*, consisted of a continuous chain on which were metal and leather discs, set at intervals, running through copper or wooden cylinders. The chain turned round a pulley wheel at deck level to another at the pump well in the bilges. It was operated by teams of several men working together at long-handled levers. In this present situation, any smaller bilge pumps available would also have been in use. The process required a huge amount of continuous manual labour.

A big ship with three tall masts should have been seen for miles, but because the weather was so bad she wasn't located, and on Monday morning Hicks with his overloaded cutter returned to Penzance. It was therefore feared that *Larkins* had foundered and the crew lost. A distraught Ingrams and his party made their way to Falmouth; they had only been there for an hour when to the delight of everyone *Larkins* sailed into the harbour. It transpired that the crew had continued to pump as best they could, and the officers, now that they knew their position, albeit the wrong one, set a new course up-Channel. The weather continued extremely hazy and signal guns were fired periodically. When off the Lizard peninsula they were heard by Falmouth pilot James James, who lay off Coverack in his small cutter *Union*. He set sail in the general direction of the firing and about three miles offshore eventually came upon the lofty spectacle of masts and sails as they appeared out of the gloom. James boarded and assessed the situation, then sent his boat back to the Lizard for further assistance, it landing at Cadgwith. Twenty eight men were quickly found in the village and sailed back to help with the pumps. The pilot James guided the ship towards Falmouth, and on the way she was also boarded by seamen from a packet vessel which had been sent out from Falmouth to search for *Larkins*.

Once in the harbour, gangs were kept working all night and the following day, managing to keep the water at eight feet in the hold. Messrs. Fox & Co., the ship's agents, organized the removal of the valuable cargo, which included cases of silks and indigo, to the safety of their warehouses. The young Robert Barclay Fox described in his journal the unloading, repairs, and negotiations between the underwriters and claimants for salvage. Also the subsequent unwelcomed bill for repairs, plus commission, presented by the Fox's to Captain Ingrams before he left on 18 December. It was not difficult to find expert shipwrights in Falmouth to undertake the repairs: several firms around the harbour were building first class merchantmen and Post Office packet vessels, and were used to repairing those damaged by storm or collision. In 1820 a dry dock had been constructed at Little Falmouth on the Flushing side of the harbour. However, if *Larkins* was too big for it, or it was already in use, repairs could be carried out on a suitable beach. All cargo, plus the defensive guns which were usually carried on East Indiamen, would have had to be unloaded, using tackles and cranes or sheerlegs.

To access and repair the damaged area of the hull, a section of the thin sheathing of copper plates, fitted ten years previously, would have to be removed. Beneath that lay an earlier sheathing of timber planks laid on tarred felt. On removal of this the damage to the hull could be repaired. The layers of sheathing could then be made good and the ship refloated, time being given for the timber to 'take up' and checked for leaks. Within a month it was reported that *Larkins* was likely to resume her voyage in a few days, a great many persons being employed in re-shipping her cargo. She obviously received a good report from the Lloyds' surveyor: for the next two years Ingrams sailed her on voyages to Madras. Other owners also took her eastwards to India and New Zealand, until she disappeared from Lloyds' List after 1854. Just after Christmas the persons principally responsible for saving the ship were given handsome rewards for their earlier efforts. The Cadgwith boatmen, 28 in number, who pumped to keep the ship afloat, received £300 to share between them. A Coastguard officer, whose men had assisted with the pumping, received a similar amount. The report included - 'Mr. James, the pilot, whose exemplary exertions contributed so largely to the safety of the ship and her valuable cargo, has been paid £100 for himself, and the two men employed in his cutter.' This windfall for James James allowed him to commission the building of a new larger cutter, and the *Alarm* took to the water from a local shipyard in 1843.

To understand how ship building and repairing may have developed on the Fal, we can speculate that from prehistoric times most naturally protected harbours around Britain at one stage or another would have held a population of fishermen, or at least farmers who also fished to supplement the local diet. The small settlements that grew up around the Fal estuary were no exception. Fishing and fowling would have been carried out in the creeks from coracles or canoes hewn out of oak logs; remains of such may one day surface from dredging operations. Later more specialised fishermen sought deep-sea species of fish in plank-made boats driven by sail and oar. Outside influences from along the coast or overseas would improve boat-building techniques, although certain features of design would have been incorporated to suit local conditions and the requirements of the user. This particularly applies to the later inshore pilchard fishing industry, where several different sizes and styles of boat were needed to capture and land the netted catch. The most well-known Cornish fishing vessel, in all its forms, that developed from the seventeenth century at least, was the lugger, although the rig was not unique to the West Country. Smaller clinker and carvel-built working boats were used around the Fal for a variety of purposes: ferrying goods and passengers around the harbour or between ship and shore; dredging for oysters with sail or oar in the wide estuary or narrower creeks. This ancient art still continues with the 'haul-tow' punts and working sailing boats, although in much reduced numbers than formerly.

As Falmouth rapidly developed following the granting of its charter, larger vessels were required to import building materials and commodities from London and the Continent; some of these same vessels might carry cargoes of local pilchards to Mediterranean ports. For the next two centuries or so many others would be carrying copper ore to South Wales, returning with vital supplies of coal. Therefore shipyards began to be established around the Fal to build and maintain such craft; shipwrights migrated from other areas, bringing new designs and building techniques. Essential supporting industries: rope makers, sail makers, mast makers, metal workers and the like, established works in the neighbourhood. Business contacts had to be developed to ensure supplies of ship's timber, sailcloth and rope, and, at some periods, guns and ammunition.

There are at least 20 sites around the creeks and bays of the estuary where ship or boat building formerly took place, discounting the lonely beaches where a fisherman may have knocked together his own boat. The sites varied from the bank of a creek where a single Truro River sailing barge came to life, to the yards around the Inner Harbour, each of which may have had several

Bottom: View by Joseph Farington, c. 1810, of tide mill pools of The Bar, with the tide mill to the left and Symon's shipyard on the outer bank. This became the town's main ship building area: vessels from barques and brigs to pilot cutters and quay punts were produced here until the 1930s.

Below: The ancient tide mill on The Bar, c.1824. An original etching by E.W. Oldham. The building was demolished in about 1900.

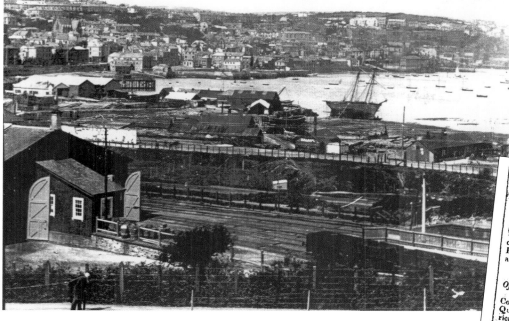

occupants, sometimes a father followed by sons, succeeding over many years. In which case the output could vary from ships of war, barques, packet brigs, merchant schooners, barges, quay punts and pilot cutters. In the twentieth century some yards were to turn to the production of pleasure yachts and sailing boats. The number of Fal shipwrights building in wood and in charge of their own yards, including father to son firms, over the nineteenth and twentieth centuries, was about 75. Working under them, the numbers depending on the size of the yard, was a workforce of shipwrights, sawyers, blacksmiths and the like. The skills were perpetuated by the apprenticeship system: from the age of 14 boys, often sons or nephews, were bound to a master craftsman for seven years before earning a full wage.

According to figures on the Bartlett Library database the number of wooden vessels built around the Fal from 1786 to the first quarter of the twentieth century was about 350. If a large number of unrecorded small craft such as work punts and sailing dinghies is taken into account that number might even be doubled. Added to this are the vessels made of iron and steel: between 1878 and 1930 G.C. Cox & Co., at their foundry adjoining Falmouth Docks, turned out 198 vessels. The list includes pleasure steamers, tugs, trawlers, and vessels for the Admiralty. Pool, Skinner and Williams, also at the docks, and W. H. Lean, close by at the Bar, produced a number of steamships and sailing vessels with steel hulls. Successful yards building a great variety of wooden vessels were at Malpas, Pill, Ponsharden, and so on, but the most prolific yards by far were those on Bar Creek, the area which from the 1930s was taken over by the development of the docks. From 1794 the Symons family built at least 20 merchant ships here, including packets. At another yard (now under the National Maritime Museum, Cornwall car park) from 1832 father and son John and Henry Trethowan built a similar number of schooners, pilot cutters and other vessels. Also on the Bar were Charles and Richard Burt, building about 30 vessels and small craft. In the first quarter of the twentieth century William Edward (Eddy) Thomas at his Bar Road yard turned out over 50 small working and pleasure craft, including quay punts.

Another successful shipbuilding site, in quantity and quality, was at Little Falmouth, a small inlet on the north bank of the Inner Harbour and close to Flushing village. One of the first to lease the site from the Trefusis family was the puritan, Richard Lobb, a successful seventeenth century merchant and ship owner, eventually becoming High Sheriff for Cornwall and M.P. for Mitchell. He was in the import and exporting business, one of the main commodities being Cornish pilchards. In common with later businessmen, the Fox's of Falmouth, he bought up catches from seines around the coast. The fish were processed and packed in barrels at his works, or pilchard palace, as such were generally called, at Little Falmouth. Cargoes typically went to Naples, Leghorn, or other Mediterranean ports. The site was later developed as a ropewalk and shipyard, but the title Lobb's Pilchard Palace persisted for generations.

Early in the eighteenth century Robert Trefusis leased the site to shipwright Peter Symons, the lease later passing to his son, also called Peter. The latter's son, Richard Leane Symons, had

Top left: The docks railway station and shipyards on The Bar, c.1910, from a similar point as the Farington view of a century before. (RCPS)

Top right: A new brig on the ways, ready for launching, a familiar scene at Fal shipyards during the nineteenth century. By J. J. Baugean, c.1814.

Above: Sale notice from the *Royal Cornwall Gazette* of July 1823, listing the vessels and materials to be found at a typical Bar shipyard of the period.

taken over the yard by about 1800. By this time Falmouth had been a base for the Post Office packet ships for over a century, the Symons yard being conveniently situated to refit and service them. In 1804 and 1805 Richard Symons launched two armed brigs for the Royal Navy, of 382 and 391 tons respectively. Six or more packet ships and other vessels followed, production was assisted by the building of a dry dock in 1820. The Trethowans took over the site in 1851, building barques, brigantines, schooners and pilot cutters. In spite of his skills as a shipwright Henry Trethowan was made bankrupt in 1876 but later continued building and repairing vessels at the Bar. Lee and Sons next took over the Little Falmouth site, building several ketch-rigged sailing trawlers for the East Coast and smaller craft. In 1928 he was followed by R.S. Burt who had been forced to move from the Bar; the site was renamed the Little Falmouth Yacht Yard, the management taking the name The Falmouth Boat Construction Company. Under a succession of owners the yard continued to repair and build pleasure craft of many kinds. During the Second World War, at this and other Falmouth yards skilled craftsmen built and repaired many naval and merchant vessels, making a valuable contribution to the war effort.

A fine study of a locally-built Falmouth quay punt off the waterfront. She is sporting the typical working rig of 'leg of mutton' mizzen, gaff mainsail, staysail and flying jib. (Cornwall Centre)

Falmouth working boat oyster dredging on Carrick Roads.

Working boat *Victory*, originally built in 1884 on Restronguet Creek as *Royal Oak* – still winning during the summer racing season.

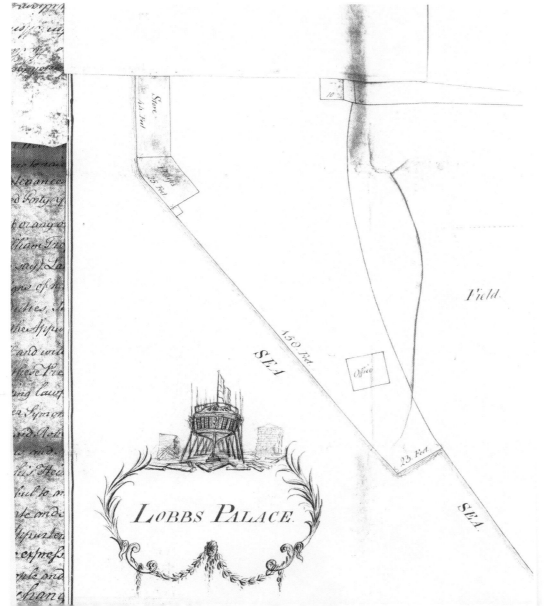

Little Falmouth, on the Flushing side of the harbour, formerly the site of Lobb's Pilchard Palace. There has been a shipyard here from the mid-eighteenth century to the present day.

An elaborate cartouche depicting a ship under construction at Little Falmouth. Detail from a plan attached to a lease of 1790 between Robert Trefusis and shipwright Peter Symons (CRO,x/727/1/7) (Courtesy of the Cornwall Record Office)

The schooner *Lady of Avenal*, moored in the harbour c.1922. She was built in 1874, a fine example from Henry Trethowan's shipyard at Little Falmouth; in trade under the ownership of E. D. Anderton until about 1920. Cargoes included Cornish granite, Welsh iron ore and coal, fish and skins from Labrador, and hides from Brazil. She was later converted as a boys' training ship, for a voyage to the Arctic, and as a yacht. During the Second World War she was laid up on the mud of Poole Harbour. (RCPS)

Right: The deck of the long-lived and much converted *Lady of Avenal*, looking aft from the bow windlass. She was photographed in this derelict state in Poole Harbour, shortly before being deliberately blown up and removed in 1955. (Poole Maritime Museum)

Far right: The 25 ton smack barge *Mary*, built by H.E. Stephens at the port of Devoran on Restronguet Creek in 1875. A familiar sight around the estuary and local coasts for the next 74 years. (RCPS)

Ponsharden dry dock on Penryn River, c.1950, with a steam yacht under repair. There was a yard here from at least 1867. Emmanuel Martin built big East Coast fishing smacks and other craft in the 1880s. Other companies followed throughout the twentieth century, building, repairing, and breaking up vessels. The site has since been covered with new development. (Derek Asquith)

CHAPTER 3
THE GROWTH OF MARITIME TRADE

TOWARDS THE MIDDLE of the nineteenth century the great advances of the Industrial Revolution brought a general increase in shipping. There was a freeing of overseas trade restrictions as industrialists demanded cheap raw materials from abroad, particularly wool, cotton, iron and timber. There was now also greater freedom for manufactured products to be sold worldwide. Restrictions were also eased on the importation of cereals, although the iniquitous Corn Laws were not totally abolished until 1849. There were to be major advances in food production with the introduction of farm machinery and the increasing use of fertilizers. One of the major sources of nitrates was found to be guano; it lay in vast deposits on bird nesting islands off the coast of Chile, South America. Here sailing ships queued up to take on cargoes of the noxious material and crews suffered the rigours of Cape Horn to bring it to the farms of Britain and Europe. However, agricultural improvements were not taken up everywhere: an increasing population meant that there were more mouths to feed, and a series of disastrous harvests led to what has been called 'the hungry forties'. The potato crop failed again in parts of Europe in 1845, and by a year later in Ireland famine had decimated the population as this staple food of the poor rotted away in the fields. The British government belatedly diverted some of the new duty-free American grain and flour to Ireland, subscriptions being raised in West Country towns and villages to help pay for it.

There was also near starvation in Cornwall: in April 1847 200 desperate Cornish emigrants joined their ship in Falmouth and departed for Canada. These were just a few of the thousands who migrated, full of hope for a better future in North America, Australia and New Zealand. Not all arrived safely at their destinations. The immigrant ships did not always live up to the sometimes

An English barque and smaller brigantine, c. 1815. An etching by J. J. Baugean.

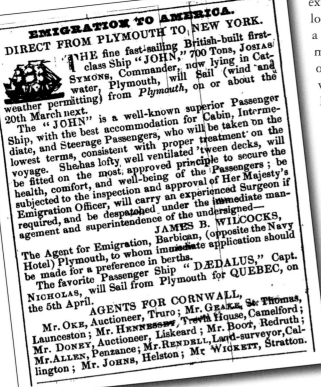

EMIGRATION TO AMERICA.
DIRECT FROM PLYMOUTH TO NEW YORK.

THE fine fast-sailing British-built first-
class Ship "JOHN," 700 Tons, JOSIAS
SYMONS, Commander, now lying in Cat-
water, Plymouth, will Sail (wind and
water, Plymouth, on or about the
weather permitting) from *Plymouth*, on or about the
20th March next.

The "JOHN" is a well-known superior Passenger
Ship, with the best accommodation for Cabin, Interme-
diate, and Steerage Passengers, who will be taken on the
lowest terms, consistent with proper treatment on the
voyage. She has lofty, well ventilated 'tween decks, will
be fitted on the most approved principle to secure the
health, comfort, and well-being of the Passengers ; be
subjected to the inspection and approval of Her Majesty's
Emigration Officer, will carry an experienced Surgeon if
required, and be despatched under the immediate management and superintendence of the undersigned—
                                    JAMES B. WILCOCKS,

The Agent for Emigration, Barbican, (opposite the Navy
Hotel) Plymouth, to whom immediate application should
be made for a preference in berths.

The favorite Passenger Ship "DÆDALUS," Capt.
NICHOLAS, will Sail from Plymouth for QUEBEC, on
the 5th April.

AGENTS FOR CORNWALL,

Mr. OKE, Auctioneer, Truro ; Mr. GEAKE, St. Thomas,
Launceston ; Mr. HENNESSEY, Trewth House, Camelford ;
Mr. DONEY, Auctioneer, Liskeard ; Mr. BOOT, Redruth ;
Mr. ALLEN, Penzance ; Mr. RENDELL, Land-surveyor, Cal-
lington ; Mr. JOHNS, Helston ; Mr WICKETT, Stratton.

An advertisement from
the *Royal Cornwall
Gazette* of 25 January
1850 for an earlier
voyage of the ill-fated
emigrant ship *John*.

extravagant descriptions in shipping agents' notices, placed in the local press to announce the intended departures of vessels bound for a better life overseas. Perhaps 200 or more souls had to exist for months in cramped conditions below decks, enduring storms, cold, or tropical heat, and possibly bad food and water. Some vessels were lost through fire, tempest, or incompetent ship handling. The latter was the acknowledged cause of loss of the barque *John*, which left Plymouth for Quebec on 3 May 1855. The following night, within hours of departure, and in good weather, she was impaled and sank on the Manacles reef, leading to the single largest loss of life on the Cornish coast, apart from the *Queen* disaster of 1814 at Falmouth. All of the *John's* crew of 19 and some passengers were rescued by local boats. Of the 263 passengers, mostly consisting of families from rural Devon, 196 were swept to their deaths in the night by rising wind and tide. Half of the total were children and infants. Eventually 123 bodies were retrieved from the sea and shore, receiving burial in a mass grave in St. Keverne churchyard.

With the collapse of tin and copper mining in Cornwall in the second half of the century, miners and their families colonised developing mining areas in various parts of the world. Many were enticed by stories of untold riches to be obtained in far-off lands, which led to the California Gold Rush in 1849, followed by that in Australia a few years later. Others had no choice in their destination: in June 1849 some ringleaders were sentenced to transportation to the colonies for seven years after serious rioting in Camborne and Pool, where the Riot Act was read after a flour store was broken into. A fortnight later a large number of vessels from foreign parts arrived in Falmouth for orders. Many came from the Mediterranean and carried corn; at last prices started to fall.

In the early 1840s there had been reductions to import and export duties on a large range of raw materials and manufactured goods, and in 1846 the Free Traders won their case for similar reductions on corn imports. Within a decade Britain was to be virtually a free trade country. Further reforms of a different nature followed: the Factory Acts slowly improved working conditions in foundries, mills and mines, particularly for child labour. There was legislation to improve water quality, sanitation and drainage in towns, and education in health and hygiene. The Navigation Acts, dating from the seventeenth century, by which English ships and crews had a virtual monopoly of trade in and out of the home country and its empire, had been partially eased in the 1820s and were to be totally abolished in 1849.

The effect of this latter legislation is clearly demonstrated in the reports of arrivals in Falmouth the following year: a number of the ships from the Mediterranean and Black Sea ports now had foreign names for vessels and Masters and presumably were manned by crews from Russia or Turkey, Italy and so on. From now the British merchant fleet had to compete for trade with ships which were owned or had been chartered in many countries; the Americans and Germans were to become particularly powerful. Nevertheless, many, if they were heading in or out of Channel ports, would still have to come into Falmouth Haven for orders, for medical attention, repairs, stress of weather, or lack of wind. This is demonstrated in a number of newspaper reports such as the list given of 149 vessels anchored in the inner harbour and Carrick Roads during one week in July 1853: English 47; Greek 7; Hanoverian 2; Dutch 7; Ionian 1; Maltese 1; Sardinian 12; Norwegian 13; Neopolitan 4; Austrian 14; French 5; Hamburg 2; Swedish 7; Prussian 6; Russian 8; Danish 3; Roman 1; Wallachian 1; American 1; Mecklenburg 2; Spanish 5.

According to Parliamentary Committee figures later quoted by shipping agent R. R. Broad in a Cornwall Railway report (*Falmouth Packet* 5.3.1859), the number of vessels calling at Falmouth for orders in 1842 was 822. In the two following years the figures were 405 and 572 respectively. Returns for three years a decade later were: 1852, 1773 vessels; 1853, 2319 vessels, and 1854, 1967 vessels.

By this later time a few of these vessels may have been powered by steam engines, but the rest, of course, were sailing ships, subject to the vagaries of the wind and tide. All had to be brought safely to anchor within the confines of the harbour under sail alone; it was not until 1858 that the

Top left: A small tug assists a barque through the harbour entrance, c. 1880. There is a westerly breeze; the pilot will be giving instructions to take in sail. (RCPS)

Middle left: The topsail schooner *Elizabeth Bennett* enters the harbour, c. 1920. Topsails are being taken in and the anchor is set ready to drop. Her cargo is probably coal from her port of Swansea. (RCPS)

Below: Shipping anchored off the town, c. 1890. In the foreground is the 158 ton brigantine *Fredericke*, registered in Papenburg, northern Germany, possibly carrying a cargo of Baltic timber. (RCPS)

first harbour tug, the steam paddler *Dandy* was available in emergencies, and at extra cost to the ship owner. Rapid sail handling was vital on entering or leaving the harbour, whether to slow the ship, which possibly displaced several hundred tons, to bring it to an anchorage, or to set sail and get way on (movement through the water) so that it could be steered out to sea. At the same time other ships at anchor had to be avoided. On at least one occasion a pilot refused to take a ship out because of safety concerns as strong adverse winds were blowing directly into the harbour crowded with shipping. After one incident the owner's complaint that the vessel had been held up for two days before reaching London was dismissed by the Sub Commissioners of Pilotage. On arrival, ships were taken to an anchorage where, depending on the draught of the hull of the vessel in question, there was sufficient depth of water at low tide for it not to touch the bottom, or 'take the ground'. Pilots had to have intimate knowledge of soundings, which varied widely over two or three square miles of useable harbour. It was not until 1870 that the newly formed Harbour Commissioners employed a Harbour Master to take control of the harbour moorings and anchorage. He had overall control, and could order vessels moved if the pilot made a mistake with the anchorage, which more often occurred at night. Vessels also occasionally went aground when sailing in or out. Most lifted off at high tide but inspection and repairs to the hull were occasionally required.

The pilots' work of bringing a vessel to anchor consisted of giving instructions to the helmsman on the course to steer, and to the officers to pass to the crew sail setting or reefing directions to assist in the vessel's course and speed. With crews from many nations entering the port language sometimes became a problem: the pilot's instructions were not always understood, and some collisions occurred. If a later inquiry found that the pilot was at fault he was liable for part or the whole cost of repairs to the damage incurred. This often involved the replacement of broken spars. The Merchant Shipping Act of 1894, and presumably previous Acts, required that all Trinity House pilots when appointed must execute a bond of £100, conditional for the due observation on his part of the regulations and byelaws of Trinity House. Thereafter he was not liable for costs through neglect or want of skill beyond the penalty of the bond and the loss of his pilotage fee for that particular voyage. In 1871 a pilot was brought before the Sub Commissioners after damage was caused to a vessel of which he was in charge, the conclusion being that he had not allowed for a strong spring tide flowing into the harbour mouth. His account of his actions was written into the Sub Commissioners' minutes and gives some idea of what was involved in, usually more successful, day-to-day ship handling by Falmouth pilots.

'I boarded the Italian barque Papa & Renetto on Sunday afternoon between 2 & 3pm SSE of the harbour 4 or 5 miles – All sail set – steered the course to bring vessel into harbour shortening sail as occasion required. On bringing vessel into the harbour took off all (sail) except 2 topsails, foresail and jib. Then took off maintopsail and the foresail, distance then 3 cables length (1 cable = 200 yards) from Lord Lyon (the ship at anchor) intending to go to the eastward of Lord Lyon, ordered the helm to port, then steady, on getting between the (channel) buoys the tide took the ship, and I sung out 'port the helm', and repeated the order, ship did not answer the helm, the foretopsail and jib were set and the mainyard brace braced by. To avoid collision let go the anchor, but that did not prevent it ...'

Generally speaking, it seems that few had reason to complain of the service they received in Falmouth. A Finnish ship Master, Captain Snellman, was to later describe his first visit, which took place in 1853. He was then Master of a small brig, having sailed to Bahia (Bahia Blanca, Argentina) from where the ship's agents had contracted a cargo of sugar to be freighted to Falmouth, there to pick up orders for its port of delivery.

'I was naturally rather excited when we approached Falmouth. Outside Lizard we were approached by a small vessel which turned out to be a pilot cutter from Falmouth. I was relieved to get a pilot on board as these waters were strange to me. He took us in and found us good anchorage on Carrick Roads.

No sooner had we entered the bay when a number of small sailing vessels left the harbour and headed towards us with considerable speed. Our pilot told me these were quay punts racing towards us; the first to reach us would have the right to handle all traffic from ship to shore during the time we lay on the roads. Already before we had dropped the anchor one of the punts had reached the ship, a man had climbed aboard and announced he was 'our punt'. It was impossible to turn down that enterprising young man, especially after the pilot had told me this was the accepted custom in Falmouth.

So, after we had secured the ship, I boarded the quay punt together with the pilot and was taken ashore. I went to see Mr Fox who was the Russian Vice Consul (Finland being a Grand Duchy of Russia). In Falmouth, as in some other places, the Russian Consul also ran a ships' agency, which meant that I would find my orders at his office.

Mr Fox duly gave me my orders. I was to take the bulk of my cargo to Amsterdam and bring the rest of the sugar all the way to the home port of Oulu on the Gulf of Bothnia.

I sent one of the crew ashore to get medical treatment while we bought some provisions (bread, butter, tar and sail cloth).

My first visit to Falmouth left me with a positive impression. We received efficient, even eager service, had a good sheltered harbour and the people were friendly which was, I presume, at least partly motivated by an attempt to create and maintain brisk business.' (From an exhibit at the National Maritime Museum, Cornwall).

Left: A fine view of the Inner Harbour from Trefusis, c. 1900. Vessels include a steam tug, barque, schooners and smacks. (RCPS)

Below: Weekly ship arrival and departure list published in the *Falmouth Packet* on 1 November 1850. Information given includes the name of the vessel, master, where from, and intended destination.

Falmouth from Trefusis.

Captain Snellman was referring to a type of small sailing bumboat which was developed to assist shipping in the port: being based at the Town Quay, they became known as Falmouth quay punts. They were open boats, about 28 feet in length, with gaff mainsail and yawl-rigged mizzen. Their masts were short to avoid fouling the yards of big sailing ships when going alongside. Their owners usually worked single-handed, sailing far out to sea in all weathers to seek incoming ships. When eventually speaking to a ship's Master bound for Falmouth, the boatman would offer his services for the time the ship was anchored in Carrick Roads; carrying supplies, provisions, messages and personnel between ship and town. As ship arrivals drastically declined in the early twentieth century these highly skilled boatmen found themselves fruitlessly cruising out towards an empty horizon. Many turned to fishing and pleasure trips for tourists. The quay punt type being a safe, comfortable boat, was to find favour with the burgeoning pleasure sailing fraternity, keeping the local shipwrights busy into the 1930s.

At the beginning of the 1850s it seemed that the worst of the social and economic problems had receded. Britain celebrated the strength and wealth generated by her home industries and overseas empire with the opening of the Great Exhibition in 1851. There was still an enormous gulf between rich and poor, but, with social reform, including advances in education, that was to be slowly filled by an emerging population of engineers, technicians, surveyors, merchants, lawyers, doctors, teachers, and so forth. All were driven by the urge to 'get on', with pride in their nation's achievements, ruled over by the popular young Queen Victoria. The increasingly affluent population meant that a greater quantity and variety of foodstuffs had to be imported; in particular a quarter of the wheat consumed in the country was shipped from North America, the Mediterranean, and Black Sea ports. The trade from the latter area received a severe knock in 1854 when the British government declared war on Russia because of its invasion of Turkey and destruction of its Black Sea fleet. There followed the two-year horror of the Crimean War, before the Russian city of Sebastopol fell to the allies. A peace settlement was finally signed in Paris on 30 March 1856.

Celebrations had followed the fall of Sebastopol when the mail coach brought the news to Falmouth in mid-September, 1855. Crowds gathered in the evening as rows of tar barrels were lit around the town and across the harbour at Flushing. There was a firework display and a tremendous bonfire on the Moor, and the militia paraded with its drum and fife band. Later a large effigy of the Russian emperor, decorated with all his orders, was processed to the quay and consigned to a bonfire. The previous day a large explosion in the harbour was a precursor of the celebratory fireworks, but happened in more unfortunate circumstances. The Master of a Spanish barque, obviously satisfied with the service he had received, thought to fire a complimentary salute to the town as he was departing for Bristol. Unfortunately the six-pound gun was apparently 50 years old and completely honeycombed with salt and rust. The charge burst it into fragments, causing damage to deck, roundhouse and mizzen mast. Most of the crew, the Master, and the pilots taking the vessel out, escaped injury. One unfortunate seaman received a severe thigh wound, and was taken to the Sailor's Home where he was operated on by two local surgeons.

Meanwhile the pilots carried on with their other hazardous offshore duties, and were often in the right place, and with the right expertise, to occasionally earn an extra bonus. On the night of 4 October, two weeks after the Sebastopol celebrations, two vessels collided to the south of Falmouth. The 98 ton schooner *Rambler*, sailing from London to Liverpool, lost her bowsprit and had serious bow damage; the barque *Cygnet*, from London to Cardiff, received damage to a bowsprit spar and the hull. The crew of the schooner, probably thinking she was going down, got on board the barque, which then limped into Falmouth. However, the schooner did not sink, and her crew were later taken out by pilot cutter no. 7, *Victoria*, to the derelict, which was drifting 14 miles off the port. With the help of Elias Chard and his crew, the schooner was safely brought into port for repairs. Chard claimed for his services, and was subsequently awarded the handsome sum of £80 by the magistrates, his crew no doubt receiving a share. After many similar previous incidents Admiralty regulations for the compulsory use of navigation lights on vessels at night came into force two years later.

Wheat had already been arriving from the Mediterranean and even from Russian ports, but noticeably on Greek ships, therefore possibly avoiding an embargo. However, in July 1856, the local papers announced that upwards of 50 wheat laden vessels had arrived from Odessa and elsewhere (probably mainly for orders), the majority being English, the first since the war. A large number were expected, and duly arrived in November, from the Black Sea, the Sea of Azoff, and the Mediterranean. This was only the tip of the iceberg of the ships calling for orders: the following January it was reported that the Custom House transient book had recorded the number of such vessels during 1856 as 1,569. Two years earlier the local Sub Commissioners of Pilotage had already recommended to Trinity House that two extra pilots should be licensed 'to meet the growing needs of the Port'.

Another salvage claim was made in 1857, this time by the pilots of the cutter *Alarm*. On the morning of 1 July they boarded the 303 ton Austrian barque *Giovanni*, which was in distress off the Lizard; the weather was hazy, with an onshore wind. The ship, which was bound from Cardiff to Venice with a cargo of railway iron, probably rails, was leaking, with four feet of water in the hold. The pilots, judging that she was in a dangerous state, sought assistance from men on shore, bringing them back to assist on the pumps and eventually brought her into Falmouth. The following December their salvage claim was brought before the Admiralty Court: in spite of objections from the owners that the ship had not been in danger the judge awarded the pilot James James and his crew the princely sum of £150 and costs. The sum was very acceptable considering that James and his shareholders had invested in a new cutter that same year. A similar amount was awarded by an Admiralty Court in April 1859 for a salvage claim by the crew of pilot cutter No. 13, *Wasp*. It concerned the 1404 ton American ship *Weymouth*, which the previous November was sailing off the west coast of Africa with a cargo of rice from Akyab, Burma, bound for Falmouth for orders. South of the Azores she ran into severe storms, losing sails and rudder, and having to jettison part of the cargo. Several thousand tons of wet swollen rice could almost certainly burst her apart. More bad weather followed as she battled northwards, finally to approach Falmouth in the second week of December. A report of the incident appeared in the *Falmouth Packet* on Christmas Day.

'The American ship 'Weymouth', 1404 tons, from Akyab, with a cargo of rice, whose arrival we announced last week, was boarded about 10 miles S.S.W. the Lizard, by Mr J. Lowry, jun., pilot-cutter 'Wasp', No.13, wind blowing strong from S.S.E., and a heavy sea at the time. On approaching the ship, the pilot saw that she had all her after canvas stowed, and cross jack yard topped, which convinced him that she was disabled. On hailing the vessel he was informed that they were bound to Falmouth for orders, from Akyab, having lost sails and rudder on the 11th of November, in lat. 31.O N., long 27.0 W., and on the 8th December she met with a succession of bad weather, and was necessitated to throw part of her cargo overboard. The pilot, after much risk and exertion, succeeded in getting a hawser on board the 'Weymouth', which enabled him to steer the vessel with the cutter for some time, when it parted; after great difficulty and danger to the cutter he again succeeded in getting a stream hawser on board, and eventually brought her in safely to Carrick roads to the satisfaction of the commander.'

A remarkable early view from the town of the coasting fleet setting sail, probably after being held in the harbour by adverse winds. (RCPS)

According to figures published in the *Falmouth Packet* in June 1858, the number of vessels visiting Falmouth had increased more or less steadily since 1850. (Few official figures are available prior to that date.) In that year there were 787 English and 752 foreign arrivals, totalling 1519. In 1857 there were 884 English and 1,188 foreign totalling 2,072. The given figures for the total registered tonnage of vessels also indicate a general rise in their size, which averaged 120 tons each in 1850 to 282 tons in 1857. The surprising statistic is that in this decade, compared to British shipping dominance in later years, foreign arrivals exceeded those of British-owned vessels. However, the figures do not include the many smaller English coastal vessels, which did not require official pilotage to enter the port and therefore were not recorded.

Falmouth had been famous as the base for the Post Office packet vessels; however, the last of the West Indian and South American vessels were withdrawn from here in 1850. The packets had generated much trade for shipwrights, provision merchants, boarding house and hotel proprietors and the like. Their presence allegedly provided employment for 2,000, and their loss threw many people out of work. However, the number of other vessels visiting the port continued to grow; the town was thriving, with new businesses providing services for a rising affluent population. The coastal trade continued, with passenger services on small steam vessels and several companies operating schooners carrying merchandise along the South Coast between here and London. A contemporary trades directory lists imports from overseas as timber (Baltic and American), guano, fruit, wines, hemp, grain, flour, dry fish and bones. The export trade was said to be inconsiderable, apart from copper, tin and lead ores, fish (pilchards), and granite. The latter cargo was exported through Falmouth from the tidal quays on the Penryn River. From the early 1800s Penryn was the principle port for the export of Cornish granite, used in the construction of bridges, docks and harbours in Britain and abroad. At peak times an average of about 10,000 tons was exported annually, representing 200 sailings for the average burthen of 50 tons for the small coasters that could reach the quays at high tide. In the 1860s it was said that there were up to 40 sailings per month.

Above left: Exchequer Quay, Penryn, c. 1910. The ketch *Penryn* was built at nearby Ponsharden in 1880 for local granite merchants Hosken & Co. To the right are the granite works and quays of Messrs. Freeman & Sons. (RCPS)

Above right: Malpas, on the Truro River, with local steam tug *Resolute* moored by the ferry crossing. Vessels such as the anchored schooners often discharged cargoes here, or waited for the tide to take them through the mud flats to Truro quays. (RCPS)

Opposite, top: Falmouth Town Quay c. 1920. Vessels moored in the basin include three motorised Penzance fishing luggers, a three-masted topsail schooner or brigantine and a smack. (RCPS)

Opposite, bottom: Unloading vessels moored on the outer arm of the Town Quay. (RCPS)

Penryn also began to be used by local merchants for the importation of live oxen from France and Spain. Some had been brought in at the height of the famine in 1847, arriving at Penzance and Falmouth. Further cargoes were brought into Penryn in the 1850s, where eventually cattle lairs were built on the wharf-side. The bulk of the imports, from Corunna in Northern Spain, lasted from the mid-1860s to the end of the century, when it is said that it was stopped to prevent the importation of cattle plague. There were also concerns about animal welfare: from 48 to up to 90 oxen would be confined in stalls in the holds of small smacks, schooners or brigantines. Over 20 vessels were involved in the trade at one time or another, owned by the Penryn companies of John Gray, Bisson and Dawe, and to a lesser degree, Mead and Mitchell. With a fair wind from Corunna voyages might take a few days, but winter storms could drive vessels miles off course, when cattle and men died, and occasionally, all were lost. However, the trade, at times of food shortages in Cornwall, was a necessary evil, apart from being lucrative: in 1870 a correspondent in a local paper stated, 'What should we do without these Spanish cattle? Beef and mutton are dear enough in all conscience already; without foreign importations we should almost be starved overnight.' Though it is unlikely that the average Cornish mining family would have seen or tasted beef anyway.

Cornish copper production was coming to a peak in the 1850s but then rapidly declined in the following decades as lodes ran out; cargoes of local ores to South Wales smelting furnaces were to be superseded by shiploads from Chile, Australia and the United States. Deeper mining for tin revived the industry for a few more decades until the collapse in the twentieth century. Meanwhile, in the 1850s the small inconspicuous coasters continued to load copper ore in Devoran, the inland port on Restronguet Creek, and slip through Falmouth Harbour on their sometimes hazardous voyages up the Bristol Channel, to return perhaps a week later with Welsh coal for the mines and domestic use. Some coal was now off-loaded into hulks in Falmouth Harbour for the bunkers of the increasing number of steam-powered vessels plying the coastal routes, although sailing ships still dominated long distance commerce. Locally, timber was always needed in the mines and for building construction as local towns expanded. Barquentines and barques from the Baltic still came up the Truro River with the tide to off-load at Malpas, from where the baulks were towed up to the timber ponds below the town.

Considering that duty had been removed from many imports by this time, the local Customs officers still seem to have been remarkably busy collecting considerable revenue, albeit on relatively few items. Tea in particular, apparently already a British addiction, received a massive 33 per cent duty at this time. The reported 1856 Customs receipts from tea, wine, rum, corn, et cetera totalled, at Truro £15,478; Falmouth £13,400; Penzance £11,567; and at Fowey £3,918. Chests of tea and other goods were probably dropped off from East Indiaman when calling in to Falmouth on their way up-Channel to London. The surprisingly large consignments destined for Truro would have been transshipped directly into Fal barges for the final few miles up the Truro River. Smuggling was still rife along the coast at this time; much rum and tea must have entered the county without being seen by

a Customs official. In November 1855 the local pilots were asked to keep their eyes open for contraband goods being handled by the crews of the small boats selling merchandise among the visiting ships. However, as the pilots had to share the harbour with boatmen who might be friends, or even relatives, it is unlikely that they would wish to 'shop' anyone. With an average of 2,000 vessels arriving each year, and the numbers rising, they would not have had much time to act as detectives.

The increasing business in the port meant higher income for Falmouth pilots; but their boats were being worked harder. Some were found to be too small for harsh offshore conditions, and with limited accommodation for extra pilots required to board all arriving vessels. The Brethren of Trinity House had fixed the number of pilot boats allowed in Falmouth at 13, and no increase was allowed. The number of licenced pilots was also controlled; at this time there were about 40 pilots unevenly spread among the 13 boats, depending on the number of qualified pilots the family, and perhaps others who bought shares in the boat, had available. There were also perhaps two apprentices, each bound from the age of 14 to one or other of the pilots for seven years. They would then continue to work on the boats until a vacancy for a qualified pilot occurred, which might take years. There were also a similar number of wage-earning crew on board for general handling and maintenance, the senior man being entitled Sailing Master.

In April 1857 the keels of three larger replacement cutters were laid down at three different local shipyards. One by shipwright James Mayn at the Bar, Falmouth, for John Chard; the second by Joseph Haly, also at the Bar, for Messrs. Andrew; the third by John Trethowan, at Little Falmouth, for Messrs. James and Partners. All three were launched the following Autumn. Other craft, which were to be indispensable to the port, were the steam tugs, some of which also later doubled as passenger vessels. The first to be used was the paddler *Dandy*; she was purchased in London by Captain Handcock in March 1858, and brought down Channel in 40 hours by pilot Collins, probably a licenced Channel pilot. This *Dandy* was replaced by another of the same name within a few years. Others followed: *Lioness*, *Wotton*, *Briton*, and so on; the later ones being screw-driven rather than paddle wheel. When *Dandy* first arrived in the port she was just too late to assist in preventing the loss in the harbour of a noble ship and her valuable cargo.

Some idea of the value of vessels and their cargoes being piloted into Falmouth practically everyday, may be gathered from the example of the 1500 ton ship *Northern Empire*. She had been built at Bath, on the Gulf of Maine, U.S.A., in 1854, and by 1858 was registered at Oldenburg, Northern Germany. At the beginning of March she was piloted into Carrick Roads and put into what was normally thought to be a safe anchorage, possibly near St. Mawes Castle. There were already 150 other vessels at anchor in the roadstead. Her crew had probably been away from home for a year or so. The voyage had taken them across the Atlantic, around Cape Horn, and northwards for another 3000 miles to Callao, close to Lima, Peru. Here the ship had taken on a cargo of 2,400 tons of nitrogen-rich guano, highly-prized in Europe as a crop fertilizer. Although heavily laden, the return voyage back around

The aptly-named harbour tug *Carbon*, burning cheap coal, towing a brigantine on a windless day. The tug was built on The Bar by George Symons in 1893 for shipping agent Robert Fox of Grove Hill House, Falmouth. (RCPS)

the Horn was obviously satisfactorily accomplished. She was well-found, and Muntz yellow-metalled, that is, the hull was sheathed with copper-alloy plates to prevent weed growth in tropical waters, which otherwise would have slowed her down. So, after a voyage of about 23,000 miles she was at Falmouth, for orders, and bound for London, a mere 400 miles away.

The wind blew up in the evening; before midnight it had built up to a violent gale, roaring down Carrick Roads from the northeast. All of the vessels rode safely at anchor, apart from *Northern Empire*. Was the anchor watch asleep; did the anchors become fouled when she swung, were they not heavy enough to hold the weight of ship and cargo? She began to drag her anchors, losing purchase as she drifted across the deep water channel in the stormy night. She struck the northern edge of the notorious Black Rock outcrop in the middle of the harbour entrance. There she stuck, battered by the gale and violent sea. Even if someone in Falmouth had seen her through the blackness, no boat could have got out to her. The inevitable sequence of her break-up began: rigging gave way under force of wind, and one or more masts went overboard; rocks penetrated the weakened hull and she began to settle. Collecting ships papers and personal possessions, the Master and crew managed to launch the longboat in the lee of what was fast becoming a wreck. With difficulty they pulled for Falmouth; fortunately their direct course was not impeded at that time by the breakwaters of Falmouth Docks, to be built two years later. They all arrived safely at the Town Quay at one o'clock in the morning.

Northern Empire lay in five fathoms, her cargo of guano seeping through the split hull and open hatches, staining the waters of Falmouth Bay and enriching the sea-life with a high concentration of nitrates. Fortunately for local reputations, the enquiry found no fault with the berthing of the ship by the pilot. The given value of the ship, prior to the disaster, was £30,000, the cargo also £30,000, and other freight £12,000. (To give an idea of monetary values of this time – Falmouth's handsome Town Hall, in Killigrew Street, finished a decade later, cost £4,000.) She lay at the bottom for a fortnight, during which time an auction was held. Ship and contents were eventually knocked down to Mr. Symons, the local shipwright, for £1,200; could he salvage her and turn a handsome profit? Barely had he begun to make plans for the massive task ahead when another gale swept across from the east. *Northern Empire*, and Symons' investment, went to pieces. Hopefully he may have recovered some freight and timber as it drifted as a hazard to shipping around the harbour.

A lithograph by Newman & Co. of the new Falmouth docks and railway station, c. 1865. (Falmouth Art Gallery)

The docks and railway station in 1900. The stippled area of shallows and ponds to the left is The Bar. There were tide-driven corn mills and shipyards here for several centuries.

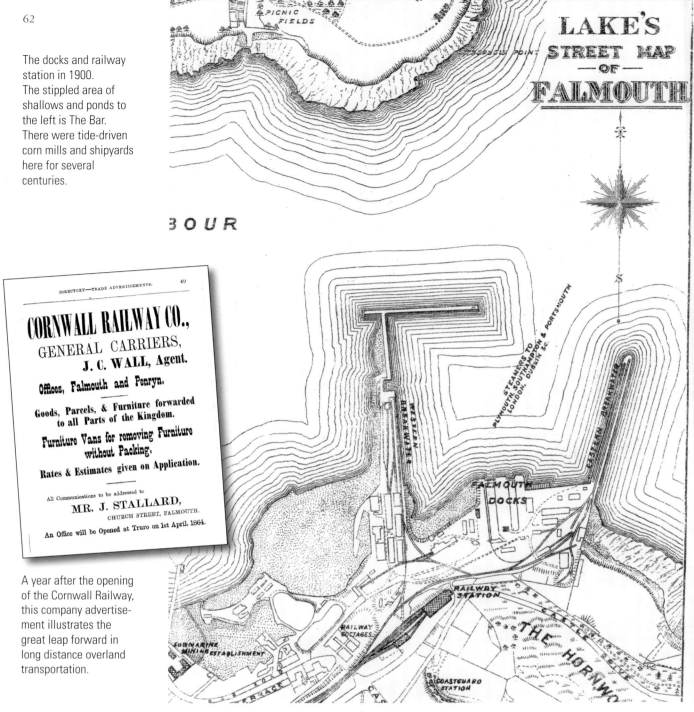

LAKE'S
STREET MAP
— OF —
FALMOUTH

DIRECTORY—TRADE ADVERTISEMENTS. 49

CORNWALL RAILWAY CO.,
GENERAL CARRIERS,
J. C. WALL, Agent.

Offices, Falmouth and Penryn.

Goods, Parcels, & Furniture forwarded to all Parts of the Kingdom.

Furniture Vans for removing Furniture without Packing.

Rates & Estimates given on Application.

All Communications to be addressed to
MR. J. STALLARD,
CHURCH STREET, FALMOUTH.

An Office will be Opened at Truro on 1st April, 1864.

A year after the opening of the Cornwall Railway, this company advertisement illustrates the great leap forward in long distance overland transportation.

Gyllyngvase, the coastline to the west of Pendennis, in about 1870; it has since been covered in suburban development. The first encroachment here was the Falmouth Hotel, some of its shareholders being the same gentlemen who promoted the building of the docks and railway. (RCPS)

The Industrial Revolution continued its relentless progress, more cottage industries giving way to the factory system. Burning coal turned iron ore to metal to make steam engines; they in turn burnt more coal to drive machines to make all things now essential for human existence. Astronomic profits were made by captains of industry and the business world on the backs of the majority of the population working in mines, foundries and factories. Much iron production went to the making of rails and engines for the expanding railway system in Britain and abroad. Heavy industrial materials, previously moved by slow canal barge, in many cases could now be transported faster and more cheaply by rail to and from manufacturing centres and ports. In 1859, Brunel's great Royal Albert Bridge at Saltash brought the railway across the Tamar into Cornwall, where

The fabulous docks company steam bucket dredger *Briton*, used to dig approach channels to the new wharfs and dry docks. Later used by the Harbour Commissioners to remove shoals for ship anchorages in Carrick Roads. (Cornwall Centre)

work on the route to Truro and Penzance had begun a decade earlier. The branch line from Truro to Falmouth Docks was opened in 1863. The construction of the docks had begun in 1860 with the building of a sea-ward breakwater, extending out into the natural harbour from the northern side of Pendennis headland. Wharves and two graving docks quickly followed, and were soon busy with imports and ship repairs.

Shipping communications were being improved by the laying of telegraph cables over land and under the seas, no doubt using a huge amount of Cornish copper in the process. A cross-Channel cable linked England to France in 1851, and another from Holyhead to Ireland in 1854. A trans-Atlantic cable was successfully laid in 1866. Meanwhile, a telegraph office was opened near the Town Quay in Falmouth in 1857, linking the port to London via an office at the new railway station in Truro; later the line was extended to Penzance. In 1872, after pressure from local shipping agents, the Post Office laid a cable from Falmouth to Bass Point on the Lizard. Vessels proceeding up the English Channel could now be reported to agents in Falmouth, from where messages from owners or Lloyds of London could be collected, either by anchoring in the harbour to wait for instructions, or by heaving to off the port and having the orders brought out by a clerk rowed out in a gig or by a pilot who had already received them from the agent.

The pilots could never be certain what the next job might entail: of what type, size and condition was the vessel that might be sighted on the horizon or appear out of the blackness of the night. And what would be the competency of the crew? On one night early in April 1861 the cutter *Alarm*, cruising off the Lizard, came upon a French sloop. She appeared to be abandoned as there was no one on deck or at the wheel. On boarding, the pilots found three Frenchmen asleep down below. On being woken they said their vessel, the *Charles et Emile*, was taking clay from Boulogne to L'Orient: they had gone below leaving the Master alone on deck and had no idea where he was. The obvious conclusion was that the Master had fallen overboard somewhere in the Channel; the sloop had sailed on westwards by herself, to be miles off course, and heading either for the rocks of Cornwall, the Isles of Scilly, or the open Atlantic. One of the pilots brought the sloop into Falmouth the following afternoon, where the crew were doubtless closely examined by the French consul.

At the end of January that year the American ship *Nonpareil* had arrived at the port for orders. Because of adverse weather she had been on passage from San Francisco for three months, laden with a valuable cargo of over 1,000 tons of wheat. But it was to be one of the last of such cargoes for some time, for within months the American Civil War began. The bitter struggle lasted for over four years, and its effects were far-reaching; such as, that apart from grain, raw cotton exports from the Southern States to Britain also ceased. Therefore one of this country's main manufacturing industries ground to a halt, and thousands of Lancashire mill workers were thrown out of work. Otherwise British industry continued to flourish, and wheat was available from Europe. During the same week of the arrival of *Nonpareil* 80 vessels arrived in two days from other foreign ports, principally grain laden. It was also reported that nearly 100 Austrian vessels were in the offing bound for Falmouth. Fleets such as these boosted the figures of vessels recorded at the Custom House over the year to 2,787. The following year the increase in earnings allowed pilot Henry Tonkin and other shareholders to commission the construction of a new cutter number 6. The existing boat had been lengthened only four years earlier, but apparently was still not adequate for the work. The 67 foot long *Arrow* was launched by Falmouth shipwright John Trethowan six months after being laid down.

It seems that there was little change in the number of ships entering the port for the next few years at least: an 1865 Parliamentary Return for Cornwall gave figures of 2,394 vessels piloted inwards and 1,755 outwards (a vessel leaving an outer anchorage often didn't need piloting to the open sea). The yearly total of fees received by Falmouth pilots was £10,131. At Penzance it was £306, at Fowey £313, and at Padstow £235.

The amount of shipping entering the port each year is reflected in the number of mariners admitted to the local Royal Cornwall Sailors' Home. Since its founding in 1852 it had provided hospital facilities, rest and care for hundreds of sufferers of shipwreck, sickness and injury in what was often a dangerous profession. The Director's annual report for 1864 gave the admittance figures for the previous year, which were fairly typical: 396 British and 297 foreign; of which 128 had been rescued and 177 were sick, including 62 suffering from scurvy, dropsy and accidents.

Among the many maritime activities in which Falmouth pilots were involved, one of the more unusual was a request for them to become spies! Early in 1864, Otto von Bismark, the Minister President of Prussia, began his programme for the unification of Germany by starting a war with Denmark to annex its southern Duchies of Schleswig and Holstein. Although pro-Denmark, Britain didn't have the resources to offer support and decided to stay neutral. Therefore it was probably illegal, or at least ill-judged, for the Prussian Ministry to have the following notice placed in the *Falmouth Packet* newspaper on 13 February that year, especially as Falmouth pilots benefited from many Danish as well as German vessels arriving in the port.

> 'Falmouth Pilots and the War. The pilots of this port and outfitters whose boats board vessels outside the harbour have received an invitation that if they board Prussian vessels in the Channel, and convey the information that Danish men-of–war are cruising in the Channel a fee of £3 for each vessel will be paid for such information by the Prussian vice-Consul at Falmouth.'

Alongside all the commercial enterprises in the town, the tailoring firms were benefiting from the rapid rise in the number of long-distance ship arrivals. Showing admirable Victorian enterprise, several began to compete to obtain custom by sailing out to tout for business among incoming vessels. If invited on board they would sell new shore-going clothes and shoes to sailors who had possibly lived in their existing salt-stained apparel for many months, and were not too concerned with the 'off the peg' fit of the suit provided. The lucrative trade had allowed the outfitters to commission the building of their own boats. These were as big and powerful as the pilot cutters, and would sail far out into the Channel, carrying a floating shop-load of garments. The boats were handled by professional skippers and crew, and carried a tailor, or his assistants, and possibly an apprentice or two, depending on who was most able to cope with sea-sickness! At this time there were three boats in the fleet: *Sally* was owned by H. Rusden; *Maseppa*, R.J. Toms; and *Grand Turk*, Messrs. Evans and Son. In October 1865 the 63 foot cutter *Star of Hope* was launched from W.H. Lean's yard at the Bar, for J.W. Eliot. These craft were just as vulnerable as any other to the perils of the sea. During August three years later, *Star of Hope* had been out for two days and was at anchor

An early view from Flushing, showing the extent of the new dock breakwaters across the harbour entrance. (RCPS)

A small part of the Southwest fishing fleet at the Town Quay, c. 1930. (Cornwall Centre)

Above left: Penzance fishing luggers setting sail off Fish Strand Quay. Craft in the background are Falmouth quay punts. (Cornwall Centre)

Above right: Prior to the building of No.4 dry dock in the 1920s the beach within the shelter of the break-waters was used to land the fish catch. It could be taken to the docks railway station within minutes. (RCPS)

on a Friday night off the Lizard, when an unexpected gale arrived. They slipped the anchor and made for Falmouth, eventually arriving at 8 am on Saturday, not before Captain S. Hughes had been washed overboard and lost in the dark. The captain's son was also aboard. The *Sally* was lost in December 1872 after a collision with pilot cutter *Vincent* off the Manacles; fortunately there was no loss of life on this occasion. Several other boats were built for outfitters in the seventies, including *Gwendolyn*, by George Symons for R.J. Toms. This proved to be a poor long-term investment, as ship arrival numbers were later to rapidly decline and she was sold off. After some years at Dartmouth, in 1906 *Gwendolyn* was to have a new lease of life as a Falmouth pilot cutter.

By now the railway network had connected many coastal towns with the expanding industrial and commercial centres of population, and where consequently there was an increasing demand for food. Prior to the building of the railways nutritional sea fish, apart from those salted or dried, were not often part of the diet for those living far inland; fresh fish did not stay fresh for very long and overland transportation was slow. Now it was possible to send freshly caught fish straight from the boat to the railway wagon, to arrive on the fishmonger's slab in say Birmingham, Manchester or London within twelve hours or so. The sea fishermen suddenly found that there was an unlimited demand for their catch, leading to a frenzy of new boat-building around the coast. The vast herring shoals of the North Sea proved to be a magnet for fishermen, and many moved to the East Coast; big fishing smacks were ordered from shipyards as far away as Cornwall, including 13 from the Fal.

In Cornwall itself, the summer shoals of pilchards had been a vital part of the diet for centuries, and were exported in their millions as far away as Naples. Now the fishermen increasingly turned their attention to other off-shore species. It is said that up to 400 new luggers were built within a few years, in the small coves and harbours of the West Country. The fishing grounds extended far out into the Western Approaches and to Ireland, catches being landed at places such as Padstow, St. Ives, Penzance and Falmouth. At the latter two harbours it took only a few minutes for the fish to be carted to the railway station for transportation to London. Farmers and market gardeners also profited by now being able to send fresh fruit and vegetables quickly to Covent Garden. The Scilly islanders, who had often lived at near starvation levels, had a new lease of life by creating a patchwork of small enclosed fields, within which they cultivated early spring flowers and vegetables. These were shipped to Penzance and thence to London by train.

While some managed to earn a living at this time, copper mining in Cornwall was soon to reach crisis point. Many mines were beginning to be worked out, although in some areas deeper lodes of tin could be reached with improved pumping. There was also to be general depression in all manufacturing industries, and demand for raw materials was to fall. Thousands of miners and their families were to seek a new life overseas. Some of those that couldn't work or emigrate, perhaps because of age or infirmity, received some support from charitable donations, which went towards running soup kitchens in the towns. Bread and coal was also handed out during wintertime, the Guardians of the Poor Law Union administering relief to 200 persons in Penryn and 400 in Falmouth. The winter of 1867 was to be particularly severe.

At the beginning of January temperatures plummeted to minus eight degrees Centigrade; a violent gale from the south-east battered the South Coast, dumping six to nine inches of snow across Cornwall. For mariners in sailing vessels trying to make their way eastwards up the English Channel, an easterly gale came from the worst possible direction. One option was to turn and run back before the wind, perhaps for a hundred miles, until the gale hopefully abated. Another was to run into Plymouth or Falmouth, to an uncertain anchorage, hoping to see the entrance in poor visibility, and perhaps with damaged sails and rigging which affected steering. A third, and perhaps the only option in some circumstances, was to run in to find shelter behind a headland, such as in Mounts Bay, and hope that the anchors would hold.

The first January gale raged for a night and a day (from Friday 4th); most vessels in Falmouth Harbour rode safely at anchor, apart from a few near the seaward entrance, where some of the huge timbers forming the new docks breakwater were ripped out. A number of vessels later had to require the dock facilities, which had been partly created for such eventualities. These vessels included a ship laden with Peruvian guano, a barque from Bahia, Brazil, and a Spanish brig with sugar. A schooner laden with china clay, which perhaps had been brought by train and loaded at the docks, went onto the rocks at Trefusis Point, where she was deliberately scuttled to prevent further damage. Later she was successfully raised. Other vessels were swept ashore in St. Mawes Creek.

A Swedish brigantine, the *Carola*, carrying coffee from Rio de Janeiro, had left Falmouth for Hamburg two days previously, but had been driven back by the gale and had again made for Falmouth. In poor visibility and approaching darkness the crew found that they had missed the harbour entrance and were being driven onto a lee shore and into the clutches of Falmouth Bay. On endeavouring to put about, the few remaining foresails were blown out, making the vessel unmanageable. The cook was swept overboard and drowned, and the captain and mate narrowly escaped a similar fate. Shortly afterwards the brigantine went on the rocks between Gyllyngvase and Swanpool beaches. Two men managed to scramble ashore and found their way across fields in the dark to the town, and to the offices of Messrs. Fox & Co., the agents. Help was summoned and the remaining crew safely landed. The next day the wreck was visited by hundreds of people, and hands were busily engaged in landing the cargo. The report doesn't say if the coffee was still useable, or if it all legitimately reached the warehouse. The wreck and stores were auctioned the following week. Meanwhile there were similar dramas in Mount's Bay.

Two months later, Falmouth's reputation as a safe haven was again severely dented when another south-easterly gale caused probably the most damage ever experienced in the port. 250 vessels were sheltering in the inner harbour and Carrick Roads. Some, at the request of their captains had been anchored by the pilots close to the harbour entrance, to enable them to leave quickly after receiving orders. It was these vessels which bore the brunt of the approaching storm. A number were to be torn from their anchorages, several being wrecked on the docks Eastern Breakwater, where eleven persons drowned. Ten were dismasted and two sunk; in some the masts were deliberately cut away to prevent the vessels from foundering. The barque *Marmion* had missed the harbour entrance when coming in during the gale and anchored in Falmouth Bay, but later went ashore at Gyllyngvase, close to where the brigantine had been wrecked two months earlier; further dramatic rescues ensued, but two crew were drowned.

The newspaper reports make distressing reading, however they do give an insight on the types of vessels and their cargoes that were passing through the port almost daily at that time. The following vessels are some of which were damaged to various degrees on that occasion. Two German brigs from Mecklenburg in the Baltic had sailed 3000 miles round the coasts of Europe, and through the Mediterranean and Black Sea to Odessa, and were returning with cargoes of wheat. Of the larger barques, also carrying wheat or barley from Odessa and other Black Sea ports, there were four English, two Norwegian, one Italian and one Austrian. An English barque was carrying cotton seed from Alexandria; a Portuguese brig was carrying palm oil from Lagos to London; an English brig carried cork from Lisbon to Exeter, and a coasting schooner had shipped coprolite at Harwich for Bridgewater.

The foregoing instances of dramatic shipwrecks emphasize the risks that had to be faced by all who went to sea in sailing vessels, especially in wintertime. The risks became less as sail gave way to steam engines, and wooden hulls were replaced by iron, and then by steel. But accidents could still happen, either through the elements, or by human or mechanical failure. Of course, many mariners in the days of sail may have been fortunate to have satisfyingly safe careers at sea. Life aboard a sailing vessel may have been hard and uncomfortable at times, but could have been worse for the average farm labourer, factory worker or miner. A diligent seaman might work his way up to be mate, and even captain his own vessel, which, if well-found, was capable of handling most storms, unless caught out close to land. There is more fine sailing weather than stormy; and nothing like the exhilaration of sailing on a good breeze, especially if blowing from the right quarter to take you to your desired harbour. With sails well-set there might be little to do but look at the sea and occasionally check the course. Nevertheless, considering the huge number sailing the oceans, it was inevitable that many merchant vessels and their crews were sacrificed in the need to carry the necessities of life between nations.

In May 1876 figures were published of the losses of British merchant vessels reported to the Board of Trade in four and a half years to June 1875. Note that the shocking figures only include consumerables such as grain, and not those carrying many other kinds of cargo, neither does it list ships from other nations lost in British waters:

Ships laden with ...	Ships lost	Lives lost
Barley, maize, oats, peas, rye or wheat	250	1006
Cocoa, coffee, rice, and other seeds	90	849
Mixed cargoes, i.e. with grain or seed part cargo	75	294
Total	415	2149

Another return was published in July 1881: ship losses of all nationalities over the previous 18 months amounted to 2,500. The monetary loss to this country alone was estimated at 150 million pounds.

From 1867 to 1872 there was a spectacular rise in the number of vessels entering Falmouth waters. The figures quoted below have been gathered from local newspaper reports and directories, and therefore perhaps not entirely reliable, however, the trend is obvious. The many coastal vessels, of 100 tons register or less, that were passing in and out of the port, were not included in the figures as they were not subject to pilotage. Only the totals for inward passages are given here.

Year	Vessels	Note
1861	2,787	Entered in Custom House
1865	2,394	Listed in Parliamentary Return
1866	2,340	For Orders only
1867	3,266	Arrived in or off the port
1868	3,726	'
1869	3,900	'
1870	3,044	'
1871	3,282	'
1872	3,945	'

In March 1868 the Sub Commissioners of Pilotage sent a letter to the Mayor requesting his assistance regarding certain permanent mooring areas in Carrick Roads, which were allocated to but rarely used by Admiralty vessels. Bad weather could bring further vessels into an already crowded harbour; a number of instances were already occurring when pilots inadvertently put vessels aground in shallow waters or anchored them too close to others, bringing a number of complaints.

'Sir, … the present crowded state of the shipping in Carrick Roads and the probability of its being increased at this usually wild season … a fitting opportunity of calling your attention to the matter with the view of your adopting if practicable such measures as may be thought expedient for increasing the present anchorage for ships … if any arrangement could be made which could secure for the Queen's ships another but equally convenient and safe place as that now occupied by the Admiralty it would be the cause of rendering available a safe and important addition to the anchorage … for merchant vessels. There is now so much difficulty experienced by the pilots in placing vessels in safety and should there be any great accession to the number of ships … it is more than probable that danger and damage to property would increase.'

Up until this time the Mayor and Customs officers were responsible for the overall administration of the harbour and its shipping. The local pilots, controlled by the Trinity House Sub Commissioners of Pilotage, were doing their best to find areas in the harbour deep enough to anchor vessels safely; harbour improvements were urgently needed. On 5 September 1870 the Mayor chaired a meeting of the Town Council, the Aldermen, Burgesses, and the premier property owner in Falmouth, the Earl of Kimberley. The object was to appoint a new board of officers, particularly those with direct interest in shipping matters, to be known as the Falmouth Harbour Commissioners. Among those appointed were shipping agents Robert Broad and Howard Fox; Falmouth ship owners chose ship builders William Henry Lean and Henry Stevens Trethowan. Byelaws were laid down, such as the collection of harbour dues of a halfpenny per ton on larger vessels. The Customs Officers agreed to collect these dues at 10 per cent commission. The many professional boatmen in the harbour, who ferried people and goods between ship and shore, or across to St. Mawes, were to be licensed and the number of passengers per boat restricted. Boat moorings were to be properly laid down and allocated. The dumping of town rubbish into the harbour was to be stopped. To facilitate such improvements a Harbour Master was appointed at £150 per annum. He was to be assisted by a deputy, boatswain, and six crew for the proposed steam powered patrol boat. The contract for the construction of this was given to Willoughby & Sons at Plymouth. This boat would be necessary for checking the anchoring of ships in Carrick Roads, and inspecting those carrying explosives or in quarantine. The *Arwenack* was delivered in October 1871. She was nearly 60 feet in length, with a screw propeller driven by a seven horse power steam engine.

The Commissioners main priority was to provide a greater area for the anchorage of vessels, that were increasing in numbers, in size, and which were therefore of deeper draught. The only way to accommodate them was to dredge away shoals and deepen the shallower edges of the Inner Harbour and the Main Carrick Roads. The objective was to aim for a minimum depth of 18 feet at low water spring tides on the main anchorage and 12 feet closer to the shore, which was adequate for coastal vessels. The first estimated costs for a major programme were prohibitive. However

The Inner Harbour, c. 1900. The steam boat in the centre is believed to be the Harbour Commissioners' launch *Arwenack*, ordered from iron founders Willoughby Brothers of Stonehouse, Plymouth in 1871. She was replaced 40 years later by a smaller vessel, built of steel by Messrs Cox & Co. (RCPS)

A busy harbour scene; the Harbour Master was responsible for ensuring that vessels were moored or anchored safely and that the approaches to the quays were kept clear. (Cornwall Centre)

an initial loan of £10,000, paid in instalments, was obtained from the Public Works Loan Commission, sufficient to begin work on the Inner Harbour. The Falmouth Docks steam dredger, known as the *Briton*, was employed, having been previously used during the construction of the docks. Six 100 ton hopper barges were also hired or borrowed, and a tug and crew contracted to tow them. Material was to be dumped close to the shore in Falmouth Bay or eastwards of St. Anthony Head, depending on weather conditions. Dredging continued for about three years, the great clanking monster of a machine eventually working up to the North Bank or shoal, being the harbour limits at the Truro Harbour boundary line from Penarrow to Messack Points. Stoppages were necessary for servicing and the replacement of buckets on the two working 'ladders'.

The Commissioners were to employ their own harbour police, who worked ashore and from rowing boats. They became quite successful in apprehending pilferers of ships' stores and equipment, deserters from visiting ships, and controlling drunken behaviour. They liaised closely with the local constabulary and magistrates court. Overall the Commissioners concerned themselves with all matters affecting the smooth operation of the port, a function which continues to the present day, at a time when there is increasing pressure to exploit Falmouth Haven commercially, and little apparent concern from business interests for the conservation of its intrinsic beauty.

A vivid picture of merchant vessels working their way along the Cornish coast towards Falmouth at this time was described by Richard Turrell McMullen in his classic book *Down Channel*. On 6 September 1867 during a voyage in his 50- foot cutter yacht *Orion*, he visited Penzance on his way back from the Isles of Scilly. He was obliged to stay moored to the East Quay for two days because of lack of wind, later complaining bitterly of the negligence of the town corporation because his yacht was covered with filth and coal dust from the quayside. On the 8th, even though the wind was blowing up to an east-northeasterly gale, he felt compelled to move out under reduced canvas to anchor in the lee of St. Michael's Mount, to windward of a fleet of vessels which had sought shelter there. The following day, after an uncomfortable night rolling in a heavy swell, and in the company of about 40 vessels, he moved in lighter but rising winds further eastwards along Mounts Bay towards an anchorage close to Mullion, and therefore protected from easterly winds by the bulk of the Lizard peninsula. The wind rising in gusts, the fleet began to shorten sail:

' All vessels in the Bay were beating up for the weather shore, between Port Leven and Mullion, under very short canvas; 1.30 a.m. anchored close to Mullion Island; from noon to 4 p.m. there was much spoondrift (spindrift/spray); 5.30 p.m. it was moderate enough to pull ashore in the boat. From the cliffs I counted sixty-four vessels at anchor, and was surprised to see how regularly they were arranged according to their ability to work off shore if the wind were to fly in. The 'Orion' was in the first line with three pilot cutters, then came sloops and yawls, and a brig-rigged steamship. Next, schooners and ketches, then brigs and barks; those in the first division were almost still on the water, the second were rolling perceptibly, the third decidedly uneasy, and the last, having no protection at all from Mullion Island, were rolling miserably. Night fine and starlight, with fresh wind off the land.

Sept. 10. – Blew hard off the land all day, with fine weather overhead. The only departure from the road was the steamship. On the other hand, the arrivals increased the fleet at anchor to over eighty sail...

...At night hoisted the boat in and prepared to leave at short notice, as the barometer was going back.

Sept.11. – The wind being moderate from E.S.E., with falling barometer, the fleet got under way and commenced working up Channel. We sailed from Mullion at 9 a.m. under very short canvas. Soon overtook the fleet, and arrived at Falmouth Harbour at 3.30 p.m., making a good but very rough passage.'

1872 was the year which saw the peak of the annual pilotage figures. *Kelly's Directory* of the following year gave the full list of vessels of all nationalities which arrived, principally for orders; and including discharging cargoes, repairs, sheltering from storm and so on. Aggregate registered tonnages were also listed, but not included here:

Nationality of Vessels	Total Number
English	1,899
German	542
Italian	352
Norwegian	218
Austrian	181
Russian	89
French	100
Dutch	112
Danish	125
Swedish	101
American	65
Spanish	92
Greek	54
Portuguese	11
Turkish	4
Grand Total	**3,945**

The Trinity pilotage for 12 months ending the 30 September amounted to £15,065 19s. 8d., above that of any other port of the United Kingdom, apart from London.

The coasting vessels of under 100 tons were not subject to pilotage and therefore not included on the above list. Without laboriously counting for a whole year the vessels listed in the weekly local newspaper ship arrivals column, the full extent of the coasting trade on the Fal could only be guessed at. Fortunately a rough estimate has been deduced from the Harbour Commissioners' minutes for 20 June 1876: it was reported that during the previous 12 months the total number of arrivals, including wind-bound ships and coasters, was 5,386. The estimated number of larger ships for the period is 2,800. Therefore the number of coasters would have been about 2,586; in other words, almost as many coasters as larger vessels.

The new Falmouth Docks were described as comprising an area of 120 acres, and consisting of a tidal harbour, graving and floating docks, with warehouses, building yards, and factories, and all other conveniences for repairing ships and taking in and discharging cargoes; the entrance was about 600 feet wide and had a depth of 20 feet at low water. A station on the Cornwall Railway was opened here in 1863; it adjoined the docks, making the transit of goods both easy and immediate. Imports at the time included Baltic and American timber, guano, fruit, wines, hemp, grain, flour, dried fish, and bones. Exports were china clay, copper ore, tin, lead ores, fish and granite. However, none could have been considered as major exports; china clay was eventually mostly shipped through Fowey, Par, and Charlestown; copper and other ore exports also rapidly declined with the collapse of Cornish mining. This seriously affected the coastal trade in ores, and although coal was still arriving from South Wales there was much less traffic at the small quays on the Upper Fal than in the 1850s. However, Falmouth was enjoying an economic boom by playing its part in Britain becoming the richest nation on earth. Industrial output was undiminished; there seemed to be no limit to the commodities that could be produced to satisfy an increasingly affluent population. Exports to the Empire saw an ample return in exotic goods and raw materials flooding into London, Bristol and Liverpool docks. With no serious conflicts around the world, trade between nations also flourished, much of it carried in ships passing through Falmouth.

By the early 1870s the value of British imports and exports had more than doubled in a decade, with a corresponding rise in mercantile shipping tonnage; a growing proportion of this being iron

A small schooner and large ketch, outward bound past Little Dennis blockhouse on Pendennis Point. (RCPS)

steamships. At this stage marine steam engines were not very efficient, being very extravagant in the use of fuel. Huge amounts of coal had to be carried in bunkers to power a merchantman across the oceans, therefore restricting the amount of cargo that could be carried in safety. It took several more decades of advances in engine technology before steamships could begin to compete successfully over long distance with the legendary American and British-built clipper sailing ships. Hull and sail design of these had improved steadily throughout the century: in the 1830s a voyage to Melbourne might take six months, whereas 30 years later one noted clipper ship took only 60 days. Generally, the voyage to or from Australia now took about three months. Steamships began to compete with sail on voyages to the east after the opening of the Suez Canal. The much shorter route via the Mediterranean was not available to sailing ships as they couldn't use the canal.

In January 1873 the Sub Commissioners of Pilotage, obviously expecting no end to the escalation of vessels to be piloted, wrote to the Brethren of Trinity House requesting to be allowed to increase the number of licenced pilots in Falmouth from 50 to 65. In February the Sub Commissioners were authorised to select ten candidates from the senior apprentices who had applied. Most of these had finished their apprenticeships ten or more years before, but had continued to work on the boats, earning a share of the income, or had been to sea on other vessels. In March Trinity House sanctioned the appointment of a further five, bringing the requested total of 65. The Masters of the existing boats were expected to find room for the new pilots, which were allocated to the various watches by the Sub Commissioners. However, boat number 12, the *Nicholas Jenking*, was quite small compared to the rest, and eventually sold off. It was replaced in 1874 by *Condor*, built for the Vincent family of St. Mawes. Accommodation for extra pilots had already been made on two of the cutters: in April 1872 John Collins received permission from Trinity House to lengthen No. 13, *Antelope*, and 6.5 feet was soon added. A month later, permission was also given to lengthen No. 5, *Alarm*, this time by nearly 13 feet. Presumably the work was done at Trethowan's shipyard at Little Falmouth where both boats had been built.

Below left: The heavily laden Plymouth-built sailing barge *Sweet May*. As trade declined on the River Tamar she was one of a number that were moved to the Falmouth area for general trading and road-stone carrying from quarries on the Lizard coast. (RCPS)

Below right: Typical small coasting vessels, seen at Padstow towards the end of the days of working sail. A Ramsgate ketch and a Falmouth registered sloop barge, *William & Emma*, lie in the inner harbour.

CHAPTER 4

THE HAZARDOUS COAST

IN 1874 THERE was little change from previous years in the number of arrivals of foreign registered vessels, apart from a rise in those from France and Germany. However, there was an ominous considerable drop of 450 recorded for English vessels, possibly indicating a general rise in foreign-owned vessels taking trade away. Other nations were not standing still: American and European, particularly German, industrial output was rising faster than British. They were now producing their own raw materials and finished goods rather than needing so much from Britain and her colonies. The initial railway boom in Britain and elsewhere was also coming to an end, causing a steep drop in the production and export of steel for engines, wagons and rails. Britain was still producing the best ships: iron hulls were to be replaced by those built of steel, and were becoming larger, with more powerful engines. They were also safer, partly due to the efforts of Samuel Plimsoll. He had campaigned for years for the introduction of limits on the maximum amount of cargo ships could carry, to prevent them from being dangerously overladen, the cause of many tragedies. The limiting load line, or 'Plimsoll Line', painted on ships' sides, was eventually introduced by Act of Parliament in 1876. Even so, for years there was still an appalling loss of life at sea. Following earlier reports, in September 1880 the Board of Trade published the figures of British losses from January 1, 1873 to May 16, 1880: 1,965 ships sunk; lives lost, 10,827.

As ships became bigger and faster, far fewer were needed to carry the same amount of merchandise across the oceans as previously. This, and the general slump in trade after the boom years up to 1872, were to be factors in the decline in the number of ships arriving in Falmouth. In 1878 a

The Manacle Bell Buoy, c. 1900. (Helston Museum)

The *Herzogin Cecilie*, built at Bremerhaven in 1902; a four-masted barque arriving in Falmouth Bay for orders. Between 1903 and 1935 she was here on 16 occasions, 12 being with grain from Australia (the 'grain races') and 4 with nitrates from Chile. (RCPS)

Three great clipper ships and a merchant steamer grace the waters of Carrick Roads, c. 1900. (RCPS)

Below: A *Falmouth Packet* shipping report of 20 September 1902. These were published regularly at this time, made possible by the advances in world-wide telegraph communications. In this example the vessels were mainly carrying wheat from the eastern seaboard of the United States and nitrates (guano) from Chile, calling at Falmouth or Queenstown for orders.

Falmouth Dock Company report stated that profits were the lowest for five years. There had been a falling off in trade at the wharves, warehouses and graving docks because of the current general depression in trade, and partly because the Black Sea imports had been interrupted due to the further war between Russia and Turkey. There were also fewer American grain ships calling at Falmouth for orders: many, perhaps bound for Dublin, Bristol or Liverpool, were receiving orders at Queenstown (now Cobh), Cork, in Southern Ireland, which was on a more direct route to those ports. Following disastrous harvests in Britain and Europe in 1879, American grain was to be needed more than ever.

The Falmouth shipping figures for 1882 confirm the general downward trend; the number of foreign vessels were much the same as ten years before, apart from a decline in German, French, Dutch, Spanish and American vessels. The only increase was in Norwegian vessels, probably indicating timber imports. Again, the largest decrease was of English vessels, which fell another 400 or so, to 1,079 out of a total of 2,454. During this last quarter of the century the trend to larger and fewer ships can be seen in the annual average registered tonnage of arrivals in Falmouth. In 1872 the figure was 410 tons per vessel, representing 76 arrivals per week. By 1890 the average vessel was registered at 646 tons, and the arrivals per week had fallen to 29. By 1900 the tonnage was 1,100 per vessel, representing 15 per week. The familiar trend continued up to and beyond the First World War; in 1913 the vessels averaged 1,500 tons, and a mere 10 per week. No further statistics are necessary to explain the drastic reduction in the number of pilots and their boats which occurred over the same period.

By the early 1900s, Falmouth shipping agents' records show that about ten per cent of vessels entering Falmouth waters were powered by steam engines. The increasing number of fast steamers on the high seas was beginning to cause problems to the usually slower and less manoeuvrable sailing vessels, especially at night. Even though all vessels were supposed to be equipped with regulation navigation lights, in poor visibility, and perhaps with an inattentive lookout, collisions could occur. The wooden-built vessel was usually no match for the iron or steel bows of a steamer, but with a tradition of centuries of sailing skills behind him, the working sailorman looked upon the dirty and smelly coal-fired steamers with the same disdain as the modern sailor might treat motorboat drivers.

Local pilots also, must have disliked the advent of steamers; new skills had to be learned to enable them to bring the mechanical monsters into port. At sea, their speed, and potential lack of understanding by helmsmen that sailing vessels were governed by wind strength and direction, inevitably led to accidents. At the end of June, 1882, while on guard at night about four miles to the southwest of the port, the pilot cutter *Vie* was run down and sunk by a steamer. This was the 915 ton *Rossini*, which was carrying a cargo of barley from Odessa and approaching Falmouth for orders. Fortunately the five pilots and crew aboard were all saved. This came at a time when the local pilotage service was trying to cut expenses, and therefore *Vie* was never replaced. The pilots were distributed to other boats. In May 1886 the large cutter, *Ida*, built locally at the Bar by Charles Burt, and owned by outfitter James Hicks, of Church Street, Falmouth, was sunk by a steamer, the *Martello*, of Hull, when cruising for custom off the Lizard. Fortunately, the four crew were saved. Some years later, in April 1905, one of the last of the sailing cutters, the *Antelope,* was also sunk by a steamer.

Homeward Bound Vessels
For Falmouth or Queenstown.

Name.	From.	Date of Leaving
Albyn	San Francisco	August 18
Bermuda	San Francisco	May 16
Brenn	San Francisco	August 31
Biarritz	San Francisco	August 19
Cardiganshire	San Francisco	July 15
Ocruna	San Francisco	July 15
Crocodile	San Francisco	June 23
Crown of Germany	San Francisco	Sept. 2
Francois	San Francisco	June 1
Helga	San Francisco	Sept. 3
Jane Gallon	San Francisco	August 16
Kynance	San Francisco	August 17
Killoran	San Francisco	July 26
Leicester Castle	San Francisco	August 23
Margrerite Miraband	San Francisco	June 7
Oliver de Olsson	San Francisco	June 19
Paul Isenberg	San Francisco	Sept. 6
Professor Koch	San Francisco	August 16
Procyon	San Francisco	Sept. 8
Rodenbek	San Francisco	June 29
Sainte Anne	San Francisco	July 24
Strossa	San Francisco	April 25
Inveroiyde	San Francisco	May 4
Inveresk	San Francisco	June 10
Jacques	San Francisco	May 18
La Perouse	San Francisco	May 28
Lydgate	San Francisco	April 29
Mylomene	San Francisco	July 9
Queen Victoria	San Francisco	June 1
St. Rogntien	San Francisco	May 19
Windsor Park	Iquique	August 21
Aldebaron	Iquique	July 7
Bablin Chevaye	Iquique	August 22
Oarioca	Iquique	Sept. 11
Dalrymple	Iquique	August 6
Dorade	Iquique	Sept. 4
Lauriston	Iquique	Sept. 6
Port Patrick	Iquique	May 23
Vincent	Pisagua	May 13
Sierra Lucena	Pisagua	June 8
Lyston	Pisagua	August 28
Falls of Dee	Pisagua	August 30
Samoa	Tocopilla	July 4
Indian Empire	Pisagua	August 9
B. Hackman	Tacoma	July 4
Pacifique	Tacoma	June 16
Braemar	Tacoma	June 12
County of Caithness	Tacoma	May 25
Dons Law	Tacoma	June 10
Ladakh	Tacoma	May 12
Peter Iredale	Tacoma	July 9
Sokoto	Tacoma	May 8
Whittleburn	Portland, O	May 17
Fingal	Portland, O	July 10
Jacobeen	Portland, O	June 4
Lord Shaftesbury	Astoria	May 31
Nomia	Astoria	July 23
Asie	Astoria	May 1
Brunel	Caleta Buena	August 9
Wynford	Caleta Buena	April 22
Alioe	Caleta Buena	July 18
Meridian	Caleta Buena	July 1
Saxon	Monte Video	July 16
Ochtertyre	Monte Video	August 11
Lazzarito	Rio Grande	August 7
Uniti	Rio Grande	July 4
Anje Berg	Rio Grande	June 28
Solstreif	Punta Arenas	August 5
Voorwaarts	Punta Arenas	July 19
Clara	Punta Arenas	August 8
Hercules	Tchio	May 29
Viduco	Tchio	June 5
Dieppedalle	Junin	July 21
Hautot	Auckland	August 2
Firth of Strossa	Rangoon	May 17
Signe	Port Blakely	May 1
Jolani	San Juan del Sur	May 9
Keirerdale	Corinto	April 16
Vidylia	Seattle	April 24
Vega	Bunbury	May 9
Les Adelphes	Albany	July 19
Cavan	Kaipara	June 17
Atlantia	New Caledonia	August 10
Mentor	Laguna	July 31
Milton Park	Laguna	July 15
Else	Laguna	August 9
Merle	Laguna	August 18
Habil	Fremantle	August 13
Mary Isabel	Savannah	August 23
Senator Versmann	Guanape	August 15
Anstad		August 6
Lucknow		

The Week's Arrivals and Sailings.

SATURDAY.—Arrived—Niobe, bk., from Freemantle, with jarrah wood; Rockhurst, bk., from Portland, O., with wheat, and received orders off port for Tyne Dock; Tacora, 4 m. sch., from Iquique, with nitrate. Sailed—Marion Lightbody, for Bristol, in tow of tug Penguin; Framnas, for Havre; Ernest Legouve, for Cardiff, in tow of tug Triton.

SUNDAY.—Arrived—Rosa, from Laguna, with logwood; Senior, from Adelaide, with wheat, and received orders off port for Leith; Ivaar Aasen, from Bunbury, with jarrah wood.

MONDAY.—Nil.

TUESDAY.—Sailed—Rosa, for London; Niols, for London.

WEDNESDAY.—Sailed—St. Aubin, for London.

By 1886, in spite of diminishing pilotage fees, the 65 pilots, plus apprentices and crews, continued to share watches around the clock on the 12 boats. Now, more than ever, they were eager to supplement their income with whatever bonuses the sea may have fortuitously brought them. The following report, published in the *Falmouth Packet* on 3 April, illustrates the efforts of the pilots of cutter no. 1, *Harriet*. In this case they not only saved lives but, with an unparalleled experience in ship handling, obviously looked towards making a lucrative salvage claim. Unfortunately this time their efforts came to nought.

'Shipwrecked Crew. – Pilot cutter No. 1, of this port, on Tuesday afternoon landed Captain Reneze and crew, six in number, of the French brigantine *Pekela*, 100 tons register, from Arcachon (France) with a cargo of pitwood for Cardiff. The *Pekela* left Arcachon on the 22nd March, experiencing rough weather soon after leaving, which caused her to spring a leak. On Tuesday she was fallen in with, about twenty miles S.S.W. of the Manacles by the pilot cutter. The crew immediately left the vessel in their own boat, taking their effects with them, and proceeded towards the cutter, succeeding in reaching her only after incurring great risk of their lives. Having safely got on board, the crew were interrogated as to the state of their ship, and, in reply, stated that she was half full of water. The vessel not presenting any immediate signs of sinking, a portion of the crew of the pilot cutter, taking into consideration the nature of her cargo, went on board – thinking there might still be a chance of saving the ship and cargo, set sail and bore up for Falmouth, the wind being from the south-west, with a strong breeze, and heavy sea running. Rapid progress was made towards the port, when, after being on board for two hours, and having run a distance of ten miles, it was perceived that she was fast settling down, so it was deemed advisable to leave her. This was not decided on a moment too soon, for the men had but just got into their boat when the vessel was struck by a heavy sea and capsized. The crew on landing were taken in charge by Mons. Emile Thomas, the French Consul.'

The following December the crew of cutter No. 5, *Alarm*, provided a further humanitarian service when they picked up the crew of the schooner *Mary Capper* off the Lizard. That vessel had been carrying a cargo of granite from Penryn, and was bound for Belfast, when it was in collision at night with a Dutch brigantine arriving from Venezuela with timber. Both vessels received severe damage, the schooner sinking in about 20 minutes. After rescuing the crew of five, the pilot boat escorted the disabled Dutch vessel into Falmouth.

The total number of arrivals for this year was to be 1,530, not much more than half the 1872 peak. A docks management report in February deplored the state of the freight markets, which had fallen to the extent that six big 'floating warehouses', ships laden with cargoes such as timber, sugar, and palm oil, were laid up on the River Fal. Three outfitters' cutters and two harbour tugs were also to be laid up. The enforced delay of the voyage of one of the larger vessels that earlier in the year had received orders to lay up in the Fal, were eventually to lead to its demise. The full-rigged iron-built ship *Port Chalmers*, of 1,568 tons register, had been built at Greenock only two years previously, when early in 1886 she entered Falmouth for orders. Her cargo was 2,500 tons of sugar, loaded at Semarang, Java. Owing to the generally depressed state of trade, and the price of sugar so low, the owners decided to discharge their crew and to lay her up on the Fal to wait for an improvement in the market. The captain and his wife, the first and second mate, the cook, and two other hands also remained. In March orders were received to proceed to Liverpool; therefore the captain engaged the services of a dozen 'runners' to help sail the ship up the west coast to her destination. On a Saturday morning a tug towed her out of the harbour where, and without a pilot, she presumably set sail westwards towards the Lands End. However, it was not until 20.30 hours, well after dark, and only a few miles from Falmouth, that the heavily laden ship ran straight onto the Manacle Rocks and began to take on water. The ship's complement took to one of the boats, staying beside their sinking ship until discovered by the Falmouth tug *Triton*.

From 1887 the newly-formed Falmouth District Pilot Boat Association (see Chapter 5), sought to improve the welfare and income of the pilots, including trying to prise higher superannuation benefits from Trinity House; however there was nothing they could do to bring more traffic into the port. With the majority of merchantmen still sail-powered, the winds played an important role in what could be seen at anchor in Carrick Roads. In April that year the local newspaper reported that owing to the prevalence of easterly winds the harbour presented a comparatively deserted appearance: very few vessels had arrived, and tradesmen whose business was concerned with shipping had suffered in consequence. From time to time a few cargoes were discharged at the docks, includ-

The old and the new in Carrick Roads: Fal sailing barges cluster alongside an anchored steel-hulled merchant-man for transhipment of cargo. (RCPS)

The steam coaster *Erimus*, built of iron at Middlesborough in 1870. By 1889 she was Falmouth registered and owned for ten years by William Lidgley of Devoran on Restronguet Creek. The next and last owner was William Bryant of Truro. (RCPS)

ing Peruvian guano. In January G.C.Fox & Co. advertised that a consignment had arrived in a Norwegian barque, giving, for the more scientifically-minded farmer, the chemical content – 10% ammonia, 18% phosphate. In March the Glasgow steamer *Tuskar* discharged 3,600 tons into the warehouse of the Anglo-Continental Company. A few steamers and schooners still delivered coal from South Wales; the well-known local schooner *Lady of Avenal* being one of several that arrived in March. That these instances were reported emphasises the paucity of such trade at the time.

In May 1887 the weather took a turn for the better; westerly winds brought in a splendid fleet for orders, occasioning much employment for pilots, tug crews and watermen. By this time, if winds were light, some of the bigger harbour tugs were capable of towing sailing vessels further up the English Channel to their ports of discharge. Time was money spent: in the face of stiff competition the quicker a cargo could be brought to market, the sooner a profit could be made. The harbour again went quiet for some time, until in July the local newspaper reported that 88 vessels had arrived in one week. A similar report appeared in August: 69 in a week, with a total registered tonnage of 48,741. This represents an average of about 650 tons per vessel. There were to be similar week to week fluctuations in vessel numbers, but over the next few years the overall annual totals of arrivals stayed at about 1,500. The rapid increase in the size of vessels is illustrated in that the total annual tonnage figure was now about one million tons. In February 1888 Falmouth had a foretaste of things to come, when the steamship *Borderer* was towed in, having lost her propeller. She was the largest Falmouth had yet seen, 3,400 tons, and 450 feet in length. Fortunately the dock company had had the foresight to build a dry dock to accommodate such vessels, and G.C.Cox & Co. had the expertise to repair her.

Kelly's Directory of this time gives an impressive list of commodities moving through the port, although much of this trade was still conducted by small vessels in and out of Penryn, Truro and Restronguet Creek, rather than the main docks. Imports were said to be Baltic and American timber, guano, grain, cattle, coal, nitrates, artificial manures, bones, phosphates, bricks, slates etc. Exports were china clay, copper ore, tin, granite, hemp and wire rope, pilchards, paper, arsenic, ochre, and firebricks. Much of the trade was being carried coastwise as well as to foreign parts. Apart from the sailed pilot cutters, now reduced to seven, there were said to be 25 steamers operating in the port, no doubt occasionally shattering the peace of the town with the shriek of their steam whistles. They consisted of tugs, passenger vessels (for the increasing tourist trade), the boarding launches of shipping agents, chandlers and victuallers, the Harbour Master's launch, and steam trawlers. The amount received by the Falmouth pilotage service in 1888 amounted to £7,464. 15s. 7d.; this was the highest in the country apart from the Port of London, but only half that of 1872.

In 1891 there occurred an incident which proved to the shipping world the worth of Falmouth, its pilots, and the port services it could offer, although there was little that could be done about the subsequent natural forces. Early in March the iron steamship *St. Andrew's Bay*, laden with a cargo of phosphate rock, was sailing up the English Channel when she ran into thick fog. She was fairly big, one of the new breed of merchantmen, 265 feet long, and registered at 1,749 tons, built at Newcastle in 1882 and with an owner based at the thriving port of North Shields. Off the Lizard, about four miles from Falmouth, she collided with the steamer *Bittern*, which was sailing from Plymouth to Cork. A nine-foot gash was torn in her starboard bow, and she immediately began taking on water; her assailant apparently sailed on. Engines were stopped, and the captain, not expecting any help, prepared to lower the boats and abandon the ship to her fate.

It appears that the pilots of cutter No. 6, *Arrow,* on duty off the Manacles, had heard the commotion and found *St. Andrew's Bay* through the fog. Pilot Edwin Richards, captain of that watch on *Arrow,* boarded the sinking steamer; he 'displayed great coolness and courage on the occasion', getting the steamer under way and piloting her through the fog into Falmouth. Here he beached her near St. Anthony Lighthouse, on the only place of comparatively level sand in the harbour, and where she could lie in safety. There she rested while engineers and divers began to make temporary repairs. Big steam pumps, their boilers and equipment, were brought from Cardiff, Plymouth, and from the local firms of Messrs Cox and Lean. 100 men and the tugs *Defiance, Triton, Eagle, Briton,* and *Pendennis,* were employed to refloat and tow her to the Western Breakwater. There her cargo was transhipped and she was then manoeuvred into a dry dock for permanent repair. No doubt there was a very expensive bill to settle, at least part, if not all, covered by underwriters at Lloyds of London, but not as much as if she had sunk. Through their solicitor, Mr. Jenkins, the F.D.P.B.A. committee later made a claim through the Admiralty Court for the contribution Richards had made towards the saving of the vessel, the owners having offered a paltry £10. The court settled the claim at £250, a very welcome addition to the meagre funds of the pilots' association.

The owners of *St. Andrew's Bay* were very lucky that their damaged vessel was safely tucked up in the docks, when, only a few days after the collision, Cornwall was hit by the legendary 'Great Blizzard'. Storm force easterly winds and heavy snow caused disruption to travel and communications across Southern England; dozens of vessels came to grief in the Channel, and many lives were lost at sea and on land. All the coastal towns and villages of Cornwall received severe damage to properties and infrastructure. The railways became blocked by snowdrifts many feet in depth; telegraph lines everywhere were torn down; communications to the outside world ceased for several days.

At the height of the storm, over 8 and 9 March, craft of all kinds were ripped from their moorings in Falmouth Harbour, and sunk or were badly damaged. They included ketches, fishing boats, the shipping agents' boarding gigs and quay punts. Also damaged was an outfitter's cutter and pilot cutter *Vincent,* hit by a wayward stone barge on her moorings at St. Mawes. Few steam vessels, and certainly no sailing vessel, could hope to beat eastwards against the storm, or even anchor to ride it out. Consequently, there were a horrific number of vessels, large and small, smashed to pieces, and much loss of life, on the south Cornish coast. At its height, the storm was too ferocious for the few rowing lifeboats to get out, but locally the Falmouth tug crews managed to tow several vessels to safety. The Coastguards and people of the coast villages did what they could; the various 'Rocket Brigades' using Henry Trengrouse's or Manby's life-saving apparatus proving to be an invaluable service.

The worst loss of life occurred just five miles to the south of Falmouth: the big steel-hulled, four-masted ship *Bay of Panama,* one of the finest clipper ships ever built, went ashore in raging seas below the steep cliffs of Nare Head, just outside the entrance to Helford River. She had been built only eight years previously at the famous Harland and Wolff Shipyard in Belfast; 294 feet in length and registered at 2,365 tons. She had arrived back in home waters from Calcutta with a cargo of 17,000 bales of jute for Dundee, her intended course being up the English Channel and northwards along the east coast. It is possible that the crew were unable to wear her round to run back before the storm, or they may have been trying to reach Falmouth.

According to the memoirs of local fisherman James Cliff, the wreck was spotted at daybreak by a farmer, out on the cliffs tending to his snow-bound sheep. The Porthoustock lifeboat crew were alerted, but the seas were so tremendous in the cove that the boat couldn't be launched. The men therefore trudged overland, carrying ropes and grapnels, meeting the men of Porthallow above the wreck. Attempts were made to pass lines across, but their equipment proved inadequate against the snowstorm and pounding waves. They watched helplessly from the cliff top as men were swept from the rigging of collapsing masts where they had sought safety. Earlier a message had been sent four miles overland to Coverack to summon the Coastguard Rocket Brigade. The crew and equipment eventually arrived after fighting through lanes blocked by snow and fallen trees. With the assistance of the locals the rocket apparatus was lowered down the cliff and set up. According to Mr. Cliff 16 or 17 survivors were successfully brought ashore by breeches buoy

Top left: Cadgwith's first lifeboat, the *Western Commercial Traveller*, arrived in 1869, being renamed the *Joseph Armstrong* a decade later. The boat was replaced by another, of 12 oars, in 1887. The photograph is probably of this second boat, which was also named *Joseph Armstrong*. (Helston Museum)

Middle left: The Porthoustock Lifeboat. A photograph possibly recording the ceremonial launching of the *James Stevens* in 1900. Most of the population of St. Keverne appears to have come down for the occasion! The lifeboat house on the left is still in use as a community hall. (Helston Museum)

Below left: The wreck of the *Bay of Panama* following the blizzard of March 1891. (Helston Museum)

Below right: A breeches buoy in operation. Once a rocket line had been fired across to the ship in distress the crew had to have the ability to haul in and attach the cable and pulley block line. (*Illustrated London News*)

and cared for at the nearby Penare House. Unfortunately a similar number had been lost to the sea, including Captain Wright and his wife. Several crew had later to be cut from the rigging where they had frozen to death. At the height of the storm local man Joseph Hendy James volunteered to take his pony to carry the news of the tragedy ten miles or so through the lanes and across the moors to Helston. Here a telegraph message could be sent to Fox, the shipping agent at Falmouth. Unfortunately the lines had been blown down, therefore, with the snow eventually proving too deep for the pony, James walked, sometimes crawling, most of the further ten miles to Falmouth with the message. (A fuller account is given by Clive Carter in *The Blizzard of '91*, David and Charles, 1971).

By mid-April the weather, and trade, had settled down; the port was busy with British and foreign vessels calling for orders. Pilots were still occasionally upsetting the Harbour Master by anchoring vessels in what he thought was an unsound berth, but any mistakes received little publicity. The *Falmouth Packet* newspaper saw them guiding big ships through a crowded harbour with their usual efficiency – 'It speaks well for the tact and seamanship of our local pilots to find the largest craft are invariably moored without hitch or casualty; only those who know the crowded state of the roads (the roadstead) at times can thoroughly appreciate the efficiency of our home sailors'.

In September the pilots of No. 13, *Antelope*, were instrumental in saving four lives. The fishing lugger, No. 60, was heavily laden, not with fish, but with nine tons of cement, probably taken on at Falmouth Docks. She was sailing round the Lizard in a strong breeze, a heavy swell running, probably bound for her home port of Porthleven, when she was hit by a sudden squall, thrown over and began to sink. The pilots, on station off Mullion, saw her go down and sailed to the spot, where the crew of two men and two boys were in the sea. The cutter Master, Charles Jenking, launched the boarding punt by which all four were rescued.

The following month another cutter, No. 8, *Vincent*, was in the right place and time, on this occasion, to perform a lucrative, rather than humanitarian service. The 165-ton, three-masted Dutch schooner *Levant* was carrying a cargo of phosphate from Ghent, bound for Cork, when she lost her rudder at some distance off Falmouth. She was seen drifting helplessly by the crew of the cutter and they naturally offered their services. They managed to tow, or otherwise help to bring her into Falmouth for repairs. It demonstrates the power of the cutter's sails and rig, that such a vessel could be towed, albeit assisted, perhaps, by her own sails. The F.D.P.B.A. put in a claim for salvage services, and eventually accepted £100. The cutters had unsurpassed sailing qualities, but were not invulnerable to heavy weather. In November hurricane strength winds hit the coast again; among the shipping casualties were three local boats. Two outfitters' cutters, still trying to find customers among the infrequent arrivals, were damaged, and pilot cutter No. 2, *Andrews* lost her main boom, sails and rigging, before she could reach the safety of the harbour.

There was a slight increase in arrivals in 1892, but thereafter the downward trend continued. In 1894 the annual figure had fallen to 1,200, 485 being British. There were very few vessels coming into Falmouth waters from across the Atlantic, and those from Europe were in no more than double figures. The exceptions were Germany, with 149, and Norway, with 271. The comparatively high figure for the latter may represent a constant demand for building construction timber in this country and elsewhere. Following the downward trend in arrivals, the 55 pilots listed in 1891 had fallen to 49 in 1896, no apprentices having been given licences. Of those that retired during this period, William Vincent was the oldest at 69; William James Lowry was 65. Several others were only in their forties, and possibly gave up through ill-health, or could see that there was little future in the service and moved to other employment.

By this time some of the cutters had been sold off, consequently in 1892 permission was granted to make internal structural alterations to cutter *Vincent* to provide berths for additional pilots serving on board. Deck hands were reduced to two per boat. There were also proposals to dispose of two more cutters, and reduce the number of pilots to 40; both objectives were achieved by the end of the century. Meanwhile, the F.D.P.B.A. committee continued to busy themselves with the care of the existing cutters. There was a regular rotation of boats being brought onto the beach for scrubbing down, re-caulking and painting of hulls; arrangements being made for the vacated guard stations such as at the Lizard to be covered by a spare boat. New equipment such as rope, chain, paint and cleaning materials was ordered when necessary, tenders being requested from local chandlers. Navigational and safety equipment was also brought up to scratch: port and starboard and masthead lights were improved, flares and foghorns issued. Two lifebelts on deck were now supposed to be standard equipment; but there is no record of them being used in emergency.

The reduction in cutters meant that the old northeast guard position off the Dodman headland had now been abandoned, leaving cutters patrolling off the Lizard, the Manacles, and off the harbour entrance. Another boat was on harbour duty, ferrying pilots to outward-bound vessels and so on. Sometimes an outer station was inadvertently left unmanned when all pilots had been put aboard ships, the deck crew or apprentices then having to sail back to the harbour for more pilots. This led to complaints from some ship Masters who might have been delayed in finding a pilot to bring them in. The Committee issued instructions that vacated stations should be covered by a spare boat whenever possible. Following the earlier alterations to *Vincent*, similar work to provide extra berths for pilots was also carried out on the *Richard Green* in 1897. Cutter No. 1, *Harriet* was auctioned and sold that year for a mere £75, but the other candidate for disposal, No. 2, *Andrews*, was possibly kept on as a spare boat until February 1900, when sold for £110.

The changes in the number of pilots working from each boat is reflected in the few surviving crew lists kept at the County Record Office, particularly in the case of *Condor*. In 1876 she had five pilots including the Master, and four apprentices on board. In 1880 there were still five pilots but apprentices were reduced to two. In 1891, four years after the reduction in the number of cutters, her complement consisted of nine pilots and no apprentices. Some further information comes from what seems to be *Condor's* last and only surviving logbook: in 1907 the names of eight pilots appear as belonging to the boat. The book was never completed; however, on further pages there are two lists of pilots for 1912, consisting of just four men apiece, reflecting the falling trade and fewer available pilots. Throughout this period there were also between one and three deck-hands employed at various times.

There was still a considerable amount of coasting trade, but many of the small schooners and ketches had been replaced by steamers of 200 tons or so, bringing larger, but fewer, cargoes such as coal from South Wales. The bunkering or refuelling of steamships at Falmouth had now become a very profitable business, owing to the port's position at the entrance to the English Channel. Some ship owners, cutting costs wherever they could, at one stage had objected to the pilots of the port charging their vessels pilotage fees when they were merely entering to refuel. However, there had been a court case in 1886 which seems to have settled the matter for a time. The captain of a St. Ives steamer, the *Treneglos*, owned by Hains and Son, had refused to accept the services of pilot William Chard, and pay the standard 'compulsory pilotage' fee for pilotage in and out, which was the standard practice of the port. Chard engaged a solicitor (this was prior to the establishment of the F.D.P.B.A.) and sued the company. Messrs Hains did not bother to attend the court hearing, and for their pains were told to pay twice the pilotage fee, plus costs, and in default to serve 28 days imprisonment. The result of an appeal is not known. While on the subject: the 'in and out' pilotage fee was also charged by the pilots for delivering orders from the shipping agents to vessels waiting 'off the port'. In 1891 it appears that both charges were reduced to the payment of inward pilotage only.

Some ship repairs and incoming cargoes kept the docks relatively busy; grain and timber being the main imports. Some cargoes still passed through to Malpas and Truro if the tide allowed. At one period towards the end of the decade a rather more dangerous commodity was arriving in considerable quantities. Cargoes of explosive had occasionally arrived for use in the mines for much of the century. But now steamships carrying dynamite from the works of Nobel's Explosive Co. Ltd., Glasgow, and the National Explosives Company at Hayle, were regularly entering and, hope-fully, anchoring at the dangerous cargoes and quarantine area at St. Just Pool, on the far side of Carrick Roads. Here dynamite was transhipped into larger German vessels bound for Hamburg and Bremen. Although probably for peaceful use, with hindsight these appear to be ominous cargoes, considering what was to follow within a decade or so. These vessels represent some of the more lucrative work for pilots, but overall their earnings were still falling. At a conference of the United Kingdom Pilots' Association in 1897, Falmouth representatives bemoaned the fall in the port's pilotage earnings from £8,500 in 1892 to £5,500 in 1896. The Trinity House pension was also complained of, being extremely low despite the many years of pilots' contributions.

In July 1898 the iconic Falmouth-built and registered clipper-bowed schooner *Lady of Avenal* was reported to have arrived in the industrial port of Swansea, South Wales. She had brought a cargo of copper ore from Newfoundland, after a remarkably quick passage of 14 days; the direct distance is roughly 2,300 miles, which equates to about 164 miles sailed per day. This voyage in a small way exemplified the massive quantities of ore imported into to Swansea from many parts of the world at this time, for refining in the smelting furnaces packed into the district. Only a few decades earlier the *Lady's* sister-ships would have only been carrying ore from Cornish mines; sadly these were now becoming exhausted of easily reached copper, and nearly so of tin.

The group of rocks known as The Manacles lie six miles due south of Falmouth. At low water they can be seen extending offshore for nearly a mile from the cliffs on the northeastern side of the Lizard peninsula. They have achieved almost legendary status because of the number of ships wrecked upon them, although perhaps that notoriety could apply to much of that coastline. Well-meaning Victorian pseudo-scientists even tried to prove that the local rocks were particularly magnetic, thereby altering ships' compasses so that in some Lorelei-like fashion they were steered onto the rocks. More prosaic reasons were lack of charts, inaccurate compasses, poor lookout, lack of visibility because of rain or fog, or the incorrect course being set or steered; most commonly, perhaps, being driven onto a lee shore by strong winds. The Manacle reef was the workplace of the fishermen of the Lizard villages, and the Falmouth pilots. Many could have named every rocky outcrop, and knew the inside passage between the main reef and the land. But even they might have experienced that awful heart-rending feeling when, perhaps at low water, they ran onto an unseen rock.

Manacle Point from Porthoustock.

In July 1838 it was reported that pilot H. Andrew was off the Manacles in his boat *Hiram,* pointing out the relevant features for the benefit of his son, who would surely follow his father into the profession. To Andrew's embarrassment, the boat hit a well-known rock, the Pinman, and quickly sank. The crew saved themselves in their boarding punt. Another incident occurred in 1851: pilot cutter *Victoria* had put a pilot aboard a ship off the Lizard and was returning to Falmouth, sailing through the narrow but familiar passage below the cliffs. By some lack of judgement or inattention, the boat ran onto one of the many rocks, was holed, and went down; the crew saved themselves in the punt. The Master no doubt had to suffer the ridicule of his peers, and the expense of replacing an un-insured boat. He also had the unpleasant duty of reporting in writing to the Sub-Commissioners at the Custom House. The letter has survived, pasted into the contemporary Falmouth Mercantile Shipping Register.

> 'Falmouth 9th December 1851
> To the Collector and Comptroller H.M. Customs, Falmouth
>
> Gentlemen
>   I beg to report that on the 25th ult. My pilot cutter 'Victoria' whilst returning to port, struck on a sunken rock on the inner passage of the Manacles and went down in 7 fathoms of water, and that on the 30th there being strong wind from the S E with great sea she broke up and came on shore and that all her papers were at the same time lost.
>   I am Gentlemen
>   Your Obedient Servant
>   Elias Chard'

The pilots, even though their living depended on seeking out incoming ships, might shelter from the force of a storm, in a small cove, in the lee of the Lizard, or perhaps by anchoring in the Helford Estuary. But even here a pilot boat's anchor cables were parted, and she was driven ashore and damaged. At the end of the nineteenth century the Manacles were the site of a number of shipping casualties. Several incidents in particular stand out, either caused by poor navigation or storm, leading to the tragic loss of many lives in spite of superhuman rescue attempts. One was a bizarre stranding, but without loss of life, more by extreme luck than judgement. It involved a huge liner, and apparently was caused purely by navigational error.

On the dark and squally night of 8 February 1890 the 1100 ton Greek Merchant steamer *Spyridion Vagliano* smashed into the Manacles reef; within ten minutes she had sunk in 20 fathoms. Two ship's boats had been launched with difficulty, and 13 crew left in the larger one; later searches found nothing of them. The captain and the eight remaining crew took to the smaller boat, managing to reach Godrevy Cove, an isolated beach within the nearby cliffs. Unfortunately the captain was drowned when the boat was swamped. After seeking help at a farm the survivors were taken to the sailors' home in Falmouth. Apart from the obvious sorrow for the loss of life there was considerable business interest in the disaster: the cargo, 19,666 quarters of grain from Novorassiyck on the Black Sea (still a major Russian grain exporting port), was to have been discharged at Falmouth docks for Redruth merchants S. and T. Trounson.

The following week an editorial in the *Falmouth and Penryn Weekly Times* tried to link the disaster to the recent reorganisation of the Falmouth pilotage service and the reduction in the number of cutters. Although the cause was thought to be navigational error, among the allegations it was said that the ship had been signalling for a pilot at the Lizard but no cutter appeared. A more general complaint was that pilots had not been so zealous in the pursuit of their calling as previously; because of poor service some ships were now calling for orders at Plymouth instead of Falmouth. Therefore local traders were losing business. George Carter, Secretary to the F.D.P.B.A., replied in a letter to the *Falmouth Packet*. He pointed out the numerous inaccurate assertions in the article, and that therefore the public could place no reliance on the allegations. The duties of the pilots were laid down by Trinity House and overseen by Sub Commissioners, 'gentlemen of nautical and commercial experience'. The newspaper editor had been looking for a scapegoat to blame for the town's declining business, rather than accepting that due to changes in deep-sea trade, the heyday of many sailing ship arrivals of two decades before had gone forever.

With an east, sou'easterly gale blowing on-shore, there was no pilot boat on station off the Manacles in the pitch-dark night of the 14 October 1898. The *Mohegan* was a 482 feet long steamship, registered at 6,889 tons gross, with four tall masts, and owned by the Atlantic Transport Company. She was in the early stages of a voyage from Tilbury to New York, carrying general cargo, 60 passengers and 97 officers and crew. After passing the Eddystone Lighthouse on her way down Channel, her course was set for the open Atlantic, theoretically to clear the Lizard by at least ten miles. It was the wrong course, or perhaps no allowance had been made for the 'windage' of the gale on her hull and tall masts drawing her northwards. At about seven o' clock in the evening she impaled herself on the Voices rocks on the outer Manacles, just inside the ineffectual Trinity House warning buoy. Her engine room rapidly flooded, therefore the generators stopped, plunging the ship into darkness. She took a heavy list to port, preventing the launch of most of the lifeboats, and sank in about 20 minutes. Distress rockets must have been heard, for the local lifeboats were called out. The Porthoustock boat, rowed through the gale, saved about 40 people, but over 100 were lost. Bodies were picked up along the coast over several weeks, some being buried in a mass grave at the village of St. Keverne, one and a half miles inland.

St. Keverne churchyard. The granite memorial and one of several headstones dedicated to the memory of those lost in the *Mohegan* disaster.

Left: An artistic impression of the wreck of the liner *Mohegan*. (Helston Museum)

The Manacles. The Wreck of S. S. Mohegan.

On 20 May 1899 a short report appeared in the *Falmouth Packet* regarding discussions by the Falmouth Harbour Board about the dangers of the Manacles. After losses prior to 1838 local shipping agents Broad & Sons had contacted Trinity House to ask for the reef to be marked. During March that year some of the Elder Brethren had an inspection cruise along the southwest coast in the Trinity yacht. At Falmouth pilot Henry Tonkin assisted them in placing a large black-painted buoy '55 fathoms southeast by south' of the outer reef. This buoy had probably been replaced several times over the years and the existing one incorporated a bell, but was difficult to see at night and in bad weather. Ever since the *Mohegan* disaster the Falmouth Harbour Board had tried to persuade Trinity House to replace the still ineffectual buoy with one also incorporating a light. The Board had recently heard that the Brethren had consented to provide a gas-lighted, automatic, sound-producing buoy that summer, or as soon as possible. Whatever length of time that might have been – it was going to be too late to prevent one of the most bizarre incidents ever to occur around the coast of Cornwall. It happened less than a week later; in the early hours of Whit Sunday morning.

The luxury trans-Atlantic liner, *Paris*, had been built in Glasgow in 1889. She was American owned, 560 feet in length, a draught of 42 feet, and registered at 10,669 tons gross. The press report interestingly added that her hull was doubled, and with 15 watertight bulkheads in the length of the ship, each rising to the height of the saloon deck. (It would be informative to compare the construction with a then proposed larger ship, the *Titanic*.) *Paris* had left Southampton on 19 May, bound for New York, calling at Cherbourg to pick up 50 of 'the peasantry class', emigrating from various European countries. By then she had on board 400 passengers, 372 officers and crew, plus mail and cargo. A rather strange course was set, for she passed right across the Channel to within sight of the Devon coast before heading down Channel. This course, set by the captain, should have carried her westwards to clear the Lizard by about 20 miles.

At one o' clock in the morning of the 21 May, the pilot boat No. 13, *Antelope* was, according to later statements, hove to a mile southeast by east of the Manacles buoy; the weather was calm, with some fog and drizzle about. Pilot Edward Ball was on watch on deck with crewman William Veale, the other five pilots being below deck. Ball became aware of a rushing sound, which he identified as an approaching steamer; a masthead light appeared through the fog about a mile away. Ball and Veale were astonished to see a huge liner travelling at speed in the direction of the rocks where only recently the *Mohegan* had gone down, its masts still rising above the water. The pilot boat had the usual masthead light, and a flare was lit and waved by Veale to warn the ship that she was running into danger. The signal flare equipment used on pilot boats around the coast consisted of a conical container of kerosene, in which was held a metal rod, on the end of which could be attached a wad of cotton waste. A protective sleeve on the rod formed the lid of the container. When a signal was required the soaked cotton waste was lit and the rod held aloft. The white mainsail formed a reflector, which could be seen for a considerable distance. Flares were supposed to be exhibited at regular intervals at night, the frequency depending on the pilotage district.

It appeared that the ship may have changed course because of the pilots' actions, but otherwise did not slow down and disappeared into the dark. A short time later distress rockets were heard and the pilots prepared to assist. It was too dangerous to take the cutter right inshore, therefore four of the crew set out in the small punt, expecting to find a sinking ship and people in the water. Instead, to their amazement, they found the intact *Paris*; by some miracle she had missed the jagged Manacle rocks and was sitting upright on the comparatively shallow and level reef of rocks

Below left:
Lowland Point.

Below right: Paris on
the Lowlands, with tugs
in attendance. (RCPS)

off Lowland Point, a little to the west of the Manacles.

At the sound of the distress signals the Coastguard boat and local lifeboats came out from the Lizard, but it was obvious that they were not needed immediately. The liner's crew dispensed tea and coffee to the passengers, and the more hysterical were calmed down. The news was sent via the Coastguards to Falmouth, requiring a difficult journey from this particularly remote spot on the coast. At daylight, naval vessels and Falmouth tugs arrived; passengers were taken from the ship by lifeboats and transferred to the off-lying tugs for passage to Falmouth. As it was out of season plenty of accommodation was found in the hotels and lodging houses, the European peasantry being consigned to the Sailors Home. Special trains later took the passengers back to Southampton to join other ships.

For nearly two months the *Paris* was a boon to the traders and boatmen of Falmouth: hundreds of excursionists arrived by rail and steamboats from Plymouth, to be taken out to the famous wreck. The local professional photographers quickly made their way to the scene, and their shops were soon besieged by ex-passengers and tourists demanding copies of their photographs. Work on salving the ship began almost immediately; but without success, until a German company provided experts and big salvage vessels previously used on similar work. Hundreds of tons of rock were blasted away from beneath the shattered bow of *Paris* before divers could temporarily patch the broken sections. She was pumped out, and on 12 July was winched off at high tide. The following day she was towed to Falmouth Docks, providing an unforgettable sight for the welcoming crowds on the waterfront. She was patched up further and towed to Milford Haven to be restored as the *Philadelphia*.

One of the many sequels to the dramatic events concerned the crew of the pilot cutter *Antelope*, who were the first to see the vast vessel driving at speed through the mist towards its apparent doom, and the first to offer assistance, however limited. Later in July the crew were assembled at the Falmouth Custom House 'looking spick and span in their neat uniforms of blue cloth relieved with gilt buttons', at the aegis of Mr. Fooks, the Collector of Customs, being one of the Sub Commissioners of Pilotage. Mr. Fox, the American Consular Agent, had requested the gathering to present the sum of £10 to the crew, which had been donated by several American passengers. Mr. Fooks' speech was full of praise for the enterprise of the crew for trying to warn the ship, and doing what they could after the stranding.

The pilots had convinced themselves and others that their actions had made the ship change course enough to prevent an inevitable sinking. After much later discussion the F.D.P.B.A. solicitor, W. Jenkins, made a claim on the owners of *Paris* of £300 for salvage services. (The value of the ship and cargo was given was £40,000.) The case was heard by an Admiralty judge at Falmouth County Court in August. The *Paris* owners were represented by a barrister, and witnesses included the captain and relevant officers of the ship. All their evidence testified that although the pilot boat flare had been seen by officers on the bridge, it did not represent a warning to them, and that no change of course had been made. (Why should it, they thought they were 20 miles offshore!) After what seemed in the newspaper report to have been rather facetious remarks by the opposing barrister, the claim was dismissed. Apparently Watkins, captain of *Paris*, was later to be relieved of his Masters' certificate for two years.

Whatever the pilots may have thought about their treatment, it did not prevent them from continuing to assist vessels in distress. In March 1901 vicious gales battered ships in the Western Approaches: a number limped into Falmouth, including several windjammers almost totally dismasted and leaky. Even in the harbour they were not completely safe: a Dutch vessel, the 1,635 ton steel barquentine *Vondel*, had been under repair in the docks for earlier storm damage and just brought out to anchor near the harbour mouth to begin her voyage the following day. Unfortunately, the wind picked up in the night and she dragged her anchors and went ashore at Castle Point, St. Mawes. At high tide in the morning she lifted off, and tugs towed her back again into the docks for inspection. Some new work obviously had to be carried out, because she didn't sail again until the end of April.

The 1880 ton steel-built sailing ship *William Tillie* built and registered in Londonderry, had been months at sea on a voyage from New Caledonia in the Pacific Ocean to Swansea. But on arrival back in British waters she was hit by gales and became unmanageable; fortunately she was found by a steamship and towed into Falmouth. It seems hardly credible, considering that there was so much medical knowledge at the time, that the main reason the ship was unmanageable was because all the crew had been struck down with scurvy. After the ship was manoeuvred to the docks by pilots and tugs, 20 crew were taken to the Royal Cornwall Sailors Home, where a number were hospitalised. The pilots of No. 12 cutter, *Condor*, who gave unspecified, but obviously valuable assistance, both to *Vondel* and *William Tillie*, were to receive £25 from the owners of both vessels, through the auspices of the agents, Broad & Co. The money was taken into the coffers of the pilot's association, who welcomed any additional revenue to boost the diminishing earnings, to help towards maintenance of the boats and general expenses.

Bass, originally Beast, Point. Its height and southerly position made it ideal for the siting of Lloyd's and Marconi's signal stations; also the Coastguard lookout, which is now occupied by the National Coastwatch Institution.

Inset: Notice advertising the opening of Lloyd's signal station, published in the 1873 edition of *Lloyd's Navy List.*

G. C. FOX & Co.,
FALMOUTH.
Merchants, Ship Agents, & Foreign Consulates.

G. C. FOX & Co., on the 2nd April, 1872, opened a SIGNAL STATION at the LIZARD, and the Government has since established a TELEGRAPH OFFICE in the same house. The Station is a white building on the highest part of Beast Point, three-quarters of a mile East of the Lighthouse, and is 20 feet high, with flag-staff attached. All vessels making the Lizard are requested to signal this Station in order that their passing may be reported to those interested.

Since August, 1871, G. C. Fox and Co. have used a new fast iron STEAMER for boarding vessels on arrival off Falmouth, and for delivering orders on board with the least possible delay. Falmouth has good dock accommodation, including Wharves where vessels discharge afloat, extensive Warehouses, and two large Graving Docks. The broad-gauge railroad runs from the Cornwall Railway on to the dock piers.

Above left: The Signal Station, Bass Point, first established by Falmouth shipping agents in 1872. The Post Office, Lloyds, and the Bilboa Submarine Telegraph Company subsequently sub-let the building. It has since been taken over by the National Trust, but not open to the public.

Above right: The restored Marconi wireless telegraphy huts on Bass Point.

Apart from pilotage in and out of the port, much revenue was also earned by some owner's orders being carried by the pilots from Falmouth shipping agents to vessels lying offshore. Much to the chagrin of the pilots, it seems a growing number of orders were now being received via telegraph at Bass Point on the Lizard, and presumably then sent out to ships by semaphore. The Lloyds' Signal Station statistics for 1886 were published in January the following year in the *Falmouth and Penryn Weekly Times.* According to the report it seems that, at that time at least, comparatively few orders were being passed from Bass Point; even so, every one represented a loss of income for the pilots.

'Lloyds' Signal Station, The Lizard, 1886 - We have been favoured by the courteous superintendent of the Station (Mr. John Prior) with particulars of the station for the past year, from which it appears that the number of vessels reported passing during the year was 10,642, of which 286 were mail steamers spotted by showing their signals at night time; 19 vessels received orders signalled to them by the station, two, or at most three, of which only would in all probability have gone into Falmouth; ten messages only have been sent direct to captains' wives, but there is little doubt that many such messages are sent away by other friends as soon as the welcome intelligence of the vessel passing is flashed by the electric wires. There was a remarkable increase in the number of private messages signalled by ships, some of the large mail steamship companies having instructed their commanders to make known to the station the number of passengers, number of sacks of mails, and at times the amount of specie which will have to be disembarked at the port of call – which information is immediately wired to the agents, who then make the necessary arrangements for the disembarkation.'

Lizard Point and the outer reefs. The light-house is behind the photographer.

Although undoubtedly valuable for communications, the presence of the signal station could impose a threat to the unwary ship Master: if a sailing vessel was steered too close, or even was hove to, in order to pass signals by lamp or semaphore, it might be swept onto the rocks by unknown currents or an onshore wind. A.G. Folliot-Stokes, author of *The Cornish Coast and Moors*, published in 1928, records meeting an old pilot, who remarked: 'If they would only sink Lloyds' Signalling Station there would be no more wrecks on the Manacles or around the Lizard Head, because captains would then give that corner a wide berth.' He would have also added that the pilots' earnings would have been higher as more vessels would have entered Falmouth!

The truth in the old pilots' words was demonstrated on 5th May 1913: the majestic clipper ship *Queen Margaret*, carrying 4,500 tons of wheat, arrived off the Lizard after a splendid voyage from Sydney, Australia. The Master received his orders from Lloyd's signal station at Bass Point, which were to proceed to Limerick. The ship was hove to off the station while the Master signalled for further information from the owners. Unfortunately an easterly wind sprang up, driving the now unmanageable vessel back to Lizard Point. Here she was soon in the clutches of the reef of rocks which extend for half a mile out from the point. She grounded on the Stag Rocks and began to take on water. With such a weight of ship and cargo holding her down it was obvious she was doomed. The Lizard lifeboat went out, first taking off the captain's wife and children, followed by the crew. Falmouth tugs eventually arrived, but it was a fruitless trip; within two days she had slipped off the rocks and vanished beneath the waves.

A further threat to pilotage revenue came in 1901 when Marconi began experiments from his new wireless telegraphy station close to Lloyds' signal station on Bass Point. However, it was going to be some years before the average merchant ship owner could afford the onboard receiving and transmitting equipment and the operator to use it. It was a different matter for ocean liners, whose passengers wanted the luxury, and it turned out, the life-saving necessity, of communication with the land or other ships. The system was not only to be used for serious business, as could be seen in a report in the *Falmouth Packet* on 8 February 1902.

'WIRELESS TELEGRAPHY. – One of the first wireless telegraphic messages across the sea has been received by Mr. James Winter, of Albany Road. Mr. Winter has a son on board the Philadelphia, and when that ship was off the Lizard on Sunday evening the son sent a message by the wireless method to the Lizard Signal Station, where it was duly telegraphed on to Falmouth, coming through in this form:- 'Lizard Signal Station, 4.40 p.m. Received Falmouth 5.16 p.m. To Winter, Albany Road, Falmouth. Philadelphia. Sunday evening. All well. Fred. Marconi wireless.'

Above left: The Lizard Light, showing the eastern operational tower and the enormous foghorn to the left. The present buildings date from the mid-eighteenth century. There were originally two lights, the western one being discontinued in 1903. The eastern light was automated in 1998; the building now incorporates a museum.

Above right: The end of the fine clipper ship *Queen Margaret* on the Stag rocks, Lizard Point, in May 1913. (Helston Museum)

Fred Winter, being a local lad, and although it was too dark to see, was probably aware that the *Philadelphia* was shortly to pass, or had already passed, Lowland Point, where, in her previous life as the *Paris* less than three years previously, she had ignominiously been marooned on the rocks. He may also have heard the news that only a month or so before he was passing this spot, another large vessel had followed *Paris* onto the Lowlands. The 800 ton iron-built barque *Glenburvie* had been outward bound from London for West Africa carrying general cargo. She was towed by tug as far as Beachy Head before setting sail and tacking down channel against contrary winds. The captain seems to have lost his way after passing the Eddystone light; on the night of 13 December 1901, in poor visibility, the barque ran close inshore and onto the Lowlands, having fortunately missed the treacherous Manacles.

The sound of distress rockets once again brought out the Coastguards with their rocket apparatus, and the Porthoustock lifeboat crew was alerted. But it was the new Coverack boat, placed there after the *Paris* incident, that got through the surf, closing with the distressed ship standing erect on its rocky platform. The lifeboat had to anchor away from the rocks, and a line was passed to the ship, whereby all 16 crew were brought to the boat and to safety in Coverack. At low tide the wreck could be reached on foot over the rocks, and within days a professional salving operation began, assisted by local fishermen. The *Glenburvie* was remembered locally for many years, for part of the several hundred tons of cargo that were salvaged consisted of 600 cases of whisky, 400 cases of brandy, and barrels of rum. The badly damaged iron hull was eventually patched up, and she was towed back to Falmouth for extensive repairs, after which she sailed back to London. The Admiralty chart of the area, published in 1900, shows the Manacles marked by a buoy fitted with a bell and an occulting (flashing) gas light, however, even though coupled with the navigation aids of the lighthouses at St. Anthony Head and the Lizard, it still did not prevent vessels large and small, especially in bad weather, from succumbing to those ancient rocks in the years to come.

In all such incidents of shipwreck over the years the fishermen of the Lizard, whether being volunteers in the local lifeboat or using their own small boats, selflessly went out to render assistance to those clinging to life on wave-battered ships. Those that were saved were cared for in humble cottages whose residents gave what they could from their limited means. When the survivors had left and the drowned buried with due ceremony the fishermen became salvors: under the auspices of the Coastguards, Customs officials or agents they may have been employed to remove the cargo where possible and strip the vessel to its bare bones before the sea took it away. Any cargo or ship material that could be spirited away unseen by the authorities was fair game, and almost the only context in which the term 'wrecking' was used, although some more serious instances were reported. It could happen, especially in the mining districts, that should a merchant ship become stranded on the shore miners and their families would descend like flocks of vultures and strip the ship, in spite of the protests from Master and crew.

The Coastguard service was created in 1822 out of an earlier coastal force known as the Preventive Water Guard. This was set up by the Board of Customs in 1809 as an anti-smuggling force which patrolled the coast from 150 or so stations around the British Isles. The force operated with shore patrols or with small inshore rowed or sailed galleys which supplemented the work of the larger revenue cutters that patrolled the Channel. At a time when the price of goods from the Continent soared because of import taxes the exploits of these men, and of their opponents, the smuggling fraternity, became a major part of the nation's folklore. From 1831 the force became a naval reserve, partly under the control of the Admiralty, with naval-style uniforms and discipline. Increased responsibility was given for coastal defence, the saving of lives, and the clearing of wrecks. Under the 1854 Merchant Shipping Act the Board of Trade issued life-saving apparatus to Coastguard stations around the coast. Although the Admiralty had been slow to adopt the marvellous rocket and breeches buoy inventions of Manby, Dennett and Trengrouse, the Coastguard 'Rocket Brigades', often operating from cliff tops in appalling conditions, were to save countless lives. In 1856 the Board of Trade passed complete control of the service to the Admiralty; Coastguards supplemented other naval forces at a time when there was increasing emphasis on coast defence because of armed conflict between European neighbours. There were improvements in the structure of the service, in wages and employment conditions; look-out buildings and rows of cottages for the crews sprung up at many locations round the coast.

In 1923 the force reverted back to the control of the Board of Trade. It had become the 'eyes and ears' of many organisations, still handling Admiralty coastal signalling and telegraphy and carrying out some Customs and Excise duties. They continued to assist ships in distress, but with the increasing use of radio communication, and little smuggling, the traditional 'watchers on the shore' that once patrolled the cliffs day and night were no longer required, apart perhaps during the Second World War. With today's modern technology and communication with shipping world-wide the service continues to provide assistance to every individual, whether at sea or on the coast, for business or pleasure. With the able co-operation of the RNLI, Coastguard and volunteer teams on shore, and other services, thousands are helped in various ways every year.

In 1900 the number of large merchantmen, sail and steam-powered, visiting Falmouth 'for orders and otherwise' totalled 779; a considerable fall compared to, say, the figure of 1200 in 1894. The overall increase in the size of vessels, particularly sailing vessels, led to problems for pilots and ship's Masters alike, and is illustrated by the case of the *Clan Graham*. She was a four-masted barque, built of steel at a Glasgow shipyard in 1893, 283 feet long, and registered at 1976 tons, one of a fleet of eight merchantmen owned by Thomas Dunlop and Sons, of that port. During the early hours of 21 February 1903, she arrived off the Cornish coast at the end of a voyage from Algoa Bay, on the Cape of Good Hope, intending to call at Falmouth for orders. She was in ballast: her steel hull higher out of the water than if she had been laden with cargo, and running before a strong south-westerly gale, in 'thick' rain and fog. The Master, Captain McIntire, believed that he was eleven miles off the land, having failed to take soundings. Unknown to him, Lizard Point had already been passed; he was only two miles off the coast and on a course for the Manacles.

The pilot cutter *Antelope*, Master Nicholas Bickford, seems to have been sheltering from the worst of the weather in the lee of the Lizard, but on sighting the ship the cutter was sailed out to meet her, during which time sail must have been taken in on the ship to slow down to pick up a pilot. On their approach, and in heavy seas, the cutter's crew launched the punt, and with senior pilot Bickford at the stern it was rowed by a boatman to reach the ship's side, on which a rope boarding ladder swung. As he had done so many times before, Bickford leapt for the bottom rungs and started to climb; but the movement of the ship and violence of the wind and waves caused the ladder to swing and twist, throwing him against the ship's steel side. He clung there in considerable peril until the ladder, fortunately with him still on it, was hauled on deck.

The pilot was incapacitated for some time, and unable to give immediate instructions to the captain. Those instructions should have been to wear ship, that is, to turn it around against the wind and bear off the land, but difficult enough to do with a big high-sided vessel in those conditions. But it was already too late: the coast was closing fast. The *Clan Graham*, and all on her, were lucky: instead of piling onto the Manacles she was steered, probably more by luck than judgement, into the bay just to the west, and ground her way to a stop on the shallows off Lowland Point, close to where the *Paris* had previously berthed herself. It was 5 a.m., and still pitch dark.

On receiving the news later in the day, perhaps from a returning *Antelope*, and as the gale eased, the steam tugs *Penguin*, *Victor* and *Triton* managed to tow the ship off at high water and took her into Falmouth. Some of her plates were damaged and she was leaking. Over the next few days some temporary repairs were made in the docks, however, there was much disappointment among the management and workers on hearing that the anticipated refit contract was given to a Newcastle company. It was even a Dutch tug that was chosen to tow her away on 7 March. The result of the Board of Trade enquiry has not been found. Statements were made by the captain and officers, and by Bickford. Following the initial report to Trinity House there was further correspondence between the Falmouth Sub Commissioners and the Brethren regarding the actions of the pilot. Failing to appreciate the extenuating circumstances the Brethren recommended that he should be given a month's suspension, representing a hefty fine in lost fees. The Sub Commissioners replied with further explanation as to why they preferred to give him what seems to have been a fairly standard rebuke for misdemeanors: severely reprimanding him, and cautioning him as to his future conduct. After further explanation of the conditions the pilot had been up against, they continued:

> 'Such an event to a man, who though hale and hearty is of considerable age, was not calculated to enable him to give his instructions as soon as he was hauled up on board, and it had a mitigating effect on the judgement that we passed. Another modifying influence was the fact that Bickford is one of our best pilots, and for 38 years his character and capacity have been unquestioned. He has undergone considerable tension as the result of the casualty, and having in view the whole case we were, and are, of opinion that discipline would be thoroughly maintained by censuring him, rather than by suspending his licence at the close of his career. We shall be glad if the Elder Brethren will give the added facts their consideration, and sustain the position of their Sub Commissioners in their relationship to the large body of Pilots here by confirming their findings at the inquiry they instituted.
>
> Your obedient servants
> Alfred Bice, A.R. Dawson; Sub Commissioners.'

At this time Nicholas Bickford was 68 years of age. He retired two years later. Dawson, in particular, was always a strong supporter of the pilots, to the extent that some time later a pilot motor launch was named after him.

The general coasting trade remained healthy, with about 1,500 vessels recorded in 1894. In spite of major improvements in road transportation small vessels still traded into Penryn and to the upper reaches of the Fal, with coal, roadstone, timber and agricultural products. In total contrast was the occasional ominous sight of flotillas of Royal Navy battleships at anchor in the bay, some of the many evil bi-products of the industrial revolution. The sight may have stirred the heart of the true Englishman, or indeed a Cornishman, but one who could have had no inkling of the horrors which were to fall upon Europe a few years ahead. For the time being the better-off worker felt safe in the knowledge that the economy was strong, although he also knew that there was strong competition from abroad, and that many products he bought for the family were imported. He could afford things undreamed of by his grandparents; instead of a crumbling cottage he now might live in a new terraced house, with gas lighting, clean mains water out of a tap, perhaps even a built-in bath and flushing toilet. Seaside places such as Falmouth were benefiting from the modern innovation that many workers were now granted an annual week of summer holiday. Families flooded into the West Country on cheap excursion trains, to escape from the smoke of factory towns and the metropolis. Thousands could be seen in Falmouth town and on the beaches on fine Bank Holidays and at regatta time. Watermen who at one time only provided services for visiting merchant ships now made their living by taking visitors on boating and fishing trips on the Fal and along the coast.

The *Falmouth Packet* reported all the events which contributed to the changing face of Falmouth, and was always concerned with the local economy. In March 1902 it decided to have a grumble about a practice which had been going on for years, but seemed to be increasing. It concerned the practice of ships laying off the port to receive their orders, rather than coming right in to anchor in the roadstead off the town.

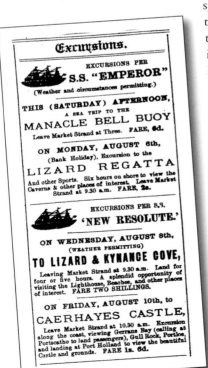

Notice in the *Falmouth Packet*, 4 August 1888. Many similar notices appeared each summer.

'Saturday, March 22nd, 1902
Ships' Orders.

On one day this week Falmouth pilots had in their possession over twenty ships' orders ready for delivery to the various captains when their vessels arrive off this port. This means that all these craft, instead of dropping anchor in Falmouth harbour for periods varying

Prince of Wales' Pier, Falmouth

Left: Market Strand Pier, with the Prince of Wales extension, opened in May 1905. Passengers board the little Flushing ferry *Greyhound* from the Strand steps and an excursion steamer at the end of the pier. Harbour tugs are among the vessels on the moorings. (Cornwall Centre)

Middle left: The excursion steamer *Victoria*, built by G. C. Fox & Co. in 1900. The full complement of passengers and the normally illegal use on a boat of the union flag perhaps signifies a special event. (RCPS)

Below: Notice from The Post Office Directory, 1892. By this time small steamers on regular timetables had replaced most of the sailing coasters.

The St. Mawes Steam Tug and Passenger Company's *Roseland*, built by G. C. Cox & Co. in 1886 and used as the Falmouth to St. Mawes ferry until 1938. (RCPS)

from days to weeks and months, will proceed straight to the port of discharge. And these are by no means isolated or rare instances; they are, unfortunately, of almost daily occurrence. Cargo owners find it cheaper to pay a substantial sum to proprietors of vessels so that, in the event of the cargo having been disposed of during the voyage, sailing orders might be put on board without delay on reaching what was intended to be the first home port of call. The practice is becoming more and more prevalent, and is likely to seriously affect Falmouth's shipping statistics, and, consequently, local trade and commerce. Other than those engaged in the shipping industry, few have any idea what the advent of a ship or steamer 'for orders' means to the port of call. Watermen, ship chandlers, agents, bum-boat people, and traders of all kinds, participate in the business that ensues, and the money thus expended by the ship's captain, crew, and owners, often amounts to a good round sum, especially if the journey has been a long one. The gravity of the matter will thus be seen, and amongst the quay folk it is causing something like a panic. Falmouth is the victim of circumstances. When steam largely supplanted sail our prosperity as a port of call was materially injured, and the comparatively new departure of avoiding all ports except the one of discharge is calculated to further impair Falmouth's chances of success as a shipping centre.'

The '*Packet*' was more cheerful in the spring of 1905, reporting that there had been nearly 80 arrivals in May, 74 of them calling for orders. The majority of them, including some splendid four-masters, brought huge cargoes of wheat from Sydney, Melbourne, Adelaide, Tacoma, Wallaroo, Buenos Ayres, Portland (Oregon), San Francisco and Port Pirie; nitrates came from Chile; jarrah wood from Bunbury; hides and bone ash from Rio Grande; sugar from Java, mahogany from Laguna, mangrove cork from Maracaibo, fustic from Punta Arenas, coffee from Santos, barley from Concepcion and jute from Calcutta. The highest registered tonnage of any one vessel was 2,882 tons. It was said that there was a great deal of pessimism about the future of sailing ships, although the May figures seemed to indicate that Falmouth was not yet finished as a port of call for these magnificent vessels.

The fall in pilotage revenue was leading to a serious decline in the standard of living of pilots and their families. The pilotage figures received by Trinity House seemed to indicate that the pilots were quite well off, until in December 1890 the Sub Commissioners wrote to try to explain that the pilots incurred considerable expenses which had to be deducted from the gross figures. These would have included earned sums for taking out agents' orders to ships waiting off the port and any salvage awards. Trinity House obviously thought that there were also other undeclared earnings, thoughts which the Commissioners were quick to try to dispel.

'...The average earnings are, by themselves, misleading, insomuch as they do not represent the actual amount received by each pilot. The cost of maintenance of the cutters and the owners' shares having first to be deducted. Taking the years 1879 and 1889 as examples, the earnings of the pilots for the former year are given as £168, and for the latter £128, whereas the amounts actually earned by each pilot was £89 and £87 respectively .... With regard to 'sums earned for taking off provisions and Channel Pilots, and assisting vessels for which there is no return made', we have no knowledge of anything of the kind, although we are aware that the pilots occasionally receive small gratuities from shipmasters.

We are. Your Obedient Servants.'

Ten years later there was further correspondence concerning the matter of income; a letter sent by the Sub Commissioners in September 1900 indicates that there was still little constructive response from Trinity House -

'Sir,

Representations have frequently been made to us that the earnings of the pilots of this District are very small, averaging only from £70 to £80 per man, and, owing to the building of larger vessels, and the consequent decrease in the number calling for orders, such earnings are gradually diminishing.

We are, therefore, unanimously of opinion that the time has arrived when a re-adjustment of the pilotage rates should be made, in order to remedy this state of affairs.

As the pilotage outwards on vessels calling for bunker coals was given up in the expectation that the number of such vessels would be largely increased, and as this expectation has not been realised, only such vessels calling as are absolutely compelled to, we would suggest that these vessels be placed on the same footing as others, viz. that the practice formerly existing be reverted to.

As vessels of over 1000 tons are generally longer, and consequently more difficult to manage in the narrow waters of Falmouth Harbour than smaller vessels, we would also suggest that vessels over 1000 tons register should be liable outwards to a charge of 5 shillings per foot of the draught of water. Vessels under 1000 tons register remaining as before. We are of opinion that the charges above indicated would add much to the contentment of the pilots, and would very little affect the shipping interests of the port, or country, and for these reasons we would ask that you would place this matter before the Elder Brethren, and ask their concurrence in our views.

We are

Your obedt. Servants

Henry Fooks, Arthur Rogers, Alfred Bice'

The general downward trend of arrivals continued up to the First World War; there were exceptional times when fleets of windjammers arrived with nitrates from Chile or grain from Australia, relieving for a few days the general gloom pervading the docks and harbour. The diminishing returns were once again concerning the pilot's committee; deputations were made to Trinity House to increase pilotage rates. Measures also being considered included trying to get a cutter more often to the west of the Lizard, thereby preventing orders from being sent out from Bass Point by semaphore or, later, by wireless telegraphy, rather than by pilots from Falmouth. Again there was discussion about reducing the number of cutters. Any argument regarding this last subject was resolved, in the worst possible way, when in April 1905 pilot boat No. 13, the beautiful *Antelope* was run down and sunk off the Lizard by the steamer *Milo*. Fortunately, the crew saved themselves in the punt, and after breakfast at Hill's Hotel, Lizard, returned to Falmouth by public transport. The pilot's committee decided that five boats were still needed, to cover times when they were beached or dry-docked for painting and refitting. Consequently, after receiving substantial compensation of £694.9s.7d. from the owners of *Milo* via Messrs Broad the agents, in November the committee purchased the big ex-Falmouth outfitter's cutter, *Gwendolyn*, which had been for sale at Dartmouth. She was re-fitted at W.H. Lean's shipyard in Falmouth, and supplied with new sails before beginning her service as cutter No. 1.

The number of arrivals in 1900 was 762; over the next decade annual numbers fluctuated but generally fell, and in 1910 stood at 568, with an average registered tonnage of 1,450 tons per vessel. The ratio between sail and steam was also changing: in 1900 about one third were steamships, ten years later it had increased to half. During the Great War sailing ships were vulnerable to attack, and many were sunk by enemy submarines, so that after the war they had become a less frequent sight in Falmouth.

In the years up to the First World War, although the number of ships calling for orders continued to decline, Britain still relied on half of her wheat consumption being imported, much of it from the colonies. Weekly sailing lists of perhaps over a hundred vessels en route for British ports were occasionally published in

Notice from Lake's *Falmouth Almanac*, 1892.

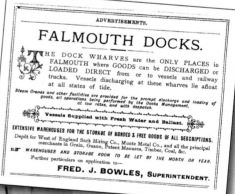

The 2494 ton steamship *Hildawell* arrived in Falmouth on 28 May 1910 for repairs in Number Two drydock. She was built and registered in West Hartlepool in 1892, one of countless tramp steamers in general trade. As such, in December 1916, during the First World War, she was recorded as missing. (RCPS)

Vessels in the two
existing dry docks in the
1890s. (RCPS)

Below left: The Royal
Navy torpedo boat
flotilla in Carrick Roads,
July 1910. (RCPS)

Below right: Ernest
Shackleton's *Nimrod*,
one of many famous
ships to visit Falmouth.
She called in on 26
August 1909 during a
return voyage from
Sydney to London
following an Antarctic
expedition. Seen
anchored in Carrick
Roads and attended by
a quay punt. (RCPS)

the *Falmouth Packet* at this time. Cargoes were being brought from all over the world, but guano from Chile and wheat from Australia, carried on the graceful clipper ships, were prominent. Little of this came into Falmouth Docks, where the main imports were maize and barley, probably the former for cattle feed and the other for beer, or even as barley bread for the poor. Exports from the Fal included china clay and china stone, brought by rail from the St. Austell area, and fish (in 1912 there were still nearly 200 Falmouth boats and 700 men and boys employed in fishing).

In 1905 the number of coasters, many now steam vessels, moving in and out of the port was about 1,200; in 1912 this had increased to over 2000. The dry docks and wharves were receiving a limited number of ships for repairs, particularly to sailing vessels with storm damage, but less so to steamers. In the foundry and shipyard alongside the docks, G.C. Cox & Co. were building a variety of small steel steam-powered craft, including some for foreign governments. Falmouth occasionally had a pall of smoke hanging over the harbour, issuing from a fleet of 30 small tugs, passenger vessels, shipping agents' boarding boats, the harbour master's launch and the like.

The number of employed pilots continued to fall, due to retirement because of ill-health or age. Three retired in 1907, leaving just 18 of the old guard who had joined the F.D.P.B.A. at its inception in 1887, plus a few new names. In 1910 the complement stood at 25; by the end of the First World War it had fallen to 15. These pilots and their predecessors, who hopefully lived in contented retirement, were the last to have seen the great days of sail. Work for the pilots had fluctuated considerably from month to month before the war: it could still be dependant on wind direction, many cargoes still being carried on sailing ships. According to the logbook of the pilot cutter No.12, *Condor*, in the particularly busy month of June 1907, her pilots boarded a total of 44 vessels, 8 being ship-rigged, 19 barques, 8 schooners, 1 barquentine and 1 brigantine; only 7 were steamships. Less than half these figures were recorded for some other months of the year; the earnings didn't reflect the many hours spent cruising off the Lizard, waiting for sails to appear over the western horizon.

There is no doubt that the diminishing number of arrivals, and subsequent lack of income, was high on the agenda at pilots' meetings. The cutters were requiring more frequent and expensive upkeep, and in 1913 it was decided to dispose of No.12, *Condor*, and she was sold to local boatman W.E. Morrison. Her condition couldn't have been too bad, because she had a second lease of life until broken up in 1942, pieces of her still lie in the Percuil River mud. Cutter No. 6, *Arrow*, was sold in 1914, and registered that year to a local owner, but not recorded the following year, and presumably broken up. This left just three in service; No. 1, *Gwendolyn*, No. 8, *Vincent*, and No. 10, *Richard Green*. This number proved to be insufficient to cope with the extra work brought by the war, and in 1915 a 35 foot wooden motor boat, the *A. R. Dawson*, was built for the pilots at a local yard, probably by W.H. Lean, who had already undertaken repair work for the F.D.P.B.A. It is unlikely that it was used out at sea, but was retained for duty within the harbour and Carrick Roads.

At the outbreak of war in August 1914 the government quickly took control of agriculture and essential industries such as coal and steel, and the production of munitions and military hardware such as transport vehicles. Britain's merchant fleet became the nation's lifeline, bringing in vital raw materials and food from the colonies, in spite of many losses through enemy attack. The smaller coasting vessels, both sail and steam, were also employed, carrying supplies such as coal around the coast and across to France and Belgium. One such was the little 58-ton ketch *Ivy* of Falmouth, built in more peaceful times by John Stephens at Point on Restronguet Creek, and owned by Norman Furneaux of Penryn. In late December 1914 she was carrying a cargo of cement and gunpowder from London, presumably across the Channel, when she received storm damage and was assisted into Ramsgate, surviving to sail another day. Vessels carrying explosives had been a common sight in Falmouth, particularly during the heydays of Cornish mining, and many used the port during the war. All had to anchor in the quarantine area of St. Just Pool, on the far side of the Carrick Roads, where transhipment was carried out.

The Port of Falmouth became a defended base strictly controlled by the Admiralty, busy with naval vessels coming in for supplies, repairs and refuelling. From October 1914 all merchant vessels in British waters were ordered into ports such as Falmouth for instructions or inspection, rather than the traditional 'for orders' from shipping agents. Only when the port officers had examined and cleared the cargo, passengers and crew was the vessel allowed to proceed or perhaps wait for a defended convoy to be organized; others were laid up on the Fal. A number of Germany-bound vessels, which had begun their voyages from distant harbours before the outbreak of war, were seized when they approached Falmouth, including two large chartered sailing vessels, each carrying cargoes of valuable nickel ore from New Caledonia in the Pacific. Passenger liners from different nations had been calling at Falmouth for years, and from early in 1915 the port was used by the great Dutch trans-Atlantic liners to embark and disembark passengers and mail, benefiting local hotels, tradesmen, tug firms and the pilotage service. The Dutch visits stopped abruptly after a large merchantman bound from Batavia to Rotterdam was attacked in the Channel. The crew, who had abandoned her, were some of many who were rescued and brought into Falmouth during the war. The ship was later towed in by patrol steamers.

Although at first scorned by the Admiralty as a serious weapon, German submarines began to inflict great damage on the merchant fleet, especially from the beginning of 1916, when all-out war was declared on undefended vessels. Submarines were seeking their victims in the Irish Sea and along the coast of the West Country, necessitating the construction of an anti-submarine boom across Falmouth Bay from St. Anthony Head to Porthallow on the Lizard. Incoming vessels, including many which may have been damaged and were being towed in by tugs, were escorted from sea through the boom at its southern end. At the height of the war the Falmouth pilots complained that tugs and navy personnel were sometimes depriving them of income, as the cutters were only allowed to work within the boom area. Even so, during the war the pilots earned a reasonable living, earnings rising dramatically in 1917, before falling again at the end of hostilities.

Pilots were certainly earning their money at peak periods; relations were not always cordial between them, who for generations had cared for shipping through the port, and the naval authorities now in command. Pilotage was particularly difficult during long dark winter nights. There was a black-out in Falmouth, and no normal navigation lights shown at sea or at the harbour entrance. Garrison searchlights operated from Pendennis and St. Anthony sometimes played across the harbour, but would have dazzled and ruined the night vision of those trying to steer a ship through the harbour deep-water channels. A glimpse of the problems encountered by all seafarers, as well as pilots, at this time, may be caught through the incident involving the *Abaris*. She was a steel-hulled vessel, built at Sunderland in 1904. A typical tramp steamer, London-owned, 330 feet in length and initially registered at nearly 300 tons. In spite of apparently having been fitted with the new 'Otter' anti-submarine or mine defence system, possibly an underwater paravane device, in November 1917 she became the victim of a German torpedo attack.

She was found somewhere out at sea in a crippled state, and shepherded towards the Falmouth Approaches where pilot James Green boarded her in the early hours of the 18th. (Following his apprenticeship, for many years Green apparently had to find other employment as crew on the cutters or elsewhere before, at the age of 50, replacing a retired pilot in 1916). The subsequent events, outlined in the following letter, instigated an enquiry, details of which unfortunately are not known. The same applies to some of the correspondence which flew between the Falmouth Sub Commissioners of Pilotage and Trinity House in London. It may have involved a claim for salvage by Green. Whatever the misdemeanour pilot James Green was alleged to have incurred, he was stoutly defended by the Commissioners. (The *Rio Verde* was London registered, similar, although slightly larger, than *Abaris*).

'The Secretary   The Custom House,
Trinity House,   Falmouth.
London

                                                                15th January 1918

    'Sir,

Agreeably to your telegram and confirming letter of December 24th, 1917 and your further letter of December 28th 1917 Pilot James Green attended the Custom House, Plymouth in connection with an enquiry conducted by Captain Clarke, Chairman of the Pilotage Committee into the alleged collision in Falmouth Bay and the grounding by request in Falmouth Harbour of the S/S 'Abaris'. We respectfully beg to bring the following facts of the case to your notice.

The Abaris a torpedoed steamer was being brought to Falmouth by the Tug 'Great Emperor' and two of H M Trawlers. The vessel was in dire distress, her engines were useless, she was deep by the head with her propeller practically out of the water, hand steerage only was available and she was continually getting deeper by the head. The vessel had her Otter Defence gear down but this fact was not disclosed to the Pilot when he took charge at 4.45am on Nov: 18th 1917.

The towing tug which should have given warning that the 'Rio Verde' was looming ahead, failed to do so, slipped her tow rope and left her tow practically helpless. The Abaris took a sheer – which may have been due to the effect of the Otter Defence gear on a slow moving vessel – and which the Trawlers used on either side of the vessel as a means of steering, failed to arrest. She struck the Rio Verde a sliding blow carrying away her port lifeboats but doing little material damage.

Pilot Green with great skill and judgement brought the Abaris into the harbour and placed her in safety on the Vilt (shallows near St. Mawes Castle), thereby winning the warm approval of the Master. We respectfully submit that the Pilot's services were not those of ordinary pilotage but were services of a salvage nature as the Abaris may have plunged at any moment and after performing such work for him to be told that his licence would not be dealt with – and we understand he was so told by Captain Clarke – implies that his skill as a pilot was in question.

We think it only just that Pilot Green should have your assurance that his skill was not for a moment detrimentally considered. The Falmouth pilots, a steady and reliable body of men, have during the past few years dealt with the situation in a most praiseworthy manner. Their record has been remarkably free from casualties when the number and size of vessels dealt with are considered and that they do not as a rule have any tug assistance. Their masterly placing of enemy damaged vessels in positions on banks from which temporary repairs have been effected is deserving of commendation.

Pilot Green attended Plymouth at personal inconvenience and we think it only reasonable that his railway fare and out of pocket expenses in connection with the attendance should not fall on the man.

    We have the honour to remain,
        Sir,
            Your obedient servants.'
        (Signed by 3 Sub Commissioners)

After being moved to the docks the *Abaris* received new engines and boilers, and sailed again.

In the years following the Great War, although Britain and her allies were victorious, she had been depleted of trained manpower and innovative ideas, and was slow, compared to her trading competitors, to take up new methods in industrial production and marketing. Throughout the 1920s Britain's export trade, and therefore the shipping infrastructure declined, leaving little for shipyards to do apart from ship breaking. Falmouth became a backwater, the creeks full of laid-up ships.

In November 1917 it was found that cutter No. 10, *Richard Green*, was in a poor state, particularly her mast, which had signs of rot. This was not the time to restore working wooden sailing boats, no matter how beautiful they were. The materials for such a project were now hard to come by, and the cost prohibitive for the depleted coffers of the F.D.P.B.A. In January 1918 the boat was sold for breaking up. By August that year pilot retirements had brought their number down to 17; there seemed to be few prospects of an increase in trade, and therefore it was decided to dispose of No. 1 *Gwendolyn*, and she was sold to a French owner. This left just cutter No. 8, *Vincent* to cruise at sea, and the launch, *A R Dawson*, for harbour duty. In October 1921 it was found that *Vincent* was in a bad condition, which was not surprising considering that she had been working almost continuously for 69 years. She was advertised and sold in August 1922.

In a letter to Trinity House in October 1922 the Falmouth Sub Commissioners gave a list of the 12 remaining working pilots, split into three watches. The regular rotation of duty at that time was given as the following:

Sea duty	10 p.m. to 10 a.m. the following day
Off duty	10 a.m. to midnight
Harbour duty	midnight to midnight
Off duty	midnight to 10 a.m.

The launch, *A.R. Dawson*, built in 1915, was recorded under the ownership of the F.D.P.B.A. as late as 1964; by 1970 she was in private hands in Flushing. In 1922, to replace *Vincent*, an order had been given to a Brixham firm for the construction of a new sailing cutter at a cost of £2,150. The *Arthur Rogers* was registered at 22 tons, somewhat smaller than her predecessors. She remained in commission until 1936 when, on 10 February during a strong gale from the south east, she broke adrift from her mooring and was driven ashore. The estimate for repairs was £300: this was deemed too much to warrant keeping her. Therefore a request was made to Trinity House to replace her with another motor launch. In August it was agreed that James Gilbert of Porthleven would build it, at an initial cost of £1,175. The final cost, including the 44 horsepower Kelvin diesel engine, came to £2,200. The new boat, named *Harry Slater*, was in service by April 1937, joining the *A. R. Dawson*. In the meantime the *Arthur Rogers* sailing cutter had been sold to

Below left: The *Cutty Sark*, brought to Falmouth in 1922 by owner Captain Dowman and refitted by ship-wrights at Ponsharden and the docks. She was moored in the harbour as a training ship for boys until 1936. (Cornwall Centre)

Below right: The ex-Royal Navy 74 gun ship *Implacable*, moored at Falmouth in the 1930s. She was bought by philanthropist G. Wheatley-Cobb as a training ship for boys, but later became holiday accommodation and a coal hulk. Her elaborate stern gallery and figurehead are now displayed at the National Maritime Museum, Greenwich. (RCPS)

96

Top right: Flushing from Green Bank, c. 1920.

Middle right: High water at Town Quay in the 1960s. These traditional timber-built pleasure and working craft were soon to be replaced by types made of glass reinforced plastics (GRP). At this time several thousand employees of the docks engineering departments were busy servicing fleets of oil tankers and merchantmen, such as those at the wharves in the background. (Cornwall Centre)

Below: Falmouth Docks, the Inner Harbour and Penryn River, c. 1950; prior to the enlargement of Number Two Drydock. The wharves and docks are packed with vessels, including a floating dock, ocean liner, and merchantmen. Flushing Village and the snow-covered fields of Mylor Parish lie beyond. (Cornwall Centre)

Abraham Hipwell of Exeter for £190. Later owners of the restored and ketch-rigged boat, up to 1955, were Robert Byng followed by Thomas Hepworth, both of London. It was later stated by Argal and Bird (*Mariners Mirror* Vol.64, 1978) that she crossed the Atlantic and was wrecked off the Bahamas.

As ships and shipping evolved throughout the twentieth century the pilots' working methods also had to change. Following the First World War, although stately windjammers occasionally graced the waters of Falmouth Bay, deep sea trade became dominated by steam and motor-driven ships. Improving radio communication meant that fewer needed to call at a port to pick up orders from agents. Neither did they often need to anchor in the Carrick roadstead to shelter from storm or wait for a favourable wind. The duty of the pilots, coupled with the local tug crews, was increasingly centred on meeting ships off Falmouth Bay and taking them directly to the docks, or between roadstead, jetties and graving docks, whether for repairs or discharging cargoes.

Between the two world wars the docks company obtained the finance to increase ship repair facilities: two new graving docks were built and numbers one and two docks deepened. Three long jetties were added to the original Western Wharf. Further dredging of the approach channel enabled some of the largest tankers and passenger liners to enter the graving docks. Large oil tanks were installed to improve bunkering facilities; this had become one of the port's most lucrative enterprises. By the 1930s the ancient ship building area of The Bar Creek, towards Arwenack and Grove Place, which gave birth to so many traditionally-built vessels, including pilot cutters, had been obliterated by spoil from the dock excavations.

During the Second World War the Falmouth district received its quota of tragedy to the population when the town, docks and surrounding area was bombed by German aircraft. As enemy forces advanced rapidly through France Falmouth, in common with other harbours on the South Coast, became a haven for every kind of craft crammed with refugees escaping from France and the Channel Isles. As in 1914, the docks and harbour infrastructure played an important part in the war effort. An endless stream of naval and commercial vessels passed in and out: disembarking casualties, undertaking repairs, being re-armed and supplied. Once again the Ministry of Shipping and the Admiralty were in charge, augmented by the United States armed forces in the months approaching and final exit of thousands of troops embarking for the D Day landings. Because of security restrictions at the time there is little evidence of the part played by the pilots during the war. However, with night-time blackouts and limited wireless traffic the local knowledge of the pilots and their boat crews must have been invaluable.

During the second half of the century the fortunes of the docks fluctuated with the ups and downs of world trade. The large Queen Elizabeth the Second dry dock, capable of taking some of the largest ships of the time, was opened in 1958. With changes of ownership and new investment Falmouth Docks have since gained a reputation for undertaking quality ship repairs to a wide variety of vessels, from fleet auxiliaries to tankers, bulk carriers, cross-channel ferries and ocean liners. A separate concern builds and services prestigious luxury yachts on the site of the old number one dock.

Over the same period the port's complement of pilots remained at about seven, employing a similar number of boatmen to handle and service the motor launches. These consisted of the little *Kernow*, 44 feet in length, which was in use from 1962 to 1978. Two 70 foot Trinity House launches, the *Link* and the *Landward* were used in the 1970s. The new Nelson class *L. K. Mitchell* was purchased in 1977 and is still in service in 2012. Following the pilots amalgamation with the Harbour Commissioners in 1988 their launch *Trelawney* was also used as a pilot boat. In December 2006 the Harbour Commissioners took delivery of a new £750,000, 16 metre Camarc pilot boat, built by V. J. Halmatic. She was built of GRP, and capable of a speed of well over 20 knots, somewhat faster than her namesake, the beautiful ex sailing cutter *Arrow*.

Deregulation of Pilotage in 1988 meant that the Falmouth Harbour Commissioners were given powers to provide the pilotage service for Falmouth Docks and the ports of Penryn and Truro. The seven self employed members of the Falmouth Pilots Partnership entered into a service contract with the Commissioners. They work on 12-hour watches with rest periods, using two launches. The pilotage district encompasses the area within the Dodman to Black Head boundary, the larger incoming ships being met at a point about three miles offshore. Work also includes the difficult navigation of small commercial vessels through the mud banks of the Truro River, or round the hazards of the Manacles to the stone quarries within the ancient cliffs of the Lizard peninsula.

CHAPTER 5
THE PILOTS

HOW DID THE FIRST Falmouth pilots originate? All must have been mariners of some kind when they took up the profession, and familiar with local waters. From early times there was a considerable pool of experienced men based around the Fal estuary, any one of which might have undertaken pilotage work, either seawards or through the tidal upper reaches. The number already working on the water is demonstrated by a parish survey of 1626, commissioned to find the mariners available to man the King's ships in time of war. On the upper reaches there were said to be eight fishermen and one mariner at Truro, and three bargemen at Kenwyn; eight fishermen are listed for the parish of Kea. There were a similar number of fishermen in Feock parish, plus the astonishing number of 27 bargemen. On the Carrick Roads and seawards, St. Anthony in Roseland had five fishermen available. In the neighbouring Gerrans parish there were 18 fishermen, probably working out of Portscatho or on the Percuil River. Across the harbour at Mylor there were 15 bargemen, some probably working on the Penryn River. Only three mariners are listed for Penryn. Budock parish, which contained the embryonic Falmouth, had a mere five sailors and four fishermen. The list for St. Just parish, which contained the village of St. Mawes, indicates a thriving maritime community: there were ten sailors, one mariner, one gunner, and 14 fishermen, one with the familiar name of John Vincent. The list is only an indication of the number working; there could be a number of reasons why men might not be on the list, official or otherwise.

We can speculate that, perhaps in medieval times, when merchant ships began to arrive in Falmouth Haven from foreign shores, a few of the local fishermen began to supplement their meagre income by guiding ships into the harbour. Some pilots were to reside in the developing town and harbour of Falmouth, where they would earn the trust and respect of shipping agents and merchants who wanted their vessels and cargoes to arrive in safety. Other pilots resided at St. Mawes, a mile and a half away on the eastern side of the main harbour entrance. In the 1530s John Leland described the place as a poor fishing village with a pier, chapel and holy well. Later in the century the castle built by King Henry VIII on the nearby cliffs must have brought some development: perhaps a few more houses and an inn or two. At that time the village was granted the doubtful privilege of sending two

Coverack Harbour,
c. 1930. (Helston
Museum)

members to Parliament. (That right was abolished under the Great Reform Act of 1832). Jurors listed in the St. Mawes Court Book in the 1740s included the familiar names of Fittock, Jenking and Vincent. The jetty protecting the little harbour was rebuilt and enlarged at this time. Nearby properties depicted on a map of 1772 included four fish cellars, three fish sheds, and two salt cellars.

The harbour and village of Coverack in St. Keverne parish was ideally placed as a base where pilots would watch for Falmouth-bound ships as they passed the Lizard. The Barker family must have operated from there long before they received official recognition in the 1809 Trinity House list of pilots. An earlier Coverack pilot was Thomas Marish, known because of a declaration made by him before John Hoblyn, Mayor of Helleston (Helston) on 6 January 1780. Marish seems to have been in dispute regarding his claim for a recent pilotage job which did not go well; no other documentation about the case is known. He declared that his age was about 58 and he had been piloting ships into Falmouth for 30 years. On Sunday 28 November 1779 off Coverack, he saw a signal flag requesting a pilot flying on a Swedish ship, the *Jungfrun*. (This was a 220 ton ship, named as *Jungfrien* in Lloyd's Register). He boarded her where the Captain, Johan Sinman, agreed a fee of four guineas for pilotage into Falmouth. After being becalmed off the Manacles adverse winds set in, driving the ship eastwards past Falmouth. Over a number of days there was disagreement between the pilot and captain about the capability of the ship to beat back against the wind and tide to Falmouth, to the extent that at one stage they were off the coast of France. They didn't arrive in Falmouth until 25 December; such were the joys of early pilotage! *(CRO.DD R03731)*.

There is no doubt that Falmouth and St. Mawes mariners were already operating as freelance pilots when Henry Vincent of St. Mawes headed the list of Port of Falmouth pilots who were granted licences by Trinity House in 1809. The Vincents had been in St. Mawes, part of the parish of St. Just in Roseland, from at least the early seventeenth century. The death of a John Vincent was recorded in 1612. It was presumably a son of his, another John, who the following year married Bathsheba Nicholas. Their children were Jane, John and Inego. The latter died in 1677, aged 53, at which time an inventory of his possessions was taken, which gives an insight into his, and perhaps his contemporaries, way of life in this coastal village. He seems to have been comfortably well off, considering that others were in debt to him to the amount of £12 (about £1000 today). His house furnishings included two bedsteads, feather bolsters and pillows, rugs and blankets. Domestic items included earthenware and pewter. Presumably he earned his living on and around the beautiful Percuil River, for his main possessions were a fishing boat and equipment and a fowling gun. He also owned a third part of a small seine (a local association with boats and nets for pilchard fishing).

In such a small community it is not surprising that later in the Vincent's family tree there were to be connections through marriage with other St. Mawes pilot families such as Andrew, Dash, Bellman, Tiddy, Lowry, Jenking and Lower. Apart from Henry, seen on the 1809 Trinity House list, Joseph Vincent, of the same age but a different family line, was a licenced pilot by 1825; his son William was to follow him. The Vincents provided at least 15 pilots over the nineteenth century. Some were to move across to Falmouth, where they joined other pilots in the terraced housing above the parish church. Here they were close to the cutter moorings off the Town Quay. The boats of the St. Mawes pilots lay on the usually more sheltered village moorings on the Percuil River.

The Andrew family, also of St. Mawes, were another prolific family of pilots, dating from at least 1809. About 12 pilots of that name have been found, although, as with some of the other families, confusion is caused by sons often having the same Christian name as the father. The 1809 list contains four pilots with the name Lowry: a total of about 15 individuals served from then until the 1930s. From the beginning the majority lived in Falmouth. One early exception, and not specifically a pilot, was W. Lowry who, in 1814, was involved in the sale at St. Mawes of the remains of a ketch which had been wrecked on St. Anthony Point. Other well-known names on the 1809 list are Collins, James, Fittock, Pascoe and Tonkin in Falmouth; Dash and Jenking in St. Mawes. The Chard family in Falmouth joined the

Below: St. Mawes Harbour, c. 1910. (Cornwall Centre)

Bottom: A view from fields above St. Mawes Harbour, with Place House in the background. Moored to the left of passenger ferry *Roseland* is an unrigged pilot cutter, possibly *Richard Green*, which was broken up in 1918. (RCPS)

service from at least 1820; up to the First World War at least 15 of them were pilots.

The only Falmouth District pilots on the 1809 list to initially reside neither in Falmouth town or St. Mawes were from the Barker and Williams families of Coverack, in St. Keverne parish on the Lizard. This was of course well inside the Falmouth pilotage area. Two John Barkers and a James Barker were on the first list. In common with many other pilots their forbears or close relations were involved in the fishing industry. At the Bodmin Quarter Sessions during 1808 a James Barker of Coverack, fish curer, was allowed relief of excise duty on 65 bushels of salt, part of a cargo of 2,000 bushels of British Fishery salt. This had been damaged in a storm during a voyage from Liverpool to Coverack and had obviously originated from the Cheshire saltworks. (Owing to lack of information on what weight of salt constituted a bushel, an estimate of 56lb., being an average bushel weight of barley and oats, has been chosen to give an estimated cargo weight of 50 tons for 2,000 bushels of salt). James Barker the fish curer must have been one of the pilots on the 1809 list, or at least a close relation, and an important member of the Coverack pilchard seine netting industry. Here, along with other fishing villages, the pilchard and other fish sustained much of the Cornish population at times when other foods were scarce. Salt was necessary for the preservation for winter storage. Mostly it was used in fish curing in the 'pilchard cellars', before packing for export overseas.

In 1809 a Henry Williams, also from Coverack, was the first of that family to be listed as a Falmouth pilot. The Barkers and Williams had close ties, probably through marriage, sharing the pilot boat *Vie* which was initially based at Coverack. The two pilot families, with their boat, eventually moved to Falmouth, possibly in about 1870. Both families had representation in the profession, as pilots or crew members, well into the twentieth century.

In 1825 there was an Act of Parliament 'for the amendment of the law respecting pilots and pilotage', and in the following year the published text included lists of current Trinity House pilots. At Falmouth District there were now 11 First Class and 24 Second Class pilots, a total increase of 10 over the 1809 list. As pilotage requirements grew towards the middle of the nineteenth century other names appeared, sometimes represented by just one or two pilots, and perhaps apprentices or deckhands. They were Angove, Bickford, Green, Jenking, Lower, Old, Richards, Sharrock and Tiddy. Followed by, consecutively into the 1880s; Ball, Carter, Coward, Hancock, Hodge, Nicholls, Sawle, Scott, Tregeagle and Watts. A list of the pilots who had served from 1887 under the Falmouth District Pilot Boat Association was compiled following its centenary in 1987. This was published by David Barnicoat in his 1998 book, *Dodman to Black Head*. Earlier pilot names may be found in the pilotage archives at the Bartlett Library, NMMC. The earliest examples of lists written into the available Sub Commissioners Minute Books are given below.

The pilots of the Port of Falmouth, as employed at 1st. January 1853.
(Edited by the author)

First Class Pilots Name	Date of Initial Second Class Licence	*Second Class Pilots* Name	Date of Licence
Samuel Lowry	15.12.1808	Nicholas Lowry Andrew	11.10.1842
Daniel Fittock	06.02.1822	James Dash	27.02.1844
Henry Tonkin	14.10.1831	James Andrew	27.02.1844
James Lowry	30.04.1833	James O. Tiddy	29.03.1845
Richard Andrew	05.06.1834	William L. M. Tiddy	03.02.1846
Nicholas Vincent	18.12.1834	Thomas Jenking	02.04.1847
Nicholas Jenking	07.07.1846	George Angove	21.03.1848
Elias Chard	16.11.1832	Joseph Vincent	21.03.1848
James James	07.01.1836	Francis Lowry	05.12.1848
John Chard	26.01.1847	Frederick Andrew	05.12.1848
John Lowry	21.02.1837	Isaac Lower	22.02.1849
John Dash	19.04.1836	Henry Chard	03.04.1849
John Barker	21.02.1837	Richard Green	23.10.1849
William Dash	06.02.1849	Peter Fittock	11.02.1851
John Barker 3rd	29.06.1841	William Vincent	11.02.1851
George Barker	23.10.1838	John Williams	20.01.1852
William Williams	30.08.1842		

A list of pilots' apprentices, in service September 1841 to March 1865

Date of Indenture	Name	To Whom Bound	Term Expired (at seven years)
13.09.1841	Henry Vincent	Henry Vincent	01.02.1848
14.09.1841	Joseph Sharrock	William Lowry	01.02.1848
31.07.1841	Joseph Barker	John Barker 3rd	05.07.1848
06.12.1841	John Vincent	William Vincent	08.10.1848
22.08.1843	Charles Jenking	Nicholas Jenking	01.11.1849
14.05.1844	John Andrew	Richard Andrew	22.08.1850
31.10.1846	William Old	Henry Tonkin	23.01.1851
02.01.1846	James Lowry	James Lowry	01.10.1852
06.10.1846	William Chard	John Chard	28.01.1853
24.08.1846	Michael Richards	Mark Tiddy	03.02.1853
06.10.1846	Elias John Chard	Elias Chard	24.04.1853
22.08.1846	John Collins	William L. Tiddy	30.07.1853
17.08.1847	Joseph Jane Vincent	Nicholas Vincent	17.08.1854
25.05.1848	Bennet Vincent	Joseph Vincent	25.05.1855
30.05.1848	Henry Nicholls	James James	30.05.1855
06.10.1848	Henry Coffin	William Lowry	06.10.1855
10.10.1848	Charles Andrew	Samuel Lowry	10.10.1855
05.12.1850	William Davey Chard	Ellias Chard	05.12.1857
04.12.1850	Nicholas William Bickford	Richard Green	04.12.1857
24.06.1851	William Dash	John Dash	24.06.1858
17.09.1851	John Fowler Hocken	Daniel Fittock	17.09.1858
15.02.1853	Charles Warren Chard	John Chard	14.02.1860
22.02.1853	Nicholas Lowry Andrew	Nicholas Lowry Andrew	21.02.1860
09.03.1853	Gustavus Lowry	William James Lowry	08.03.1860
20.07.1853	William Henry Jenking	James O. Tiddy	19.07.1860
19.08.1853	Jonas Jenking	Thomas Jenking	18.08.1860
08.11.1853	Richard Andrew	Richard Andrew	07.11.1860
09.10.1854	Joseph Dash	William Vincent	08.09.1861
07.02.1855	Edward James Andrew	Frederick Andrew	06.02.1862
19.02.1856	John Lowry Jnr.	John Lowry	18.02.1863
19.02.1856	Joseph Dash	William Dash	18.02.1863
02.09.1856	Henry Tonkin Jnr.	Henry Tonkin	02.09.1863
26.02.1858	Charles J. Chard	Elias Chard	26.02.1865
05.03.1858	William J. Hicks	William Vincent	05.03.1865

In common with most trades at the time, before becoming a pilot the applicant had to serve an apprenticeship under an existing licenced pilot for a term of seven years. In this district the apprentice was often the son or a close relation of the pilot, and started his term at 14 years of age. (There was at least one instance when the pilot preferred his son to go to another boat!) During, or at the end of the term, the apprentice had to serve at least a year at sea on a square-rigged vessel, for as a pilot he would have control of such ships when bringing them to an anchorage within the port. Often, before a vacancy for a new pilot occurred, full-term apprentices may have had much sea experience before they reached the top of the list of candidates, for instance: in March 1855 John Vincent, who had finished his apprenticeship in 1848, gained his licence after six years as crew on a pilot boat and another year on voyages to Quebec and the Mediterranean.

As children, the applicants for apprenticeships would have had much experience playing or fishing on small boats around the harbour. They may have already been known to the Trinity House Sub Commissioners of Pilotage when they came before them to be examined as to their suitability. Such meetings were sometimes recorded in the Minutes, as in June 1853: Nicholas Lowry Andrew, Second Class pilot, prayed to be allowed to take his son, of the same Christian names, as an apprentice. 'The Sub Commissioners examined the lad on Reading, Writing and Arithmetic and found him properly educated according to his station.' The future was not always plain sailing: the following month an apprentice, who had served his seven years with pilot George Bickford, was struck off the list for his 'intemperate habits'.

The number of licensed pilots on each boat was governed by the number required to cope with the amount of work expected and the amount of each pilot's share of the revenue earned by the boat. Obviously, if too many were employed individual earnings would be reduced, making the job uneconomical. Trinity House also restricted the number of licences issued, reaching a maximum of 65 for the 13 boats at the peak of maritime trade in the early 1870s. Therefore Falmouth boats generally carried an average of five licensed pilots each, including the Master. Consequently there was strong competition among those apprentices who had already served their seven years and were waiting to apply for any vacancies that might occur.

Having completed his term satisfactorily, on applying for a post as pilot, the candidate would be examined by the Sub Commissioners. They would take into account his appearance and character and his knowledge of all aspects of navigation around the district; tides, depths, transits, navigation marks, anchorages and so on. Likewise, his knowledge of ship handling, cargoes, ships' papers and logbooks was tested. Knowledge of general navigation and local byelaws was required, particularly in relation to the pilotage rates to be applied to any particular ship and over what distance. A pilot had to negotiate with ships' Masters, shipping agents' boarding clerks and so forth. Diplomacy was essential during negotiations, sometimes difficult when dealing with foreign vessels and language problems.

After the recommended application had been accepted by Trinity House in London, the successful applicant was granted a Second Class licence. The receipt of such a note as the following, sent by the Sub Commissioners, would doubtless lead to celebrations in the local hostelry:

To Mr. Wm Pascoe,

You are hereby directed to proceed on board No. 11 Pilot Cutter and authorised there to act as a 2nd Class Pilot pending the receipt of your licence from the Trinity Board,

    Custom House Falmouth, 8 April 1873

    (Signed by Sub Commissioners)

The licence, when received, and for which the pilot had to pay a fee, was supposed to be carried by him when he was working. The text of the document, in this case issued to James Lowry, Junior, is as follows:

    To all to whom these Presents shall come, We, The Trinity House, send Greeting. Know Ye, that in persuance of an Act of Parliament, made and passed in the 17th and 18th year of the Reign of Her present Majesty, Queen Victoria, called 'The Merchant Shipping Act 1854', We, The Trinity House, having received a satisfactory Certificate, under the hands of Frederick Swatman, James Caddy, William Robinson Esquires, the Sub- Commissioners of Pilotage, by us appointed for the Port of Falmouth (being within the Trinity House 'Outport Districts') that they have examined into the qualification of James Lowry Junior Mariner (the Bearer hereof, whose description is endorsed on these presents) to act as a Pilot for the said Port, and the adjoining coasts thereof, and, that he is duly qualified to act for such Port and Coasts. Do Hereby Appoint and Licence the said James Lowry Junior to act as a Pilot within the Limits hereinafter mentioned, that is to say, In and out of Falmouth Harbour, St. Just, Carrick Road and Helford Sound, along the Coast from the Dodman to the Lizard and in and out of all Ports and Places within those Limits. And this License (if the same shall not be revoked or suspended in the meantime, as in the said act is provided) is to continue in force, up to and until the 31st day of January next ensuing the date hereof, but no longer, unless the same shall be renewed from time to time by Indorsement hereon.

    In Testimony whereof We have caused our Common Seal to be hereunto affixed this twenty ninth day of June in the Year of our Lord 1858'

The reverse of this document was countersigned annually by Sub Commissioners up to 1864, when Lowry received a First Class Licence.

On the commencement of his service the pilot was obliged to begin contributing a percentage of his earnings to the Trinity House Superannuation Fund, which was presumably administered through the Sub Commissioners. The scheme seems to have been badly managed in London: after running costs had been deducted, the pension a pilot received on retirement was very small, leading to calls from the Pilots' Association for reform. In the middle of the century the pension could be a paltry £10 *per year*. If a widow made a request for the pension on the death of her husband in service she might only receive half of that. William James Lowry (possibly brother of James above) seems to have been the victim of petty bureaucracy, causing him to write to the Sub Commissioners on 17 December 1892:

Top left: Pilots and crew aboard *Richard Green*. Personnel altered over time and identification is uncertain. There are surviving crew lists for the boat in the County Record Office for just four years between 1889 and 1899, the theoretical period for the taking of the photograph; therefore those portrayed might include any of the following: pilots (in uniform) – Charles Andrew (Master and managing owner), W. H. Jenkins, Fred Watts, Richard Green, Sampson Williams, Charles Fittock, Thomas Jenkins, Charles Jenking, Fred Handcock, James Dash, Richard Andrew. Crew – Charles Green, James Green, Alfred Pascoe, Charles Andrew, Richard German. Others may also have manned the boat before her end of service in 1918. (Photo – Tim Knight)

Middle left: Pilots and crew in working clothes aboard the *Richard Green*, moored off St. Mawes. Boat features include the saloon skylight and stove chimney. The loose-footed trysail is stowed on the lowered gaff yard. (Chris Pollard)

Bottom left: The *Richard Green* off Trefusis Point; this beam view emphasises her size. The patchwork on her big trysail may be repairs undertaken by sailmaker Prior in December 1903. Inexplicably the bowsprit bobstay has not been tightened although the jib is set. The dinghy in the foreground seems too small to have been a boarding punt. (Tim Knight)

'Gentlemen, May I ask that you will kindly move the Trinity Board to cause the rate of my pension to be altered to £16 per annum, instead of £14. I was licenced as a pilot on 1 February 1853 and should have completed my 40 years service on 31 January 1893. I was under the impression that as I was licenced up to 31 January 1893, and the licence paid for that period, I was entitled to claim the rate of pension for 40 years service. If the Trinity Board will not take this view I ask that my licence may be returned to me until the expiration of my period of 40 years, or, otherwise, I shall lose £2 per year, and this with my small means is a great consideration to me. I have paid much more to the Superannuation Fund than I shall ever receive back from it.'

At Falmouth the Second Class licence allowed pilots to take control of the majority of merchant vessels that came into or left the port. Because of the depth restrictions in some parts of the harbour, Second Class pilots were only supposed to bring in ships with a maximum draught of 17 feet. Over that draught, only a more experienced First Class licenced pilot was entitled to navigate such ships and claim the higher pilotage. However, there were some instances when a senior pilot was not available, and then a Second Class pilot was justified in taking the job. Apart from the Master of the cutter, the several other pilots on board had joined it on mutual agreement with him, perhaps being a relation, and even having shares in the boat. Others may have been allotted the position by the Sub Commissioners, sometimes for a short period such as when their usual boat was laid up for refitting. In what could be hazardous and uncomfortable working conditions, perhaps at sea for a number of days at a time, it was imperative that the men were outgoing and of reasonable character to work together. Any conflict between them was quickly resolved if brought to the attention of the Sub Commissioners. In February 1856 John Vincent had been told to move from cutter number 8 to number 11, but had begged to be excused from moving because of 'want of cordiality' from the Master of the latter vessel. The two men were brought before the Sub Commissioners: the Master was reprimanded, and then expressed his willingness to be on friendly terms. A warning was given that if it was heard that the quarrelling continued action would be taken, 'for the good of the service'. In other cases of misconduct, reprimands might just consist of being told to be careful in future. Larger penalties, if administered through the Trinity House Head Office, could consist of the removal of a pilot's licence for three months or more, preventing him from earning a living for that period.

In September 1867 the pilots of number 10 complained of the 'unbearable demeanour' and general conduct of the Master. A report went to Trinity House: his boat licence was taken from him and issued to two other pilots from the boat. The licence was returned two months later. The Master may have had some medical problems, as he died two years later, aged 45. Throughout the years there were occasional reports of pilots being drunk or at least belligerent, either ashore or when working on the boat. In the latter case this could cause severe problems for the rest of the crew and embarrassment to the service if witnessed by ships' Masters or shipping agents' employees. Generally the pilots were of excellent character and a number were teetotallers.

Understandably, in a small community such as St. Mawes the occasional conflict between neighbours, who may also have been relatives, was hard to avoid. One such conflict was to lead to an incident the newspaper reporting of which was worthy of being made into a Victorian melodrama. In the 1860s two sisters, of the well-known Peters family of St. Mawes boat builders, had married two local men: Margaret married William Henry Jenkins, who received his first-class pilot's licence in May 1867, and was generally a well respected family man. The other sister, Elizabeth, married William Lower. Although at least two members of the Lower family had been pilots he had remained a boatman; early in 1881 being crew on cutter No. 2, *Andrews* on which Jenkins at that time was a pilot. However Lower had since been dismissed for drunkenness. For a long time there had been major differences between Lower and his wife, leading to periods of separation when she went to live with her sister at Jenkins' house, the latter on occasion trying to mediate. It was a trying time for him: apart from the sister-in-law there were six children in the house, and wife Margaret was soon to have another. Lower was blaming him for his wife's absence over the previous five months and in public had threatened to do him harm, which apparently no one had taken seriously.

In the late evening of 5 July, William Jenkins had returned from an excursion trip on his small steam boat *Wotton*, both sisters being among the passengers. On his way home alone he found Lower waiting for him in an alleyway; Lower raised a revolver and shot him in the head. Incredibly the bullet, seemingly a lead ball, glanced off Jenkins' skull, leaving him dazed and bleeding from a wound over his right eye. As he was then being chased by Lower a second and third shot missed.

He reached safety at the Fountain Inn, by which time William Thomas, a St. Mawes sailmaker, and John Sparks, engineer from the *Wotton*, had disarmed the assailant. They were soon surrounded by a large crowd where Lower was arrested by Police Constable Crews. At the subsequent trial at Bodmin Summer Assizes witnesses confirmed that Lower had openly said that he wanted to kill Jenkins; it took the jury seconds to find him guilty of attempted murder. Considering the gravity of the charge the sentence, for the time, seems lenient: 15 years penal servitude, although Lower was 47 years old, and would be an old man if he survived to his release.

Pilot William Henry Jenkins, a patriarch of St. Mawes society, with his family in about 1893. His wife Margaret (nee Peters) sits on the opposite end of the middle row. William was to retire in 1897. (Tim Knight)

Apart from Royal Navy ships and the small coasters, which did not require piloting, under the Act of 6 Geo.IV.c.125 all vessels entering Falmouth, a compulsory pilotage port, were subject to charges depending on where the pilot had met them at sea. According to Directories published in 1846 and 1862 the charges had remained the same over that period, namely: if a pilot boarded the ship at or further out than the Lizard the charge was £3-3 shillings; the charge was the same if conditions were such that the pilot boat had to run before the ship to calmer waters before the pilot could board. For boarding a ship outside the line drawn from The Manacles to Dodman Point the charge was £2-2 shillings. For boarding outside the line from the entrance of the Helford Estuary to Gull Rock (off Nare Head, to the east of Gerrans Bay) £1-10 shillings and 6 pence. There were usually lesser charges for outward pilotage.

In addition to these charges, if vessels were taken to anchorages within Carrick Roads, St. Mawes or the Inner Harbour the Master was liable to further charges, which varied depending on the draught of the vessel, for instance: a schooner drawing no more than 8 feet of water was charged £1-4 shillings; thereafter the charge rose foot by foot to a charge of £6 for a full-rigged ship drawing 22 feet of water. Port of Truro vessels arriving from abroad were charged half rate. These charges increased and were calculated in different ways later in the century, including, in 1897, payments for pilotage within the harbour, and if the pilot was kept on board for some reason. For the latter service there was a scale of charges, from 10 shillings and 6 pence for 6 hours to £3-3 shillings for 72 hours. Vessels were also liable for harbour dues, for shipping ballast, and so forth. Vessels entering the Falmouth Docks, constructed from 1860, were subject to the docks company charges.

It is unclear whether the appropriate pilotage fees were given by the ship's Master in cash directly to the pilot on the completion of the job, or collected later from the relevant shipping agent, who dealt with all the financial matters of the ship when in port. The latter is likely in most situations, although there were instances of pilots asking for, or being given, cash in hand payments above the normal fixed rate for the job. This was allowed if extra services were carried

Pilots and crew servicing *Vincent* on Grove Place Beach on a warm summer's day. The boat is held up by substantial 'elephant's foot' beaching legs. The clinker-built boarding punt is beached on the right. (National Maritime Museum, Greenwich)

Arrow and her boarding punt on Grove Place Beach. The confusing amount of rigging means another cutter is beached behind her. In the background lies the Bar ship building area. (National Maritime Museum Greenwich)

out which justified such payments. Apart from the normal pilotage, lump sums were occasionally earned by the boat as a result of salvage claims, usually assessed by the courts, whereby the pilots had prevented the loss or damage of ship and cargo. Other income was earned by the common practice of taking letters containing ship's orders from the Falmouth agents to deliver them to the appropriate ship offshore, thereby negating the need for the ship to come into port. For this service the pilots usually received a payment equivalent to the 'inwards and outwards' pilotage charge, and was paid by the ship's agent. For all such transactions the agent would be reimbursed, adding his commission, by the owners of the ship or cargo.

Such transactions as the above were occasionally recorded in a ledger of shipping agent William Broad & Co. for the years 1867 – 70 (*CRO X 225*). On 23 March 1867 the owners or agents, George Marshall of London, were issued a bill which included a cash payment to pilot J. Tiddy for putting orders off the port on board the *Patrician* - £5, plus 14 shillings and 6 pence for the boat hire to the pilot cutter (plus commission for Broad – 10 shillings and 6 pence). On April 26 George Marshall were billed for £5 cash paid to pilot Andrew for putting orders on board the ship *Winchester*.

The following invoice (*CRO.FS3/426*), dated 21 July 1842, issued by G. C. and R. W. Fox & Co. to Captain Charles Shirley of the schooner *Kara*, reveals the extent of the expenses, including pilotage, that a Master (who in this case was probably the owner) was likely to incur on entering Falmouth Haven at that time, with a relatively small vessel. As it had been put into the quarantine anchorage of St. Just Pool it had probably come from an area suffering from one of several epidemics prevalent at the time.

	£	s	d
Paid pilotage into port and distance money	4	4	0
Anchorage 2 shillings 6 pence, Harbour Light 5 shillings			
8 pence		8	2
Boat hire to quarantine with provisions		4	6
John Edey butcher	1	2	3
Barnet Falck for sail cloth	2	6	8
Paid for supplies in quarantine 8 shillings 8 pence, fish etc.			
5 shillings		13	8
Pilotage to sea	2	6	0
Paid him cash (the pilot?)	3	0	0
Stamp for draft and postage		4	0
	14	9	3
Commission in advance, clearing at Customs etc.		10	6
	14	19	9

Detail from a unique painting by local marine artist Alexander Brander, circa 1895. It depicts a Falmouth shipping agents' gig, probably owned by Lloyds' agents Broad & Co., passing Little Dennis blockhouse on Pendennis Point on a course to meet an inbound ship. As the wind is advantageous a lugsail has replaced the more usual six oarsmen. Some may be on the windward side, hidden by the sail, helping to balance the gig. (The Lander Gallery, Truro)

In July 1877 Fox & Co sued the owner of the schooner *Lutha* for non-payment of harbour costs. She was a 124 ton vessel owned by T. L. Seaton of Padstow; this was his only vessel: in other years he had owned larger ships involved in taking emigrants abroad and returning with cargoes such as timber. *Lutha* had arrived for orders in Falmouth with a cargo of maize from Mazagan, on the west coast of Morocco. The report of the subsequent court case is a further example of the financial arrangements made between captains, shipping agents and owners, which was the usual 'custom of the port'. When merchant vessels, other than small coasters, approached the harbour, they were usually met by a boarding clerk in a Falmouth shipping agent's gig, in most cases an employee of Messrs Broad or Fox & Co. The clerk then offered to take the captain to the Custom House where he was obliged to report his ship's arrival. That agent thereby gained the right to handle the ship's port expenses, for which he was paid a commission. The bill was either settled by the captain before the ship sailed or obtained later from the owner.

In the case of *Lutha* the amount was for pilotage fees in and out of the harbour; Light Dues (a standard fee for the maintenance of lighthouses), telegrams, and Mr. Pope's chandlery bill. The total amount, including commission, was £12, 10 shillings and 4 pence. When time came to settle the bill the captain said that he had no money. In court, through a solicitor's letter, the owner disputed the claim, stating that the captain, Hawker, should have had enough money. The captain in turn said that the chandler's bill was to make the vessel seaworthy. The Judge gave the verdict against the owner, who should settle the Fox claim.

It may be of interest to make a small digression into the affairs of the Fox family. Apart from their prominent position in Falmouth as ship owners and agents, in common with many Quakers they were involved in many aspects of the Industrial Revolution. They had business interests in mining, owned the local Perran Foundry and an iron works at Neath in South Wales. Daughter Anna Maria founded the Royal Cornwall Polytechnic Society, which sought to foster improvements in all aspects of science and technology. Along with other local businessmen, the Fox's promoted the building of Falmouth Docks and the Cornwall Railway. We know much about the family through the eyes of the son, Robert Barclay Fox, who was born in 1817. After an excellent and undoubtedly privileged education, he became fully involved with the shipping business from the office near the waterfront. Robert's diary, or journal, written between 1832 and 1854, gives fascinating details of contemporary social and economic affairs, and many of the events, both mundane and dramatic, which occurred in and around Falmouth Harbour. His references to pilot boats are unfortunately few and very brief, but nevertheless are relevant to their history:

'*29 September 1836. Pope's pilot boat was wrecked last night near Crab Quay by missing stays* (when tacking) *and driving on the rocks.*'

Pope was not a pilot, but presumably owned the boat. The Popes were shipowners, sailmakers and chandlers in Falmouth. They were later to be the main shareholders of cutter number 6, *Water Nymph*, built in 1844, Philip Pope the accountant being later involved with *Arrow*, also number 6. Perhaps the wrecked boat was also number 6, the name of which unfortunately was not given.

'*20 March 1837. Had a most glorious sail out of the harbour on board the Havre, the magnificent French brig. It was blowing fresh and I came home in the pilot boat, gunnel under.*'

Oh to have been there! The exhilaration of being aboard a graceful boat, thrashing through choppy waters, sails possibly reefed down, the sea surging against the bulwarks as she leaned to the wind.

'*27 August 1838. Engaged a pilot boat to take Cousin Edwin and the rest of the Mission to Scilly. My father being leader of the party ...*'

The 'Mission' may have been an excursion by the Society of Friends, taking the Word to the unenlightened inhabitants of Scilly. The influential Fox's were then able to employ a pilot boat on any occasion they wished, and it would have been very lucrative for the pilot and his crew. As the port became busier later in the century it is unlikely that the Sub Commissioners would have sanctioned such a cruise.

There seems to have been no objection to cutters occasionally being used as 'water taxis', bring passengers into Falmouth from off-lying ships. At the beginning of August 1860 the cutter *Alarm* met the *Kent* about 26 miles south of the Lizard. The ship, with 230 passengers on board, was homeward bound, probably for London, after a passage of 97 days from Melbourne. Twenty-three people requested to be taken into Falmouth, and were crammed aboard the cutter and taken in with the mail. Several such instances were reported in 1862: in mid-May the Australian ship,

Prince of Wales hove to off the port, having sailed via the Cape of Good Hope rather than round Cape Horn. This was the time of the American Civil War and merchant ships were being harassed by American privateers on the latter course. The ship had a cargo of wool, hides, tallow, copper ore and gold, plus 180 passengers. Pilot boat no. 13, *Wasp*, managed to cram 50 people, plus the mail, on board (on one trip?!) and brought them into Falmouth, presumably taking a fare from each. 'Some of them were just in time to catch the afternoon mail omnibus, which was crowded to excess'. A fortnight later another Australian ship, the *Verulam*, with wool and copper ore, was met by boat no. 4, *Telegraph*, and Master John Chard brought in ten passengers. And a week later the troop ship *Agamemnon* was in the Channel, being en route to London, with time expired and invalided troops from Calcutta. She was met by cutter no. 12, *Nicholas Jenking*, and Mr. Evans' cutter, *Grand Turk*, who between them brought in 14 passengers and the mail.

Pilots and crew aboard *Vincent*. Seen in the photograph is the massive mainsheet block to the trysail, the iron 'horse' across the counter, the small hatchway to the saloon, and the edge of the boarding punt to the right. The pole strapped to chocks on deck is probably the mainsail boom. (National Maritime Museum, Greenwich)

Vincent off the Lizard. Features include the boarding punt, loose-footed trysail, merchant ship-sized mast and massive shroud tackle and halyards. The out-of-focus object in the foreground is a rope made off on the bowsprit knightheads. (Opie of Falmouth, pub. *The Medley of Mast and Sail*, vol.1. Teredo Books, Brighton, 1976)

Some pilots obviously thought themselves financially sound enough to be able to make a small investment towards the construction of Falmouth Docks that were being promoted at this time, particularly by merchants such as the Fox family. In January 1859 the initial subscription list of persons purchasing shares in the new company included five pilots: Elias Warren Chard, Elias John Chard, James Lowry and Richard Green, all of Falmouth; and Nicholas Vincent of St. Mawes. Each paid a 10% deposit on one or two £25 shares, which was the amount generally invested by local shopkeepers and the like, among the 174 initial subscribers. The docks were successfully completed and were soon busy with ship repairs and use of wharfage. However, the company had shaky financial times later on, and were taken over by the Public Works Loan Commissioners, the debt not being cleared to 1914. The early shareholders did not receive any return on their investment.

Pilots usually bought shares in the product they knew about, boats, particularly their cutters. They probably also invested in trading vessels owned and worked by relations or friends within the close-knit communities on either side of the harbour. In 1869 St. Mawes pilots William Henry Jenking and Frederick Andrew were two of the four shareholders who purchased the 64-foot iron steam boat *Wotton*, taking over from an earlier steam passenger service between Falmouth and St. Mawes. A Falmouth guide book of 1877 states that the ferry ran several times a day all year round from Market Strand, fare to St. Mawes and back six pence. According to the Mercantile Navy List, Frederick Andrew was the managing owner of the vessel from 1870 to 1896. At times *Wotton* was used for private pleasure cruising, such as in July 1881 when pilot William Jenkins took his wife and friends on a round trip to Fowey regatta. The company also competed with the several other passenger boat services, with excursion cruises in the locality. In September 1882 a large notice was placed in the *Falmouth Packet* advertising *Wotton* trips to Coombe plum gardens on the Upper Fal, to Gerrans Bay and the Helford River. In common with some of the other steam boat companies, outside the tourist season *Wotton* may have also operated as a tug.

As merchant sailing ships faced increasing competition from steamers, Masters tried to keep their time in harbour to a minimum, therefore an increasing amount of towage work was required around the harbour. In adverse winds the big sailing ships such as the windjammers might request a tow in or out of the harbour, or from an anchorage in Carrick Roads to the docks.   The tugs were especially valuable when crippled ships were in the offing in foul weather. Usually this didn't negate the ship Master's obligation to call for a pilot and pay the pilotage cost as well as a charge for towing negotiated with the tug Master. If a pilot was not available the ship Master could still proceed, not paying pilotage, accepting full responsibility for his ship but relying on the skill of the tug Master to take him to a safe mooring.

At many ports around the United Kingdom merchant ship Masters had the option of accepting or refusing to take on a pilot. On the other hand, for historical reasons, at London's Trinity House Outport Districts such as Milford Haven, Dartmouth and Falmouth, pilotage was compulsory, and had to be paid for. This applied to all large merchant ships; naval ships and coastal vessels under 60 tons (later 100 tons) register were not included. A ship Master could refuse to take on a pilot but still had to pay the pilotage charge inwards and outwards. Some disputes over the charges arose from time to time, such as when one particular steamship came in merely to recharge her bunkers with coal, and was not trading. The Master refused to pay, but the owners were later found liable. The payment of pilotage gave shipowners some assurance in the case of damage to that vessel or other property while under the control of a pilot. If it was proved in court that such damage was the fault of the pilot, he was liable for the cost of repairs. However, Trinity House, in later years at least, were of the opinion that the Master was still ultimately responsible for the navigation of his vessel. In extreme circumstances he could be justified in countermanding the pilot's instructions. Of course, the pilots were not wealthy, and not insured, apart, possibly, by the £100 bond they had executed to Trinity House when receiving their licence. The proposed 1884 Shipping Bill brought in by Joseph Chamberlain sought to eliminate compulsory pilotage. Spirited petitions by the Port of Falmouth, and presumably by the others involved, were sent to Parliament, and their case won the day: compulsory pilotage stayed.

As previously noted, from the beginning Trinity House, through its Sub Commissioners, exerted considerable control over the pilots, particularly in staffing, disciplinary, and financial matters. However, the actual working of the boats at sea was left to the pilots, who, after all, owned the boats. The main concern of Trinity House was that vessels were met, and efficiently and safely brought to Falmouth, or where necessary taken to other ports further east by Channel pilots. Officially, only the licensed pilot cutters, flying the pilot flag, could be used to approach shipping to offer pilotage services, but occasionally, when ships may have been missed by the cutters out at sea, they could be boarded by pilots who may have been watching on shore, say, at Coverack on the Lizard, or even from St. Mawes Castle within the harbour. In this case gigs or other rowing boats, with pilot flag hoisted, were also used. This method may have been used frequently in the harbour for ships that were intending to depart.

With their work encompassing ships and crews from many nations, the pilots could never know what situations might occur while performing their duties. An incident in August 1885 illustrates one pilot's courage while helping to stop a serious altercation between crewmen on board the 172 ton Dutch brig *Albatross* he was piloting out of the harbour. During a quarrel, the Dutch cook drew a knife on a German seaman, but the latter, a more powerful man, wrenched the knife away. A fist fight ensued, until they were parted by pilot Richard Dash. Back in his galley, the cook seized an iron belaying pin and dealt the German a blow, which laid open his forehead. He was stopped from striking again by the pilot, who managed to take away the weapon. After the injured German had received attention, the captain, who seems to have played little part in preventing the fracas, paid off the cook, who was sent ashore in the pilot boat.

Pilots worked in an unpredictable environment, and in the days of sail, when ships were moved by the inconstant winds, families at home had to remain stoical if their menfolk did not appear when perhaps the boat returned without them. Hopefully wives may have received a message through the grapevine to be told of their husband's whereabouts. All to the good if a lucrative pilotage contract had been obtained to take a ship further eastwards up the English Channel. But sometimes such passages were unintentional: in late January 1860, somewhere to the west the pilot Richard Andrew boarded the barque *Norma*, homeward bound from Honduras. By the time he had brought her close to Falmouth the weather 'came on very boisterous'. The ship was driven off, and had no option but to continue up Channel. Andrew and the barque were not heard of again until about two weeks later, after she had arrived off Deal in Kent.

It could be worse for the wives of the independent 'Channel pilots', a number of whom lived in Falmouth. These were licensed by Trinity House to guide vessels along the English Channel and also perhaps towards Irish ports and Liverpool. Their income depended on the number of vessels that required a pilot for such voyages and therefore could be very irregular; they could also be away for considerable periods. This sometimes led to social and financial problems for their wives at home, which in one case had tragic consequences. In January 1864, it was reported that while Channel pilot William Angove of Falmouth was away at sea his wife, 48 year old Mary Ann, had received goods from a packman, or tallyman. Subsequently she could not keep up the repayments and the tallyman had taken out a summons against her. The County Court bailiffs had since removed furniture from the Angove home in lieu of payment. Apparently Mary Ann could not face her husband when he returned, staying with a neighbour or even living rough, and had taken to drinking. She later went to the local druggist to buy a pennyworth of oxalic acid, which she said was for cleaning but was advised that it was a strong poison. Shortly she went to another neighbour's house to ask for water; her behaviour alarmed the neighbour who went to find her husband. A search later found her dead in a backyard. The inquest jury were to return a verdict of death due to temporary insanity, at the same time recording that they strongly condemned the tally system which had brought the anxiety and shame to cause the suicide.

Throughout the nineteenth century the Falmouth port limits remained as laid down by Trinity House in 1809, that is: from the Lizard in the west to the Dodman Headland in the east and all ports within, including the Helford estuary. However, from the middle of the century as more seaworthy cutters were built, the pilots began to cruise far and wide for custom, particularly to the south and west. Until the inauguration of the F.D.P.B.A. there was no station within the District that a cutter had to keep to. Presumably it was known by experience, on the time of year, and wind and weather conditions, from which direction ships were likely to appear. Competition between the crews frequently took them to Scilly and beyond. In one incident in 1855, involving a drunken and belligerent pilot, reported in the Sub Commissioners Minutes, he had met and boarded a ship at a distance of 40 miles to the south of Scilly. Cutters could be away for several weeks, depending on the time it took to put all their pilots aboard incoming vessels, returning home for repairs and provisions, then away again seeking ships.

As ship numbers declined into the 1880s, the fewer but larger steamships replacing the many of sail, competition between pilots became even more fierce, bringing bitter complaints from Scilly pilots of incursions by Falmouth cutters into their district. The Scilly pilotage service was mainly concerned with putting pilots on board sailing ships going eastwards up the English Channel or perhaps northward through St. George's Channel.   Such traffic had considerably declined, and by 1884 there was only one pilot cutter, the *Agnes*, left on Scilly, and the few pilots were finding it difficult to make a living. They were understandably upset when the Falmouth boats hove in sight to poach in their waters. Jenkins quotes from the 1884 logbook of *Agnes*, in which such incidents were recorded: on the morning of 6 April three Falmouth cutters were in sight. By 10.00 hours cutter number 2 (*Andrews*) was close alongside; they were then seven miles northeast of Scilly. The *Agnes* pilots managed to speak to an Australian ship, after which they were then followed by cutters number 2, number 7 (*Victoria*) and number 13 (*Antelope*), to the northeast (a rather unexpected direction) for 35 miles. They each tried to board ships ahead of the *Agnes*. Number 7 gave up, but later several other cutters were also in the Scilly area. Over the next two days they harassed the *Agnes*, trying to put pilots aboard ships before her.

During pilots' committee meetings over several years there had been proposals for saving expense by reducing the number of boats, pilots or crews, and the setting up of some sort of pilots' union. In November 1886 the Falmouth solicitor W. Jenkin was asked to draw up a document outlining a 'scheme for the reduction of pilotage expenditure', the draft of which was accepted at a meeting of the Sub Commissioners of Pilotage. With few exceptions it seems to have been adopted by the pilots as laid down:

A Scheme for the Reduction of Pilotage Expenditure

It has been decided by a majority of 9/10 (nine tenths) of the Trinity Pilots of Falmouth that a reform is absolutely necessary for their better working and remuneration. We beg leave to submit the following scheme for your consideration and approval.

First, Amalgamation, second, Reduction of Expenditure, third, Raising money to effect the same.

Amalgamation.

By amalgamation we mean that every pilot shall have an equal interest and bear an equal share of the responsibility in the proper carrying out of the pilotage duties. We propose to form an association to take over the whole of the cutters and to frame rules (subject to the approval of the Trinity Brethren) by which every pilot shall be obliged to take his regular turn, to a fine unless prevented by illness for which he shall have to produce a medical certificate. To dispose of five cutters and to work the remaining seven as follows. Two cutters to cruise within a radius of twenty miles from the Lizard, one cutter stationed at the Lizard, one cutter cruising between the Lizard and Manacles, one cutter between Manacles and Dodman, one on Harbour duty, one in reserve in case of emergency. The above subject to any alteration the Trinity Board or Sub Commissioners may deem advisable.

Reduction of Expenditure

Owing to the falling off of the Trade of the Port, pilot's earnings have been seriously diminished, and by the reduction of five boats, we should save thirty shares which would probably enable us to live whereas under existing circumstances we find it utterly impossible to do so. It is our opinion that under the proposed plan we should be enabled to do our duty with more satisfaction to shipping and safety to ourselves than under the present system.

By having less opposition we shall be able to rig our craft lighter and consequently make our cutters more efficient in bad weather.

Raising money to effect the above.

It is proposed to have an impartial valuation of the cutters to determine the amount necessary for purchasing the same. To borrow the money to purchase the whole of the cutters, five to be sold the proceeds of which sale to be handed to the Bankers. The remaining seven cutters to be mortgaged in addition to which we give our personal security for the proportional part owned by us. In the event of a pilot dying or leaving the service, the association shall pay to him, his executors, or assigns the amount already paid by him in liquidation of this debt, and shall take over his responsibility and interest in the Pilotage Service. In the event of the owners not coming to an amicable arrangement, the Boats to be valued by impartial surveyors, one to be appointed by the shareholders and one by the Association. Should they not agree they are to have the power of calling in a third who must be accepted by all parties and whose decision shall be final.

The only serious objector to the scheme was Nicholas Lowry Andrew, principle owner of No. 5, *Alarm*. He agreed to accept £250 for the withdrawal of the Trinity House licence for the cutter, and was allowed to retain the craft, but no longer for pilotage use. There were two Nicholas Andrew's, father and son; the latter had been drowned four years earlier. Nicholas senior survived his son, and was now about 65 years old and therefore due for retirement anyway.

The first meeting of the new Falmouth District Pilot Boat Association was held on May 2, 1887; eleven pilots attended as committee members, Samuel Collins being voted in as chairman, and George Barker as secretary. Over the next few days they were busy with processing pilot's applications for membership, a register of which had to be sent to the Sub Commissioners at the Custom House. All the pilots, a total of 59 at the time, signed up. There had been no new licences issued for several years, and although the 34 apprentices were listed, it was unlikely that the majority would ever become licenced pilots. With the forthcoming further reductions in pilot boats, most would eventually find other employment.

All the cutters, except *Alarm*, were purchased from the respective owners of the shares of each boat, for total amounts varying from £200 to £525, depending on the boat's age and condition. The seven best boats were then mortgaged to the Cornish Bank Ltd. No. 1, *Harriet*; No. 2, *Andrews*; No. 6, *Arrow*; No. 8, *Vincent*; No. 10, *Richard Green*; No. 12, *Condor*; No. 13, *Antelope*. Although the boats were now owned by the Association a list of newly appointed 'managing owners' was then registered at the Custom House. Some of the new 'owners' had previously been major shareholders in the same boats they took over again. It was next proposed that the remaining four boats must be sold off, at less than their earlier estimated value: No. 4, *Telegraph*, for £150; No. 7, *Victoria*, for £200; No. 9, *Dash*, for £150; No. 11, *Nautilus*, for £120. In July arrangements were made to auction *Nautilus*, followed by *Telegraph* in September. *Victoria* was kept on until the following August, then being bought back by the Chard family, being registered to John until 1904. *Dash* was sold to a St. Mawes resident. *Nautilus* remained registered to the Association until 1889.

Prior to 1887 each cutter Master seems to have been in charge of all the revenue collected by the pilots of each boat from ship Masters or their agents in Falmouth. Shares of this money were then re-distributed to the pilots at fortnightly 'settlings'. Apprentices, depending on their length of service, were also given a percentage, and deckhands were paid a wage. The shareholders of the boats also expected to receive a return on their initial investment. Enough money had to be kept back for boat maintenance materials, and major replacements of rigging and sails. All such financial matters were now to be the responsibility of the committee of the F.D.P.B.A. At the meeting on 21 May it was proposed that £347. 10s. cash was to be drawn from the bank for the payment of crew wages and pilot's shares (of the pilotage fees, presumably taken over the previous two weeks). The crew's wage bill was £52. 10s. and the pilots' shares totalled £297, pilots each receiving £5. In the years ahead wages and shares continued to be paid fortnightly. The amounts set at committee meetings varied considerably, depending on the trade into the port and number of pilots.

On all ships approaching from the westward, to enter the English Channel, Masters expected to make a landfall, or see first, the Isles of Scilly, or more optimistically, the Lizard peninsula. At

The 2008 ton steel four-masted barquentine *Beethoven* arrives for orders on 20 June 1906, carrying a cargo of nitrates from Pisagua, Chile. Anchors are hung low, ready for dropping. Even though towed in by local tugs the ship would have been boarded by a Falmouth Pilot to guide her in, but accepting a reduced pilotage fee. (RCPS)

night, and in bad weather, especially if visibility was bad, if he knew he should be near the land, the Master would be anxious to pick up a pilot. This was also the wish of the owners of the ship and cargo, merchants, agents, victuallers, shipwrights, sail-makers, watermen, innkeepers, tailors etc., all of which might benefit from the news that a ship had arrived safely off the Lizard and was being piloted into the port. Therefore, Trinity House kept a close eye on its pilots, wherever they served, and ensured that they remained aware of the great responsibility they bore. On their part, pilots had to support their families and therefore, except in the most extreme conditions, went to sea to seek out those incoming ships. Masters that had been flying a signal requesting a pilot were quick to complain if they hadn't been approached by the time they got into Falmouth Bay. This did occur occasionally in very poor visibility, and at busy times when a cutter's complement of pilots had boarded ships, and the deck crew had sailed back into port to pick up more pilots. The Sub Commissioners' view was that the cutters should remain on station, pilots having to find their own way back to the boat. This seems unrealistic, especially if the cutter was several miles out to sea. Perhaps one method employed was for a gig crew to row them out.

In all but extreme weather a pilot was expected to board the ship he was attending. In his mind he had to assess the accessibility of the deck of the ship, the wind strength, wave height and movement of both vessels. He also had to consider the safety of himself and the crew member who was to row him across. On seeing an approaching customer, be it a trans-Atlantic windjammer or a small European brig, the cutter would be steered towards it until it could be seen if it was flying a signal flag requesting a pilot. This was either the code flags P.T or G, or the pilot jack, which consisted of the union flag within a white border. Equivalent lights were shown at night. If so, the cutter would close up until the question could be asked: 'Do you want a pilot to Falmouth?' If the answer was in the affirmative, the Master would already have given orders to reduce sail. He was obliged to slow his vessel down to assist in the boarding process, although not expected to slow down to the point where steerage way was lost so that his charge became unmanageable. It is also unlikely that in bad weather a big ship would be brought into the wind and hove to to assist a pilot.

For the pilot to board: the cutter would be closed up on a parallel course until in the sheltered leeward side of the ship. The boarding punt, a clinker-built dinghy of about 15 feet in length, may have been on tow in fine weather, otherwise it was kept on the deck of the cutter. To launch it a section of the bulwark was lifted out and the punt slid overboard stern first, its bow painter controlled by someone on deck. The pilot and one or two rowers would climb aboard. Ideally the cutter would be taken close to the ship's side as the punt's painter was let go, leaving the rower

A barque, believed to be *Magwyn*, photographed when calling for orders, either in May 1902 on a voyage from Chile, or November 1903, from South Australia. She is attended by the Harbour Commissioners Launch *Arwenack* (11) and a passenger tug. (RCPS)

only a short distance before gaining the boarding ladder. After the pilot had reached the deck, the punt was rowed back to the cutter, which was waiting astern. The crewman may have been able to pick up a line from the cutter, to be pulled back alongside to where the punt could be heaved back aboard. If short-handed, a tackle may have been used to assist in the lift. Even though the cutters, and the punts, were eminently stable craft, and the pilots and their crews some of the best in the world, in rough conditions the whole procedure, which may have had to be done a number of times every day, was fraught with danger.

When ships at anchor within the harbour required a pilot to take them out to sea to continue their voyage the usual signal for a pilot was hoisted. A pilot was put on board either from a gig or a dinghy (usually referred to as a punt) rowed out from Falmouth or St. Mawes by an apprentice or boatman employed by the pilots. It is likely that the ship towed the boarding boat out until clear of the land, where the pilot re-boarded it and was rowed back to the harbour. This supposed scenario has been corroborated by a dramatic report published in the *Falmouth and Penryn Weekly Times* in June 1861.

At this time there were various armed squabbles among European neighbours which, although Britain remained neutral, brought about the formation of a national volunteer defence force. Locally, this included the re-arming of the Tudor forts of Pendennis and St. Mawes for the defence of Falmouth Harbour. It gave the Coastguards and other volunteers the opportunity to act like soldiers and sailors by indulging in sessions of practice - firing the antiquated fort guns at artificial targets off the harbour entrance. The lack of consideration for the safely of users of the harbour led to many complaints of poorly aimed shots coming close to boats in the Bay. The St. Mawes battery was firing on the 28th, when about noon: '...William Pascoe, a waterman of the town, was bringing Mr. (George) Barker, a pilot, in from the bay out of a vessel he had just piloted to sea; when a nearly spent shot from the guns struck his boat, she being at the time outside the Black Rock, crashing through her starboard bow and passing out on the other side abaft the midship thwart, striking poor Pascoe, who sat on the thwart, in the thigh and knocking him almost senseless in the bottom of the boat, occasioning serious contusions of the parts struck and breaking one of his fingers. Some of the splints of the boat struck Mr. Barker, who sat in the stern, knocking his hat overboard, and cutting his lips and otherwise disfiguring and injuring him...' One can imagine the scene on the small boat, as Barker tried to make Pascoe comfortable and then row the half mile or so back to the town to get the casualty to his home and summon medical assistance. The newspaper expressed its indignation at this 'homicidal practice', particularly as there was another near miss to a pilot boarding boat within an hour or two of the first. Barker was fortunate to escape with his life on this occasion; other members of the family were not so fortunate when on pilotage duties.

Whether living in Falmouth or St. Mawes the pilot families were probably seen as reasonably well-off members of Victorian society; the occupation engendered a certain respectability, although invariable there was the occasional black sheep. Family group photographs depict the men in smart suits and the womenfolk dressed in the height of fashion. As a matter of course the social scene included a weekly visit to church or chapel. Although some pilots were teetotal, no doubt for some a drink with neighbours was not out of the question at one or other of the pubs on the waterfront on either side of the harbour. Some inkling of other activities may be gathered from an item published in *the Falmouth and Penryn Weekly Times* on 8 February 1890. It concerns a social gathering of the St. Mawes Brass Band families and friends, with some pilots obviously taking an active part in the proceedings.

'BRASS BAND:- On Wednesday night the members gave their annual supper, in a barn lent by Mr Pomeroy. The guests numbered about fifty, including Rev. H.E. Carlyon and Mrs. Carlyon, Rev. W. E. Postlethwaite, Mrs. Christoe, Miss Beauchant, Mr. And Mrs. Gilbert, Mr. Hicks, Misses Hicks (2), Miss Tiddy, Mr. Fittock, Miss Green, Messrs. W. Andrew, Collins, Angove, and Hodge, and did justice to a substantial spread. The repast over, the floor was immediately taken possession of by several couples, dancing, interspersed by singing, being freely indulged in. Mr Fittock sang 'The warrior bold' in his usual style, followed by Miss Tiddy's rendering of 'Caller Herrin' and 'Now', both of which were loudly applauded. A Cornish tale by Mr. Sara was much appreciated. Mrs. Christoe's singing of 'Twickenham ferry' followed by Martin's humourous song 'Killaloe', sung by Mr. W. Andrew, added to the pleasure of the evening. A vote of thanks was accorded to Mr. Pomery (conductor of the band), who, with Mrs. Pomeroy, undertook the responsibility of carrying out the wishes of his committee in order to ensure a successful evening.'

CHAPTER 6
PILOT LOSSES

IT IS A FUNDAMENTAL law of the sea that some of the people who venture onto it will be drowned. Thankfully, in today's world of safety equipment, sophisticated communications and rescue services, that statement does not have the same impact as it may have done in previous centuries. The Man against Man carnage of war apart, in the days of the wooden sailing ship there was an inevitable considerable loss of life amongst the peacetime sailors of the merchant fleets of the world. Winds are essential to the sailing ship, but winds, and the waves that they bring, can sink you, as can human failings of the incompetent use of navigation aids and sailing in unsound vessels.

The nineteenth century Falmouth pilots and their crews do not appear to have used lifejackets; the cork jackets that were eventually manufactured would have been too cumbersome for the work they had to do. Even if some could swim, their winter and wet-weather gear included the use of heavy coats and boots that were not conducive to survival if they fell in the sea. It was only towards the end of the century that the Minute Books mention the requirement for life buoys to be kept on the decks of the cutters.

Before the publication of local newspapers from the beginning of the century, there is no doubt that there were unrecorded losses among the early pilots. Later on, even if there were such incidents during the Napoleonic War, and at other times of national crisis, editors would have had little space left to include them as an important item of news. With the growth of shipping trade into Falmouth, the papers began to place greater emphasis on general maritime affairs. Among the many reports of loss of life when ships were wrecked on the coast, accidents to pilots and their crews began to appear. Some reports are very brief, others more comprehensive: the Victorian reporter might report what he had been told by the participant or observer, but he or the editor might add or subtract material for the sake of the story. However, some of the reports, apart from expressing regrets for the loss of life, sometimes give family details, and useful insights into the working practices of ship crews and pilots, or the failure of such, at the time. The original reports of the incidents described below may be found in the contemporary newspapers within a week or so of the approximate dates given. (All are on microfilm at the Cornish Studies Library, The Cornwall Centre, Redruth.) Exact quotes are marked as such, otherwise, the reports have been edited or expounded by the author.

The first report relates to an accident caused by a basic lack of communication, which fortunately in this case did not lead to a fatality. When a pilot attended a vessel, the Master of such had an obligation to play a part in the safety of the pilot boat and the boarding punt. In the case of a sailing vessel, there was usually plenty of time for the punt to get clear as the ship got under way again. Such considerations were not apparent in the case of at least one of the new-fangled paddle steamers when they first began to hiss and clatter into Falmouth Haven. The *Soho* was a 510-ton paddle steamer, first registered in 1828 and owned by the London and Edinburgh Steam Packet Company. In January 1838 she was in Falmouth harbour, having taken a pilot on board. Apparently the boarding punt was tied alongside in order to take him ashore. Aboard the punt were pilot Samuel Lowry (probably Samuel Junior who appeared on the 1809 Trinity House list) and crewman Richard Warren. For some reason the steamboat got under way so quickly that the punt was towed under and the men thrown into the sea. The *Soho* captain had a boat lowered and both men were rescued from the icy waters. They were landed at St. Mawes, presumably as the vessel's paddle wheels were churning it out to sea.

August 1842: it had been a successful regatta day. There had been a good turnout for the pilot cutter race, the *Spy* of St. Mawes being a competing boat. At 10 p.m., after being ashore, perhaps for evening celebrations, the skipper, pilot George Bickford Junior, and William Real Richards, who was a pilot or crewman, went out in the darkness to a vessel in the harbour in a small boat called a dipper (probably used in the local pilchard fishery). They never returned that night. Their families may not have been unduly concerned, supposing that they had acquired a lucrative pilotage job. The boat was found adrift the following day; their bodies were recovered later. Bickford left a widow and five children; Richards a widow and four children. Eight years later, it was probably George's son, Nicholas William, who became an apprentice, to carry on his father's name as a Falmouth pilot. Also, it may have been Richard's son, Michael, who was to become an apprentice in 1846.

At the beginning of July 1846 there occurred a very unpleasant, although fortunately not fatal, accident involving the pilot boat *Harriet* and a foreign vessel. The circumstances described in the report were a classic example of the 'wrong way to do it' when today's yachtsmen, and professional mariners alike, are learning the maritime law concerning 'Collision Regulations'. A modern Court of Law would sort out who was in the right in this case, but at the time the Master of the Belgian ship involved seems to have got away scot free. The *Harriet* had been sold to the Jenkings only two years previously. A replacement boat was built for Nicholas Jenking in 1847.

'*Falmouth Packet*, 4 July, 1846.

Collision at Sea. – An accident occurred in the bay outside of Falmouth harbour, on Tuesday afternoon last. The pilot boat Harriet, Jenking master, was standing towards land on her way to harbour. The Hortensa, a Belgian brigantine, bound to Liverpool, was on the other tack. The pilot-boat finding they could not weather the brigantine, put her helm down and eased off her head sheets, thinking to drop to leeward. The captain of the brigantine, however, instead of putting his helm down as was attempted by one of his crew, ran abaft, put it hard up, and ran right aboard of the pilot boat, striking her amid-ships and she sank immediately. The crew had scarcely time to get on board the brigantine, by climbing over her bows, the captain refusing the assistance of a rope; and when on board the Belgian would not even get out his boat to put them on board of a trawler close by. They were eventually taken out by the Prince Albert, trawler, and landed at Falmouth. The pilot-boat belonged to three brothers and a widowed mother, and had only been recently purchased, the cost of which and her outfit for the employment absorbed all their hard savings for many years.'

A decade later a deckhand was drowned while attempting to haul the boarding punt back on deck. Circumstances which contributed to his loss included the rough sea, and that the cutter was short-handed; pilots had been put aboard their ships and there were too few crewmen employed to cope with an emergency. No life jackets or life buoys were carried. From this and following reports it seems that it was a frequent practice to have two oarsmen in the punt when taking the pilot to a ship. In this case leaving just one pilot to control the cutter. The accident happened on the *Vie*, owned by the Barker and Williams families. Apart from the two hands, the cutter could have left Falmouth or Coverack that day with five pilots: two Williams and three other Barkers.

'*Falmouth Packet*, 18 October 1856.

Melancholy Accident. – We are extremely sorry to state that a fatal accident occurred on Wednesday last, off our harbour. A punt from the pilot boat Vie No. 3, had boarded a barque, and put a pilot on board. On returning, one of the men, named Francis Barker, when assisting to haul on board the punt, slipped his foot and fell headlong into the sea. The other man immediately pushed off the boat, and therefore being obliged to scull, it blowing at the time a gale of wind, he unfortunately could not manage to reach him, although he was seen for some time after the accident occurred. There was only one person (another pilot,) left on board the Vie, who, as a matter of course, could not leave the vessel to assist. The deceased was much respected by all with whom he was connected, and we are sorry to hear that he has left a wife and young family to lament his loss. It has not, we are happy to say, been the case, for many years, that we have had occasion to notice a loss of this kind.'

Naturally some pilots were lost through circumstances other than drowning at sea: 33 year old John Ralph Williams of Coverack, pilot on the family boat *Vie*, died at home on 20th December 1858 from 'consolidation of the lungs'. He was probably a victim of influenza: the parish records reveal a significant number of deaths across the age span around this date, perhaps indicating a local outbreak of the disease. The closeness of the Coverack Williams and Barker pilot families is demonstrated in that his fellow pilot, 42 year old George Barker, was at his bedside when he died.

The families were able to finance the erection of an impressive headstone over his grave, close to the west wall of St. Keverne Church.

In October 1859 Edward Ball was drowned following another collision close to the harbour. The *Vincent* sailed out in hazy weather to meet an incoming French brig. Poor visibility was later said to be the cause of the two vessels colliding, leaving the cutter taking on water. The pilots and crew, believing that their boat was sinking, were taken aboard the brig. Ball then decided to regain the cutter, and a ship's boat was lowered for him. It seems that there was too much haste employed: there were no oars in the boat, and no plug in the drain hole in the bottom of the boat. As it filled and eventually capsized Ball was thrown into the sea. Attempts were made to reach him, but he sank and was lost. He was said to have been a worthy and much respected inhabitant of St. Mawes, supporting a wife and a number of relatives before his untimely death. There was a later Falmouth pilot with this name, but having no apparent family connection with this Edward Ball, who does not appear on the contemporary list of pilots, therefore he was probably a deck hand.

On 12 March 1860 St. Mawes pilot Thomas Jenking was lost. It is hard to conceive the rough sea conditions into which the cutters were sometimes taken, and that the crews in the diminutive boarding punts were still able to deliver pilots to the high-sided ships; 'all in a days work' to earn a living. Thirty eight year old Thomas was on the family boat *Nicholas Jenking*; they were four miles off the Lizard, having delivered a pilot on board a ship bound for Falmouth, and had just recovered the punt. The cutter must have been pitching and rolling, and suddenly took a heavy sea on deck which tore away the after bulwarks and the punt, taking Thomas with it. At the same time the rope holding the boom jaws to the mast broke, making the sail unmanageable. Without the punt no rescue attempt was possible, during the few moments that Thomas was still seen.

Two weeks later another deck hand lost his life close to Falmouth, in the first of several tragedies that were to befall the Bellman family. Again, the accident occurred during the manhandling of the boarding punt on the deck of the cutter, in similar circumstances to the loss of Francis Barker.

> *Royal Cornwall Gazette* 22 March 1860. 'We regret to record that ... a young man called Bellman, of St. Mawes ... drowned outside in the Bay; one of the crew of pilot cutter No. 13 (*Wasp*) when assisting on deck with the cutter's punt, which had been employed in placing a pilot on board the ship *Richard and Harriet*. The pilot cutters always carry their punts on deck, and when to be put in requisition the (bulwarks) gangway board is removed, and the boats are launched into the water; when to be stowed are again taken up and hauled by hand on the deck. It was when so employed that the deceased was thrown over from the deck with the cutters punt, and by a tremendous sea striking the cutter at the moment; and he could not be recovered by the crew.'

1860 was a bad time for the service: within a month three more lives were lost, again from the Lowry boat *Wasp*: 33 year-old pilot Joseph Sharrock and two deck hands, John Rowe, and Henry Coffin. The latter was an experienced man of about 26 years, who had carried on as crew on the boats after completing an apprenticeship five years before.

> '*Falmouth Packet*, 7 April 1860.
> Three Men Drowned. – A most lamentable accident, attended with the loss of three lives, occurred off the port of Falmouth on Monday forenoon. The pilot Joseph Sharrock, belonging to No. 13 cutter, attended by two men named Henry Coffin and John Rowe, was in the act of boarding the Dutch schooner 'Catharina' from Rio de Janeiro, for the purpose of piloting her into port, when the boat was struck by a sea and upset. Sharrock and Coffin, although they apparently clung to the boat, soon disappeared after the 'Catharina', close-hauled, had passed them on her weather side and thrown them a rope. Rowe managed to hold on by the boat for upwards of half an hour, during which time the most strenuous efforts were made by the pilot cutter to reach him, though blowing a heavy gale with a high sea running. On their first tack they fell short of him, but so close that they heard the poor fellow call 'Mind you reach me next tack'. On coming up again, they were able to throw over him a rope but from exhaustion he was incapable of laying hold of it, and at the same time he was engulfed by the heavy swell. Sharrock and Coffin have left widows and children.'

Other pilot families were to mourn in 1871. The beautiful *Antelope* had replaced *Wasp* the previous year, taking up the boat number 13. The omens were not good; perhaps those around the harbour with superstitious natures may have pointed out that the number had proved unlucky for *Wasp*.

But officialdom may have insisted that the numbers should run consecutively. The new principle owners, the Collins family of Falmouth, didn't seem to mind. There were two young apprentices on board: Henry James, about 18, son of pilot James James; and William John Collins, son of the Master, John Collins. Early in February, off St. Anthony's Head in a strong southwesterly breeze, they both went out from *Antelope* in the punt to put a pilot aboard an English brig. As they returned towards the cutter they were capsized by a large wave. These were tough lads, but the sudden shock of striking the sea in mid-winter is not conducive to survival. The cutter approached the spot as quickly as possible, and a rope thrown towards the lads; Collins managed to grasp it and was drawn to the boat and safety. Before the crew could make further efforts to reach Henry James he had disappeared beneath the waves.

The following April the Barkers lost a second member of the family from their boat *Vie*. They were about eight miles south of the Lizard, carrying the full boomed mainsail, and in freshening winds the time had come to take in a reef. James Barker, the sailing captain, head of the deck crew, was stopping the reefing pendants on the boom, when the mainsheet blew away from its cleat. The boom flew out to leeward, pitching Barker overboard. He dropped into the sea and quickly disappeared. He was the nephew of the Master, and left a wife and four children.

A few days before Christmas, 1874, fate again dealt a cruel blow to the crew of number 13, *Antelope*.

'*Falmouth Packet/ Royal Cornwall Gazette*, 19 December 1874.

Three Falmouth Pilots Drowned. - On Wednesday evening the Falmouth pilot cutter Antelope, No. 13, left the harbour with a crew in search of vessels entering the port. They sailed some distance in the bay, and about half past two on Thursday morning Mr. John Collins, pilot; his son, John Collins, pilot's apprentice; and Joseph F. Bellman, a seaman on board the *Antelope*, left her and went into their punt for the purpose of boarding a steamer which was then some short distance off, proceeding for Falmouth harbour. On approaching the steamer the boat was capsized in a squall, and the three were drowned. It was blowing a very strong gale from the north at the time, and cries were heard by those left on board the *Antelope*; but the darkness of the night and the gale which prevailed prevented their being seen or rendering any assistance. Mr. Collins, the pilot, who is about 52 years of age, leaves a wife and four children (three sons and a daughter); his son is about 21, and was about to be married in a few months. Bellman, about 28, belongs to St. Mawes, but has been lately residing at Falmouth; he leaves a wife and a child; the latter is about two months old. Collins and his son are well known and respected at Falmouth. They are both teeto-tallers and members of the Wesleyan Society. Great sympathy was felt in the town on the sad occurrence being known.'

A few months later another Bellman family was to suffer a tragic loss. No direct family connection has been found between Joseph Bellman and the young crewman with the surname Bellman who was lost from the cutter *Wasp* in March 1860. The same applies to Richard Bellman, although the other Bellmans would have grieved his loss, as would everyone in that tight-knit St. Mawes community. Richard was born in 1835, the son of John Bellman, a cooper, a skilled tradesman making barrels and casks, most likely for the St. Mawes pilchard industry. By 1851 Richard was listed as a fisherman, and ten years later a mariner. He would have either been working as a merchant seaman or perhaps a deck hand on a pilot boat. The latter case seems most likely, as in 1871 he bought four shares in the cutter *Antelope*. At some stage he became an apprentice pilot, gaining his second class licence in March 1873. In 1860 he had married local girl Phillipa Peters; by August 1875 she had given birth to four children and another was on the way.

Since becoming a licensed pilot Richard had worked on the *Vincent*, sharing watches and taking regular turns in piloting vessels into Falmouth. On about 8 August, somewhere off the Land's End, he boarded the *Eurica*, an Italian barque heading for Falmouth for orders. She carried a cargo of beans, loaded at the Portuguese port of Mazagan (now El Jadida), Morocco. At nightfall there was little wind, and banks of fog brought poor visibility; the *Eurica* sailed eastwards at a mere five knots. Suddenly a large vessel, sailing on the opposite course, appeared out of the gloom and struck the barque violently on the port bow. The other vessel, which proved to be the emigrant ship *Samuel Plimsoll*, drew off, apparently undamaged; it would have taken some time to come about in the dark to assist the barque, which rapidly took on water. She sank in about ten minutes; in the resulting panic the Italian Master and crew had no time to lower boats. It took several hours for the *Samuel Plimsoll's* boats to find their way back in the darkness to where the barque had gone down. The Master and nine crew were eventually plucked from the pieces of wreckage to which they had clung; but two crew members and pilot Richard Bellman were not found. The ship hove to until morning, when she was approached by pilot cutter *Arrow*. She took the Italians on board and headed back to Falmouth, where they were taken into the care of the Royal Cornwall Sailors' Home. Someone then had to take the sad news of Richard Bellman's loss across the water to St. Mawes.

Early in November 1881 there occurred another familiar accident involving the boarding punt, this time, fortunately, without fatal consequences. The cutter No.7 *Victoria* was cruising off the Lizard, when she met and spoke to the Italian barque *Tiro*. The punt was launched and a pilot and two crew proceeded towards the ship. Sea conditions must have been bad, because the punt capsized. The cutter number 10, *Richard Green* was cruising in the area and managed to pick up one man. The other two were in the water for at least 15 minutes before they were eventually rescued by sailors on the barque.

Within a few days of this last incident another maritime tragedy was to hit the Barker family, although it was not to be through pilotage service. First class pilot Joseph Barker, originally from Coverack, was now residing in Falmouth. One of his sons, Joseph Henry, had not become a pilot, probably because his father had already taken on his elder brother Anthony as an apprentice. Instead Joseph Henry had trained in Falmouth as a joiner. At this time residents of ports such as Falmouth would have been some of the first to hear of the beginnings of the mining boom in South Africa. Single, with no ties, in search of better employment, and no doubt adventure, 23 year old Joseph junior decided to head for the Dark Continent. He was joined by two friends, William Spargo and Charles Hocking, both joiners. With four other men from Falmouth, all signed up to work their passage to Natal on a new iron-built steamship, the *Jackal*, built that year at Preston, Lancashire. She was a small vessel, 89 feet in length, with a gross tonnage of 115 tons. The registered owner was John F. Hitchens also of Falmouth. Presumably they all made their way to Lancashire to join the vessel, whose Master was to be Captain Downer FRGS, who incidentally had accompanied Dr. Livingstone on a previous expedition. The new vessel had received a satisfactory report from the surveyor, however as they sailed southwards along the Welsh coast the crew grew uneasy as her low freeboard made her liable to take on water. A coastguard officer at Fishguard Bay later opined that she was unfit to make a long winter passage. And so it proved: she put into Padstow owing to stress of weather, where some crew members told locals that they would go no further than Falmouth. Soon after leaving the shelter of that little port she went down off Trevose Head, with the loss of all aboard her. In St. Keverne churchyard stands a simple but elegant headstone dedicated to the memory of pilot Joseph Barker, of 13, Guerdon Place, Falmouth, who died on 1 February 1895, aged 70 years. It had further inscriptions; to wife Mary, and to son Joseph Henry, who was drowned by the foundering of the *S.S. Jackal* off Padstow, 10 November 1881.

The hand of fate was now to rest on the shoulders of the Andrew family. On 21 April 1883 the *Falmouth Packet* reported that at about 5 a.m. the previous Wednesday the pilot cutter *Alarm* was on duty somewhere between the Lizard and the Longships lighthouse. While running before the wind she was struck by a heavy sea; at the sudden lurch (possible a jibe?) pilot Nicholas Lowry Andrew (junior) was pitched overboard and never seen again. He was said to have been a much respected man, about 43 years of age. Having previously lost their mother, his three children were now orphans. Hopefully there would be some provision made for them, partly from his Trinity House superannuation contributions.

At the beginning of September that year, the Southwest was hit by a severe southerly gale. A deluge of rain fell, mountainous seas battered the coast, causing great damage to property, especially at Penzance, where the promenade and town streets were flooded. Many vessels at sea were sunk or damaged, some eventually limping into Falmouth with sails shredded and boats and bulwarks smashed. Previously, somewhere to the west, the barque *J. D. Jones*, of Newport, Monmouthshire, en route from Bull River (possibly Georgia) with a cargo of phosphate, was boarded by pilot James Andrew, and was heading up Channel towards Falmouth. Few could have expected such a severe gale at that time of year; as it built up the barque was driven towards the coast. According to the survivors, towards nightfall Andrew realised that they were not going to clear the Lizard, and turned her in an attempt to make for Penzance; they were in the grip of Mount's Bay, with nowhere else to go. It was soon seen that Penzance was out of the question, and as a last resort two anchors were dropped on 80 fathoms of chain. Neither held, and she was driven onto Cudden Point, a long narrow promontory of jagged rock, close to Prussia Cove. The Master, his crew, and the pilot, tried to cling on to life as the masts went overboard and the ship began to break up. By this time the valiant Coastguard Rocket Brigade had struggled through the night to arrive at the top of the cliff. A number of lines were fired across the ship but no one on board was capable of hauling in the breeches buoy cable. As waves swept the decks, most of the crew, and James Andrew, were taken by the sea. There were only two survivors, a man and a boy: they were washed onto the rocks and saved by a group of women, who waded out in the night to drag them from the violent waves.

As the number of merchant ships calling for orders fell towards the end of the century, there was a fortunate corresponding fall in accidents to pilots and crews. However, another typical, although non-fatal, boarding punt incident occurred in 1892. Early one morning at the beginning of December, *Harriet* was off the Lizard when she met with the Swedish barque *Livingstone*, from the River Plate to Falmouth for orders. The pilot, Thomas Coward, approached the ship in the punt, rowed by deckhands E. Lowry and William Andrew. (These were both from well-known piloting families, but, as there were few prospects by that time of them becoming pilots, they had opted to work as crew.) There was a strong sea running from astern of the ship; as the punt ran alongside the ship's quarter a wave picked it up and turned it over. Coward managed to catch the bottom of the boarding ladder, the others a rope and a chainplate. From these precarious positions they were rescued by the ship's crew. The punt was retrieved by the tug *Triton*. Presumably Coward recovered sufficiently to pilot the barque into Falmouth.

On a fine clear morning off the Lizard in April 1905, the luck of cutter number 13, *Antelope*, finally ran out. She was hove to on the Lizard Station, some of her pilots having already been taken to incoming ships, leaving on board pilots Edward Ball, Henry James and deck hand O. Dash. On such a morning they hadn't thought it necessary to keep a good lookout; with little warning the cutter was violently hit on the starboard bow by the large coasting steamer *Milo*, and began to sink. Dash abandoned ship by climbing over *Milo*'s rail. The two pilots managed to launch and escape in the boarding punt as the cutter and their possessions vanished beneath them. They joined Dash on the steamer, and were put off on the Lizard, having to find their own way back to Falmouth on public transport. The sequel to this incident is described elsewhere.

The last tragic event involving the boarding punts of the sailing pilot cutters happened in January 1908. Compared to the brevity of some previous reports, the *Falmouth Packet* took up almost a whole page to describe the occurrence, together with witness statements and photographs of the gentlemen involved. The cutter No.8, *Vincent* had once been based at St. Mawes, but with the reduction of boats in recent years was now moored in Falmouth. All her complement of pilots and crew also resided in the town. The cutter had left for the Lizard station one Wednesday morning with four pilots and two deck hands, one of which was brought back the following day feeling unwell. The cutter then returned to the Lizard with one remaining deck hand. Later, in a fresh breeze and strong sea, between the Lizard and Black Head they met the German three-masted schooner *Eduard*, making for Falmouth for orders. Following her signal for a pilot, it was the turn of 62 year-old John Andrew to pilot the ship into Falmouth. The remaining deck hand, Richard Greet, was to join him in the punt, accompanied by 61 year-old pilot Richard Green, who had volunteered to take the place of the missing deck hand.

As the punt was launched, and departed, there were two pilots, James Dash and James Williams left to handle the cutter. As they worked on deck they were made aware that the punt had suddenly disappeared and two men were struggling in the sea. It seems that a wave had capsized the punt before it could be brought head to wind. John Andrew had disappeared beneath the waves almost immediately. No assistance came from the schooner, but boatman Harry Morrison was nearby, single-handed in his new Falmouth quay punt, one of the sturdy and versatile local sailing bum boats. He sailed to where Green and Greet were clinging to the upturned punt and managed to get a rope to Greet. He was wearing heavy clothes and boots, but through a great feat of strength and seamanship Morrison managed to haul him aboard to safety. Meanwhile the two pilots had sailed the cutter near to Richard Green and threw him a rope. However, he proved too weak to help himself, and after being hit by the punt as it tossed about in the swell, he too disappeared. Andrew left a widow, five sons and four daughters; Green a widow, one son and two daughters.

This is believed to have been the last serious loss to the service during the days of the sailing pilot cutters. However, there were at least two later bereavements to pilot families. Truro River pilot Elijah Burley was drowned one January night in 1921. While engaged in piloting the *Salcombe Packet* down river to Falmouth, he was in a dinghy taking a rope to a buoy, when it was upset and he was drowned. In September 1974 the *Falmouth Packet* reported the loss of the much respected pilot L. K. Mitchell, who fell from the ship's ladder while boarding the Southampton to Lisbon ferry, which was approaching Falmouth for repairs to storm damage.

CHAPTER 7
THE REGATTAS

MAN IS A competitive animal, and has always enjoyed beating others to a particular goal. Sailors are no different: a major factor in ship development was the quest for speed, to gain the upper hand over adversaries, either in battle, taking a cargo to market, or even a pilot out to a ship. There would always have been informal racing, purely for pleasure, among fleets of working craft, in any port or harbour around the globe. In England, one of the earliest recorded sailing vessels to be used for pleasure was the *Royal Escape*. She was originally the Brighton brig *Surprise*, on which Charles II escaped to France in October 1651. After admiring yachts in Holland, Charles later bought her and she was re-rigged as a gaff sloop or cutter yacht for pleasure cruising. He was so taken with her he had others built, beginning a royal tradition that lasted until recent times. There were already hundreds of sailing and rowing craft, from small wherries to huge state and livery company barges gracing London River, particularly seen on royal occasions. Charles' enthusiasm for yachting caught on among the gentlemen of the Court and more yachts were built for them; a new fashionable pastime was born. Sleeker cutter and schooner-rigged craft were gradually developed to cater for the new market. It was only the affluent who could afford to have a yacht built purely for their own pleasure, but shipyards used to turning out small working and fishing craft were increasingly being asked to build pleasure craft as well. By the mid-eighteenth century the first sailing clubs had been established, at Cork in Southern Ireland, and on the tidal River Thames. Membership consisted almost exclusively of well-off gentlemen with plenty of time on their hands. However, the crews that manned their high quality and often luxurious boats in the summertime yachting and socializing season were generally professional sailors and fishermen.

In the early 1800s other clubs were founded at Southampton and at Cowes on the Isle of Wight. Through their influence, and the regattas they held, there were major improvements to yacht design. The building of such craft was only possible because of the availability of high quality timbers and other necessary materials such as cotton for sailcloth imported from overseas. As the sport developed and became more popular, clubs attracted royal patronage, some adding the prefix 'Royal' to their titles. In the west, the Plymouth Yacht Club had become the Royal Western by 1827. In July 1826 some enthusiastic 'respectable persons' at Falmouth chartered the steam packet *Sir Francis Drake* for a day's cruise to watch the Plymouth Regatta. The vessel was to depart from Falmouth at 11 a.m., and for the return voyage from Plymouth at 6 p.m.; tickets were available at 3 shillings. By 1845 the club boasted 333 members and listed 95 yachts. During the season some of the more dedicated of the racing fraternity were taking their boats to compete in a series of regattas along the South Coast and Ireland.

In common with pleasure boating on inland waterways, particularly the Thames, the growth of an affluent Victorian middle class brought off-shore yachting within the pockets of a wider public. Coastal cruising in small family-sized yachts became the vogue. Those potential sailors working on a tight budget might convert an ex-fishing boat or ship's lifeboat, while those with the money might approach a local boatyard, where they might be persuaded that the yard's latest design was really the only one for them. So the love of the sea, and some of the skills of sailing, albeit for pleasure rather than commercial reasons, were passed to future generations. For the Victorians, sport in all its forms was to be encouraged, generating a healthy youth that would be of benefit to country and empire; sailors would be particularly useful for the Royal Navy. All around the coast, at harbours large and small, amateur rowing and sailing races were enthusiastically organized.

A notice for one such local event appeared in the *Royal Cornwall Gazette* on 10 September 1823: entries were invited for a Truro Boat Race, to be held on the 23rd. Silver cups and other prizes were to be presented to winners and runners-up of two classes of boats. There was to be an 8 a.m. start; around high tide; the course being from Truro to the Black Rock at the harbour entrance

A regatta scene off Trefusis, possibly in the 1920s. The vessels dressed overall appear to be visiting naval sail training brigs. (RCPS)

and back to Malpas, the organizers obviously estimating that there would not be enough tide to reach Truro on the return. The total distance is about 14 miles. Six sailing boats competed: three in the 24 foot to 15 foot class, and three smaller boats under 15 feet in length. According to the subsequent newspaper report, the race was followed by enthusiastic spectators, who were treated to some very competitive racing, particularly by the larger boats. No doubt at times oars were resorted to in the narrow upper reaches where the high tree-clad hills cause winds to be fickle. Towards the finish at Malpas first one and then the other of the leading two contenders took the lead, both occasionally getting stuck on mudbanks. Mr. S. Williams' *Peverel* was finally beaten by Mr. T. Bate's *Chevy Chace*, whose owner climbed onto the bowsprit to touch the finishing buoy to claim victory.

In the nineteenth century there were often so many sailing vessels coming and going that the pilot cutters were seldom noticed as they went about their business; and much of their trade went on during the hours of darkness anyway. Certainly they seem to have been seldom pictured by Victorian photographers. However, on Regatta Day, from 1836 into the 1880s, the pilots were able to proudly show off the capabilities of their craft to the general population. This was not always successfully achieved: the regatta was funded by subscriptions contributed by local dignitaries; occasionally the organizing committee failed to raise sufficient funds to run it or to offer reasonable prize money. Sometimes the weather on the day was not conducive to good sailing; perhaps only a few cutters could take part because others were on duty out at sea. The Falmouth annual regatta was one of a series of such events held around the locality, other smaller versions were held at Penryn, St. Mawes and so on. It became a major event in the town's social calendar, especially as there was plenty of après-sailing activity. The following week, while reporting the results of the sailing and rowing matches, the newspapers were usually most appreciative of the part the pilot cutters played in the success of the day. The first annual regatta was held in August 1836. There had been other festivities before, such as when a new ship was launched from a local yard and, no doubt, sailing and rowing matches between watermen and fishermen. However, this was to be a two-day event, funded by the town council and local dignitaries, and organized by harbour officials, naval and Post Office packet personnel. The contributors to the prizes were headed by Lady Basset and the Earl of Falmouth. It began a tradition of annual regattas, which, apart from the two world wars, has lasted until the present day. *The Falmouth Packet* newspaper later printed an enthusiastic description of the events, beginning with the morning of the first day.

'Flags and banners were suspended from the windows of several houses, the Falmouth band paraded the town, giving forth 'sweet sounds', and every thing and every body bore a cheerful aspect. Strangers arrived in quick succession from all parts of the county in every description of vehicle, and the harbour presented a beautiful animated appearance; the surface, on which the boats were about to make trial of their speed and qualities, was gently ruffled by a steady breeze ... His Majesties' packets and revenue cruizers in harbour were dressed in colours of every hue and nation, which glittered in the sun ... Every place from which a view could be obtained soon became thronged with people, and at half past 10 o'clock a gun from the *Active* revenue cruizer called the first class sailing boats to take their stations.'

Compared to much grander events further up-Channel, this was a very local affair, but the committee were to be congratulated for organizing an interesting programme for the many spectators. This, and further regattas, were showcases for all the local amateur and professional seafarers that belonged to the area and could only enhance the reputation of the port. On the first day there were matches for four classes of yachts; those competing were mainly from Falmouth, but a few individuals had arrived from Looe, Plymouth and Penzance. The course was held within the harbour and Carrick Roads. Boats proceeded from the Inner Harbour to the north of Bar Point (where the docks were later built) around Black Rock; around a boat moored off St. Mawes Castle; around the *Astraea* frigate (an Admiralty depot vessel moored in the Inner Harbour from 1823 to 1851), to St. Just Pool. Then around the hulk of the *Aurora* frigate, returning to the Inner Harbour and the *Active* revenue cutter; some classes going round the course twice.

The results published in the newspaper were followed by an observation which could just as well be applied to the present annual Falmouth 'Classics' day: 'The boats ... were so intermingled ... that we could with difficulty follow the course of the several boats, and therefore we abstain from any observations on their sailing. So many pleasure boats skimming the surface of the water gave great beauty to the scene.' The yachts were followed by races for four and six-oared gigs, with four boats in each event. Unfortunately the course was not described, but may have been out of the harbour to the open sea. For both races it was a long slog for the rowers: all of the boats finished the course, taking from just under four and a half to nearly five hours for the slowest.

The second day began with the Subscription Cup race for all boats belonging to the port, under 40 feet in length. Only six took part, four of which were pilot boats; the winner was *Friendship*, followed by *Harriet*. There next followed another race for six-oared gigs: six boats competed, over a shorter course than the previous day. The winner, taking just under two and a half hours, was Pope's *Exquisite*, in spite of the stroke oar collapsing two-thirds of the way round the course (or as the reporter noted – 'fell from his perch'). A female crew from Saltash, probably led by the legendary Ann Granville, competed unofficially in the same race, in a four-oared gig. They astonished the whole harbour by achieving fourth place, ahead of three of the larger boats, including shipping agents Broad & Sons' *Fighting Pig*. The day ended with a race between nine watermen's boats and a novelty gig and punt race. Evening activities included a dinner for dignitaries on board the *Active* revenue cutter, accompanied by a band playing on deck, and a ball for 200 at Pearce's Assembly Rooms.

The success of the first regatta had generated considerable interest among the South Coast yachting fraternity: the following year's two day event included a race for larger yachts of up to 50 tons; it engendered entries from Southampton, Poole, Teignmouth and Plymouth. There were four other classes for sailing boats, and races for the gigs and river barges. The Subscription Cup race had generated the most prize money: the first four places were to receive from £8 to £2. The open boat *Friendship* was again the winner, but closely pressed by the patriotically-named *Victoria*, which had just been launched by John Trethowan at The Bar, Falmouth. His yard was to produce the best of the pilot cutters over several decades. Only four cutters took part in the race, which must have disappointed those who raised the subscriptions. This may have been the reason that the pilots were not asked back the following year. There may have been other reasons, mentioned in the 'Amacus' letter quoted in chapter two.

The 1839 regatta programme followed that of previous years, well supported by the owners of yachts, barges and sailing punts. The rowing events now also included gigs from the packet ships and cutters from other ships in the harbour. The pilots came back with eight boats; there might have been more, but the wind was said to be too strong for the smaller ones. It was a handicap race, one minute per ton being given. The course was not described, but it must have extended out into the bay, as the fastest over the course, the new boat *Spy*, took 4 hours 43 minutes.

The year 1840 brought even greater support and prestige to the regatta, for it had now received royal patronage. The *Falmouth Packet* report on August 15 began with an enthusiastic description of the preparations:

'In consequence of the very general support which the Falmouth Regatta had hitherto received from all parts of the county, the committee this year deemed it advisable to change its name to one more strictly in unison with the localities of its patrons. By so doing, they have united the aquatists of the county to one point, which naturally produces a galaxy of fashionables, and a perfect combination of amusement, where otherwise there would only be a partial and indifferent display. Moreover, it has received the royal patronage, and numbers amongst its officers some of the most distinguished lovers of the briny deep. Unfortunately, however, this year, the regatta came off on the same day as several others along the coast, as did also the Cork Regatta. Every arrangement had been made with the committees of these Regattas to avoid such an occurrence, but circumstances have since arisen, which rendered it otherwise impossible. The origin of these circumstances were as singular as they were annoying, and it need scarcely be told that in consequence there were less yachts entered for the race than had been previously anticipated. Nevertheless, the affair went off admirably, as will be found from the sequel.

Tuesday, First Day.

Early in the morning, the whole harbour was studded with small yachts, and the din of preparation pervaded every nook. At eight o'clock a signal was made from H.M.S. Astraea, for the packets to hoist their colours, and the precision and uniformity with which this was executed by each vessel had a very pleasing appearance. All the yachts were also decorated in their gorgeous apparel, and the merchant-ship and the coast-trader paid homage to the day by a like exhibition. All the public offices and the residences of several of the inhabitants had also colours hoisted of various hues. About nine the Falmouth Band perambulated the town, playing most enlivening tunes. Strangers arrived from every part of the county, in every kind of conveyance, from the jostling van to the open barouche and four, and by the time the 'tug of war' was to commence, all the headlands round the harbour, and Quays and slips along the shore, - indeed every point which could command a view of the proceedings, - were all well covered with spectators. Nothing occurred to delay the amusements of the day beyond the given hour: the weather was beautifully fine, with a smart breeze from the N.W.'

On the first day the yacht classes were followed by a six-oared gig race, and then one for four-oared boats rowed by the crews from some of the packet ships in port. Ten boats took part, over a long course, at the end of which all came home within four minutes of each other. The winner, a boat from the depot ship *Astraea*, took four hours 25 minutes. It is impossible to judge what distance that time represents, but it would be an interesting experiment to find out how modern gig rowers, or even university oarsmen, would cope when racing for the same length of time.

The report of the second day's events began with praise for the pilot boats: 'Falmouth may now boast of having within her port fine and effective a class of pilot boats as ever swam, and we must sincerely trust that our townsmen will ever patronise and encourage their weatherbeaten owners …' Ten boats took part in the pilot boat race, varying considerably in tonnage, therefore it was another handicap race. The *Victoria* came in first, but due to handicapping the small boats took the prizes. For the next two years the race was split into two classes. After the racing Captain Plumridge and other naval officers provided a lavish supper and entertainment for the gentry of Cornwall and local dignitaries on board the *Astraea*.

The Royal Cornwall Regatta continued to thrive throughout the 1840s, during which time the older and smaller pilot boats were replaced by eleven new cutters; six of these were produced by John Trethowan, at The Bar, Falmouth, and two by his neighbour, James Mayn. The fleet was now more equally matched and considered seaworthy enough so that, in at least one year, the course was set to take them as far as the Manacles Buoy.

The regatta of 1850 was pronounced to have been the best yet. The many merchant ships in the roadstead were decorated with flags; thousands of spectators congregated on the hills surrounding the harbour and on Pendennis Head. All the local boats were engaged by spectators to watch the racing. Gentlemen's yachts arrived from other regattas at Teignmouth and Plymouth. The programme was similar to previous years: races for yachts and sailing boats, punts, lighters and gigs. Finishers were greeted by a local band playing on a barge anchored near the committee boat.

The pilot boats raced for donated prize money of £8 to £2 for the first four over the line, and £1 for all finishers. There was a splendid breeze from the N.N.E.; the course was set from the Inner Harbour; to a boat moored off the Helford River; to a boat moored southeast of St. Anthony Headland; round a buoy off St. Mawes Castle and a boat off Trefusis Headland. Back in the Inner Harbour, and before reaching the committee boat, the cutters had to go round the frigate *HMS Aurora* (which was a coal hulk, being broken up in the harbour the following year). There were to be two rounds of the course. The reporter enthused over the pilot cutters as they assembled before the race: '... a beautiful squadron of pilot yachts ... no other name would fairly indicate their character and appearance.' They were lined up on starting buoys, superintended by H.M. Customs officer J. Shelley Esq., Commissioner of Pilotage. All 13 started, sent away by a signal from a pilot jack flag and a gun, followed by the cheers of spectators. The estimated distance given for the course was given as 70 miles, which seems a considerable exaggeration. Even so, it must have been a hard slog for the winner, *Harriet*, which took 6 hours 52 minutes; *Gem* finished only 40 seconds behind. They were followed within half an hour by *Nicholas Jenking*, *Water Nymph*, *Wasp*, *Dash*, and *Victoria*. The other six failed to complete the course.

There seems to have been several years during the 1850s when no regatta was held. At other times comparatively few cutters raced: this could occur when there were many ship arrivals and pilots were obviously out at sea. On more than one occasion, when the weather was so miserable, or there was insufficient wind, the pilots declined to race. However, there were successful events in 1851 and 1853, all 13 cutters taking part in each. There was indubitably some stiff competition between boats: they raced so hard at times that gear was broken, sheets or halyards carried away. However, their sailing skills were such that even when in the confines of the Inner Harbour, there are no reports of serious collisions. The importance given by the pilots to their annual exhibition race is demonstrated by the preparations observed prior to the 1860 race:

'During the week ... the splendid class of pilot cutters ... have already commenced to refit ... several have discharged ballast for restowing, the bottoms of the craft are being carefully overhauled, and some new mainsails are already bent for stretching. The spirited owner of No.13, is likely to set his usual example of eficiency, and we doubt not the beautiful cutter will be in first rate order for the day. At St. Mawes, our neighbours are not a whit behind hand, and the various yacht-like boomers, are beached on either side of the river, and the crews are indefatigable in doing all they can to make their craft faultless.'

The crews had to watch the tides when putting the cutters on the beach: in one year several were not taken off quickly enough and were stranded as the tide fell, consequently missing the race. By this time the course for the race had been changed again: to a boat moored three miles off St. Anthony Head, round a boat off Rosemullian Head in Falmouth Bay, and back to the Inner Harbour and around *HMS Russell*; twice around the course. There was now very handsome prize

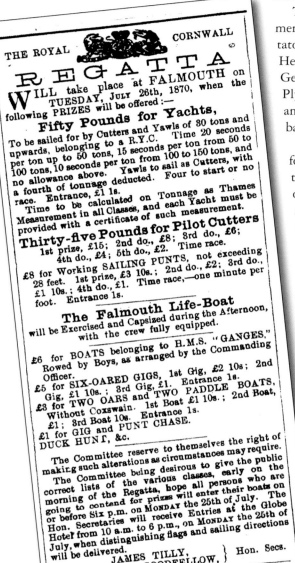

Regatta notice published in the *Falmouth Packet* on 25 July 1870.

THE ROYAL   CORNWALL

REGATTA

WILL take place at FALMOUTH on TUESDAY, JULY 26th, 1870, when the following PRIZES will be offered :—

Fifty Pounds for Yachts,

To be sailed for by Cutters and Yawls of 30 tons and upwards, belonging to a R.Y.C. Time 20 seconds per ton up to 50 tons, 15 seconds per ton from 50 to 100 tons, 10 seconds per ton from 100 to 150 tons, and no allowance above. Yawls to sail as Cutters, with a fourth of tonnage deducted. Four to start or no race. Entrance, £1 1s.

Time to be calculated on Tonnage as Thames Measurement in all Classes, and each Yacht must be provided with a certificate of such measurement.

Thirty-five Pounds for Pilot Cutters

1st prize, £15; 2nd do., £8; 3rd do., £6; 4th do., £4; 5th do., £2. Time race.

£8 for Working SAILING PUNTS, not exceeding 28 feet. 1st prize, £8; 2nd do., £2; 3rd do., £1 10s.; 4th do., £1. Time race,—one minute per foot. Entrance 1s.

The Falmouth Life-Boat

will be Exercised and Capsized during the Afternoon, with the crew fully equipped.

£6 for BOATS belonging to H.M.S. "GANGES," Rowed by Boys, as arranged by the Commanding Officer.

£5 for SIX-OARED GIGS, 1st Gig, £2 10s; 2nd Gig, £1 10s.; 3rd Gig, £1. Entrance 1s.

£3 for TWO OARS and TWO PADDLE BOATS, Without Coxswain. 1st Boat £1 10s.; 2nd Boat, £1; 3rd Boat 10s. Entrance 1s.

£1 for GIG and PUNT CHASE.

DUCK HUNT, &c.

The Committee reserve to themselves the right of making such alterations as circumstances may require.

The Committee being desirous to give the public correct lists of the various classes, early on the morning of the Regatta, hope all persons who are going to contend for prizes will enter their boats on or before Six p.m. on MONDAY the 25th of July. The Hon. Secretaries will receive Entries at the Globe Hotel from 10 a.m. to 6 p.m., on MONDAY the 25th of July, when distinguishing flags and sailing directions will be delivered.
                                  JAMES TILLY,   } Hon. Secs.
                                  B. M. GOODFELLOW, }

money for the first three finishers, of £20, £10 and £5. This year only six boats competed; the winner was the Plymouth-built *Vincent*, with a time of 4 hours 20 minutes, followed by *Harriet*, the third boat of that name, just beating *Victoria* (the second of that name); all three were built in 1852.

During the 1860s the regatta programme continued as before, however, the committee was probably disappointed that it failed to become as prestigious as other regattas along the South Coast. The high prize money of £30 was offered to attract the big classic yachts of up to 30 tons to compete, but although one or two occasionally attended, Falmouth was too far to the west to compete socially with other places such as Cowes. Invariably, therefore, the pilot cutters afforded 'the best race of the day'. By now the regatta crowds were swelled by numbers arriving by cheap excursion trains on the new Cornwall Railway branch line from Truro, which opened in 1863. The racing course now had to take into account the construction works for the new docks: the arms of the breakwater now extended for a considerable distance over what had been open water. From 1866 the sailing course was re-arranged to include passing round *HMS Ganges*, the big training ship for boys, moored in Mylor Pool, about two miles along Carrick Roads.

In 1870 local enthusiasm for the regatta remained undiminished. The lower part of the town was converted into a small fair, with various booths set up. According to a visitor, the Reverend Francis Kilvert, 'the town was very lively by reason of the regatta, stirring music of fifes and drums, all the Falmouth people out upon the narrow winding streets in their best clothes and gayest colours, the crowds marching along with the fifes and drums, and the town crier, a tall greybeard man in semi-uniform and high hat, stalked in solemn majesty with his bell, making proclamations …'

Although the day was fine, there was a strong breeze from the north, whipping up white horses in Carrick Roads. In spite of this at least some of the rowing and sailing matches were run, although with diminished numbers starting. Of the working sailing punts, up to 28 feet in length, four of the seven entries started, going thrice around a course from the Inner Harbour and around the Black Rock and the *Ganges*. In spite of some damage to gear, three out of the four completed the race. All of the pilot cutters had entered for their race but only four started. Four were unable to get off the beach after cleaning; *Arrow* was on duty at sea; another four took up the starting buoys but failed to start. This left *Vie*, *Richard Green*, *Alarm* and the boat just completed by Mr. Trethowan, *Antelope*. The course was to take them twice into the Bay, to Rosemullian Head, a boat off St. Anthony and round the *Ganges*. The Reverend Kilvert obviously enjoyed watching the event, and as a visitor unfamiliar with the sights, his graphic description of the race outshines the usual well-informed newspaper report -.

'There were all sorts of races but the great event of the day was a fine race between four pilot boats, Nos. 13, 3, 10, 5. They started from the Committee boat, went out of the Harbour far out to sea, round two boats moored and then home, passing in and out through the shipping and round the man-of-war guardship Ganges. It was a first rate race, and the two leading boats No.13 and 3 started well and got away very close to each other. No. 13 tore along through the water under every stitch of canvas she could hold, heeling over and the sea boiling and foaming past her bows as she flew. No. 3 was pressing close upon her, coming up hand over hand as if she meant to take the wind out of her rival's sails. It was beautiful to see the boats straining every nerve as if they had life, now one gaining, now the other, as each of the fine vessels tried all she knew to win. They had been over the course once, and were just sweeping through the shipping in the Roads and gliding out of the Harbour for the second round when at a critical moment as No. 3 seemed to be gaining, her peak halyards snapped and down came her top sail. A groan of pity and disappointment ran through the excited people who lined the cliffs as they saw the accident. No. 13 instantly sprang ahead, though No. 3 recovered herself gallantly in the third and last round. She never quite made up her lost ground and came in second. She got the first prize though, we heard afterwards, because she was a smaller boat than No. 13. No. 10 was third and No. 5 last. They both sailed well these two last boats, but they were never in the race for first or second places, they only steadily kept their distance.

It happened fortunately that the race was over just in time for us to see the finish, as the leading boat glided past the goal and the gun was fired, the white puff of smoke almost clearing away from the Committee boat before we heard the boom of the gun across the Harbour.'

Pilot cutter *Antelope* in serious racing rig: sporting a 'proper' topmast and topsail, boomed mainsail, extra large staysail and jib, plus a jib topsail. A spare jib topsail is poled out to starboard in 'goosewinged' fashion. The helmsman and crew had to be highly skilled to keep the rig under control. (Sketch based on a photograph, c. 1880, courtesy of Helston Museum).

A number of big cruising yachts were now passing through Falmouth during the summer season, and in 1871 the regatta committee were able to persuade some from South Coast yacht clubs to enter for an ocean race from Dartmouth to Falmouth, to arrive before and take part in the annual regatta. Due to light winds, for the few that entered, it became a slow cruise rather than a race. However, on regatta day six big yachts, being cutters, a schooner and a yawl put on a brave show for the public, the 129 ton cutter *Condor* breaking a topmast in the process. Following the success of the regatta, and with the encouragement of a few notable visiting yachtsmen, some members of the regatta committee decided it was time to establish a Cornwall Yacht Club, based in Falmouth, and for following years to organize a separate club regatta. This became entitled the 'Royal Cornwall Yacht Club Regatta' after the Prince of Wales had agreed to become Patron of the club.

In 1872, possibly to avoid confusion, the Royal title was dropped from the name of the traditional regatta, being at first renamed the 'Falmouth Quay Regatta', followed the next year by the 'Town and Quay Regatta'. It now consisted of races for the smaller classes of sailing punts, barges and novelty races. The club regatta was held shortly afterwards in the year; the Ocean Race from Plymouth was abandoned because of gale-force winds, but otherwise the varied programme was a great success. It consisted of some classes from previous regattas, including yachts and gigs; the highlight again being the pilot cutter race, although only four were able to start. The following year the two regattas were temporarily combined; all the usual events took place; three big yachts completed the Channel Race from Plymouth, and seven pilot cutters raced.

For the rest of the 1870s there were separate events: the 'Town and Quay', and the yacht club regattas, both held within weeks of each other in July or August. The pilots opted to race in the club regatta, where the total prize money usually allocated to them was £30 from Borough Members, and £10 from the club, split among the first four finishers. The yachts and pilot cutters still used the course which took in a mark off Rosemullian Head, a boat three miles to the southeast of St. Anthony, and the *Ganges* training ship in Carrick Roads.

Only a certain few of the Masters of the pilot cutters seem to have had a real thirst for racing, and appear most frequently in the regatta reports. Over a ten year period *Victoria* managed to line up in every race, *Antelope* in nine, *Richard Green* in seven, *Nautilus* and *Harriet* in five; the rest in four or less. Even if they had entered, the pilots could never be sure if they were going to be able to compete on the day. It took time to prepare the boat for racing, and there was always the chance that expensive breakages could occur in the heat of competition. With the chance of 50 vessels or more arriving for orders in a single week, as was once reported in 1876, their work at sea meant that the number of boats free to compete in the regatta at that time was limited.

Prior to the Royal Cornwall Yacht Club regatta of 1877, some of the yacht club members, and no doubt the pilots, were shocked to see that the cutters had been omitted from the printed programme. This was said to be due to John Mead, Chairman of the programme committee, who considered that the cutters were not yachts and the pilots not Corinthian yachtsmen, inferring

Elegant gaff cutter yachts, possibly in the 10 ton class, racing in Falmouth Bay, c. 1890. (Cornwall Record Office)

Racing off the town in the 1930s. A working ketch is being used as the committee boat. (Cornwall Centre)

Below: J Class yachts racing in Falmouth Bay, c. 1926. Between then and 1936 various wealthy industrialists and gentry brought their magnificent vessels westwards to compete against each other at the Falmouth Regatta. (RCPS)

that they were not good enough to be associated with the club. The prize money, he said, could be better spent on races for yachts. At a special club meeting that decision was overturned, and £40 was again allocated for the pilot race. There were no big visiting yachts for the club regatta; the programme went ahead with the usual sail boat classes, and the pilot boats. Although only five started, as usual it was a hard-fought exciting race, in a good breeze. At one point, towards the end, *Antelope* was being caught by *Telegraph*, which of course couldn't be tolerated. She therefore hoisted a jib-headed topsail, and consequently carried away her topmast. Not to be outdone, a jury topmast and a gaff topsail was set, bringing her home in second place, just behind *Alarm*.

It was probably by mutual consent that in the following years the pilots sailed in the Town and Quay Regatta, rather than with the club. In the early 1880s this became the 'Port of Falmouth Regatta'. With the rapid downward trend in merchant ship arrivals from that time, there began to be discussions among the pilots about reducing the number of working cutters. It is understandable that the enthusiasm for racing was not as it had been. Four cutters competed in the last pilot boat race, held in the 1884 regatta. It was won by *Antelope*, closely followed by *Richard Green*, *Harriet* and *Victoria*.

Rounding the mark off Trefusis Point on Classics Day during Falmouth Week in the 1990s.

'J' class yachts *Ranger* and *Lionheart*, chased by a commotion of small craft, racing in Falmouth Bay on 30 June 2012. *Valsheda* and *Rainbow* also competed. This was the first time the class had taken part in a regatta at Falmouth since the 1930s. (Lynne Vosper)

CHAPTER 8
THE SAILING PILOT CUTTERS

TO PUT THE Falmouth pilot boats into the general context of the Southwest maritime community, some of the other pilotage services of the region should be mentioned. Over the centuries many different types of vessel were used for piloting, depending on ship developments at the time, the distance covered to seek out incoming ships, and the number of pilots that might be sharing a boat. Generally, it seems that port pilots around most of the coasts of Britain preferred to work independently, in their own boats. They used their skills of seamanship to beat their fellow pilots to a ship to gain the right to bring it into port. The boat had to be able to cope with all expected sea conditions, but small enough to be economical to maintain. It had to be fast, but with sails that could be easily handled by the minimum number of crew. Costs might be kept low by taking on a working apprentice, or having a family member to share the work. In estuaries or on sheltered coasts, where it was not necessary to go far out to sea, a rowing boat could be adequate, but although the cost of maintenance was low, it was necessary to have perhaps six or more rowers available at any time, and who, of course, would have to be paid.

In the West Country, specially-built sailing pilot boats may have been few and far between in the eighteenth century. Fishing boats could well have doubled as pilot boats. Otherwise, four-oared watermen's boats could have been used in favourable conditions. Many such craft, of differing styles and dimensions, had been used around the coasts of Europe for centuries. By about 1800 the more powerful and sea-worthy 30 feet-long six-oared gigs were being developed, it is said by the Peters family at their boatyard in St. Mawes. One of the first to be documented is the *Newquay*, built in 1812, which was used for some years by the Falmouth shipping agents, William Broad &

An early chart depicting the domain of the Falmouth and Scilly pilots. Depths given fathoms.

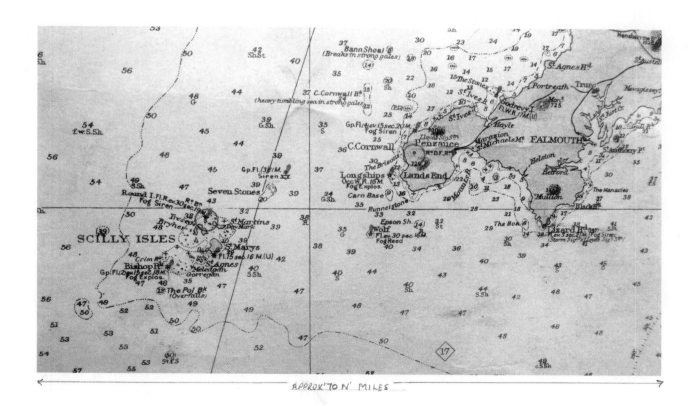

APPROX 'TO N' MILES

Honorabilis Franciscus Godolphin de Baylies in Com: Buch: Armiger hanc tabulam impensis suis aere incisam suo nomine decorari voluit.

Above: A view over Hugh Town Harbour on St. Mary's to the Northern Isles of Scilly, 1752.

Right: Hugh Town harbour, St. Mary's, Isles of Scilly, c. 1930.

Co. Gigs were soon to be seen in many harbours around the Cornish coast and on the Isles of Scilly. They were particularly useful in the islands, for inter-island transport, fishing, smuggling, and as pilot boats.

The pilot gig has become the iconic craft of Scilly. Well-rowed, it could reach a ship offshore far quicker than a sailing boat if winds were light, but was also vulnerable in rough seas. Some incredibly brave feats were performed by the men of Scilly while attempting to rescue shipwrecked mariners from those dreadful outer rocks, and many essential island bread winners were drowned in their attempts. Pilots and boatmen were also lost from over-laden boats when trying to reach ships waiting offshore for pilotage. One of the worst of many similar instances occurred in December 1816 during severe weather: a large cutter, the *Mary*, bound from Brazil to Liverpool, was seen off Scilly in apparent distress, although in fact the captain had had the mainsail boom unshipped in order to reduce sail. Two sailing boats and one large rowing boat, with pilots and crews on board, went out to assist the ship, but the rowing boat, holding 16 men, was swamped by a heavy sea. Some survivors were picked up by the other boats but seven men perished; 'four of them leaving widows with large families plunged in the greatest distress and immediate want by the lamentable catastrophe.' The *Mary* was later driven ashore by the gale and totally wrecked, although the crew were saved. Bags of mail were recovered and sent to London via Penzance, but the cargo of wool and cotton was lost. In January 1833 ten St. Martin's men in a rowing boat were proceeding out past the Lion Rock, at the northernmost limit of the islands. There they were struck by a heavy sea and the boat turned over. Six were drowned, some leaving widows and children. That the men were prepared to gamble with their lives to earn a few pilotage fees accentuates the desperate living conditions the islanders often faced.

To the occasional summer visitor the islands may appear to be idyllic, but for past generations of Scillonians life was a continuous battle for survival, especially on the outer islands. By the early nineteenth century the inhabitants were supporting themselves by growing potatoes and corn in small walled plots, and raising a few cattle on rough grazing among the granite boulders. Shellfish, particularly limpets, were gleaned from the foreshore, and net fishing carried out from small boats. Some little money was obtained from mainland contractors by the primitive back-breaking industry of kelp burning. Seaweed by the ton was cropped from the surrounding rocks, to be burnt in open pits.

After much tending, this produced potash and iodine, which was used in soap and glassmaking. The islanders always had an eye on the ocean, for there was no telling what might end up on the beaches after a storm. The isles are a notorious graveyard for shipping: a wrecked sailing ship could give up enough timber and fittings to build an entire farm. Every ship that approached the islands also brought the possibility of trade, even the chance of bartering a few fish, eggs or garden produce for some meat. A small packet boat or pilot cutter bringing mail and a few supplies from Penzance was practically the only contact with the mainland, and even that ceased in bad weather.

In 1812, not for the first time, the islanders faced possible starvation. The summer fish catch was normally salted down to provide enough food to last through the following winter. Because of the French War, salt, used to preserve the fish, and much of it produced in Brittany, was very difficult to obtain; because of the high duty it was also very expensive. Fortunately the islanders' plight was noted by the Bishop of Exeter, who arranged for the Treasury to supply enough salt free of duty and at low cost. Another crisis was looming six years later: in common with other parts of Europe the vital potato crop had failed. Zealous Customs and Excise officers were also attempting to stamp out smuggling. The trade was a valuable part of the economy; up until then the authorities had turned a benevolent blind eye. Help again came from the mainland:

money was collected by subscription to purchase new fishing gear; an 'Industrious Society' organized the islands' infirm and aged, and the distressed widows and orphans, to produce goods that could be sold in Penzance. This involved teaching them to spin, knitting stockings and straw plaiting. Girls were imported from Mousehole and Newlyn to teach net making. In later years encouragement was also given to revive the kelp industry, the product from Scilly not being of good quality. Such was still the case in 1834, when it was reported that the industry had fallen into disrepute, and there was much distress on the islands.

In common with Falmouth, in 1809 the Scilly pilotage service had come under control of Trinity House, a move which was hard to accept by the free spirited islanders. Only half of the 76 freelance pilots around the islands were given

A full-rigged ship escorted by Scilly pilot cutter No. 5. A traditional woven wool picture by Scilly shipwright Thomas John Pender (1852-1926). (Isles of Scilly Museum)

Thomas John Pender, Scilly shipwright and artist, in 1909. Generations of Penders were fishermen, shipwrights and pilots. (Isles of Scilly Museum)

licences. However, many others still continued to operate, and, no doubt, still continued to take their boats on smuggling trips as far as France. Apart from the gigs, which could be sailed with lugsail rig as well as being rowed, larger sailing cutters were coming into common use by the early nineteenth century. The building and maintenance costs were high compared to gigs, therefore they were funded by shareholders among island families, and merchants and businessmen on the main island of St. Mary's. Their advantage was that they were much safer, and with just two hands to work the boats, the larger vessels could take out perhaps up to eight pilots. Some of these would be Channel pilots, guiding ships along the English or St. George's Channel. They did not generally stray into the Falmouth District, although the reverse was not always true. Although designs obviously varied, their cutters were of the same size, and rigged and worked in a similar manner to the Falmouth boats.

The islanders hand to mouth existence had led the pilots to adopting methods aimed at extracting all that they could from the Masters of ships to whom they offered their services. The methods some used could have received the severe disapproval of the Brethren of Trinity House. In *The History of the United Kingdom Pilots' Association*, Harry Hignett assumes that Scilly pilots are referred to when quoting the mate of the yacht *America*, which in 1851 had just completed a trans-Atlantic crossing en route to the Solent for the famous 'Cup' race. The skipper was a New York pilot.

'This Channel beats everything and all conception that I had of its extent and magnitude. The pilot boats beggar all description, they are about 40 foot long, sloop-rigged or cutter as they would call them. Most of them carry only one or two pilots and these are as dirty as chimney sweeps. The first thing they ask is 'Do you want a pilot?' If answered in the affirmative they ship over the side a small boat and board you. The pilot steps aft and is introduced to the Captain. They make a bargain as to the amount (pilotage fee). He next asked, 'Have you a bottle of spirits on board for the boat?' … the Captain said 'No!' 'Have you any pork?' The Captain told the steward to get some of each kind and give it to the boat: 'Could you spare some tea and coffee? Have you any bread to spare? We have been out this trip three weeks last Tuesday.' Here the Captain filled away (set sail) and the boat had to leave. The pilot told me that he spoke and boarded every vessel he met and asked the same questions. He told me that he supplied a ship last Wednesday with 200 pounds of beef and pork, besides other things, for which they received £3 sterling. They are without exception the damnedest beggars I ever fell in with.'

On a visit to Scilly in 1861 yachtsman Richard McMullen thought that the islanders' way of life had not changed from that described by William Borlase a century before. Even on St. Mary's the inhabitants' primitive appearance and simplicity of dress and manner prevailed everywhere. It was

The St. Agnes pilot gig *Slippen* and crew, possibly photographed in December 1907, after they had rescued the two sole survivors clinging to Hellweather Rocks, following the wreck of the massive American schooner *Thomas W. Lawson.* (Gibson of Scilly)

difficult to get meat, or anything but stale Penzance bread and butter. However, on his next cruise there in 1868 things appeared to have changed considerably. Now good quality food was available; the women wore fashionable clothes and the children had jewellery. He puts the improvements down to the introduction in 1862 of a beautiful little screw steamer, the *Little Western*. This was now bringing mail, passengers and cargo on four-hour long passages, three times per week from Penzance, 'where London fashions are very fierce'. Good crops of potatoes were also being produced, to be sent on the steamers to Penzance, en route to London. McMullen enthuses about the beauty of the islands, but with a sailor's eye, remarks on their vulnerability in stormy weather. The pilot cutters, owned at all the chief islands, have 'ponderous' moorings in the snuggest spots to be found. Even so, they have sometimes succumbed to westerly gales. This connoisseur of sailing boats, having sailed all round the British Isles, reckoned the Scilly pilot cutters were some of the finest in England. Unfortunately very few illustrations of these craft exist.

Some other examples of pilot craft operating from other Southwest ports should also be mentioned: Plymouth District had at least eight cutters operating from the port in the mid-nineteenth century, one possibly based at Cawsand. Five of them were built in Plymouth. Registered tonnages ranged from 54 tons down to 31 tons, therefore they were generally larger than Falmouth boats, presumably taking more pilots on board. In 1857 the *Surprise*, registered at 36 tons, made a foray into Falmouth territory to take part in the regatta pilot cutter race, which it won. This naturally upset the locals, who protested that its size put it outside the class. As a sort of compromise the race committee eventually gave it the second prize. To rub salt into the wounds, *Surprise* returned in 1865, and won again.

At the smaller ports around the Cornish coast gigs became the dominant pilot boat. Only rarely are larger sailing pilot boats recorded, although many gigs, which in some places were beamier and more heavily built than today's 'standard' version, could set a lugsail, mizzen and jib sails. The Penzance District extended from the Lizard to the Land's end. In 1809 Trinity House granted pilot licences to 12 Penzance men, most, if not all, would have been fishermen. No doubt they were thoroughly examined for their competency as pilots, but unofficially, in those hard times, their first priority was to make a living. Sometimes altruistic considerations, at least where no danger to life was involved, might succumb to the chance of making a profit. In a report published in September 1818 the *West Briton* was furious about one such incident:

> 'The sloop *Jones*, of Dartmouth, bound to Bridgwater, during the gale on Monday last, made for Penzance Pier, which not being able to weather, she came to anchor outside it, and made a signal for a pilot. A boat put off to her assistance, but, according to custom, the persons on board determined to extort as much as possible for this aid, and refused to come on board the sloop unless the Master promised to comply with their exorbitant demands. During the delay occasioned by the proceedings, the sloop parted her cable, and immediately drove on shore. She sustained considerable damage, but fortunately was got off next tide. Is there no mode of punishing such conduct on the part of pilots?'

The Newlyn lug-rigged gig *Polly*, sailing from the harbour c. 1920. Wide-beamed gigs such as this were used for fishing and piloting in Mounts' Bay for generations. (National Maritime Museum, Greenwich)

There was always a price to pay: two years later, in January 1820, the *Royal Cornwall Gazette* reported that three men were returning in a small punt to their pilot boat after speaking to a Swedish ship in Mount's Bay, when the punt was upset in a heavy sea. Two men sank without trace, the third was rescued, but died before the boat reached the shore. On a happier note: Master S. Higgs, of the small Penzance pilot cutter *Gorilla*, dared to enter the Falmouth regatta race in 1864. In slackening winds, only one round of the race across Falmouth Bay was held. *Gorilla* was eighth of the nine finishers. Where there are reports of sailing pilot boats in the western districts, it is more likely that they were owned by fishermen who sometimes acted as pilots for local ports. Most pilot boats probably evolved in this way. Three of the lugger fleet at the tiny village of Mousehole, to the west of Penzance, came into this category. The lugger *Marquess of Wellington*, patriotically named after England's hero of Waterloo, was one such vessel. Two other luggers appear in a report in the *Cornish Telegraph* in February 1867: pilot boat *Nautilus* met a Penzance schooner 12 miles out to sea; on the same day the *Weatherall* was towing some spars and rigging of an unknown wrecked ship into the harbour. No doubt some use could be found for the wreckage, or even a profit made from its sale.

'Around the corner' of the Land's End and into St. Ives Bay on the north coast, where the industrial port of Hayle lies deep in a tidal inlet in the southernmost part of the bay. In March 1831, while trying to tow the sloop *Unity* through the entrance channel, a pilot gig with seven on board was upset in the surf over the notorious sand bars; two of the crew drowned. It is possible that the gig and crew belonged to the nearby fishing village of St. Ives. The harbour there consists of little more than an open beach, a small southern part being sheltered by a headland and pier, built by Smeaton in 1770. This was originally only about 100 metres long, not being lengthened to its present size until 1890. The harbour is still very exposed to winds from the north and west, and was even more so before the pier was extended. However. the harbour thrived as an important fishing centre, with a large fleet of pilchard seine boats and offshore luggers. All of these could be hauled up high on the beach in bad weather. A few coastal vessels once used the harbour, bringing in coal and general goods; some slate and ores were exported. Otherwise sailing vessels were advised to avoid these coastal waters or risk being driven onshore by the prevailing westerly winds.

The St. Ives fishermen, as at Penzance, carried out limited pilotage work and assisted in rescue and salvage of vessels. In December 1836, pilots in a gig saved several lives from a coal smack that was aground on the beach near the pier. Two years later a very similar incident occurred: a dramatic report appeared in the *Royal Cornwall Gazette* on 28 December 1838, concerning the rescue of five crew of the brig *Rival*, stranded in heavy seas off the pier. Pilots and fishermen, in gigs and seine-netting boats, made repeated strenuous efforts at rescue, until eventually successful. All later received a portion of the award raised by subscription for the 'noble conduct of pilots and fishermen'.

In late February that year, during a period of stormy weather, it was heard that vessels were in distress at the Land's End. Seventeen St. Ives men, in the pilot boat *Caesar*, went out in tempestuous seas; about 15 miles off the land they came upon an abandoned French brig, sails lost and in a near sinking condition. Eventually they managed to bring it into port. Six survivors were later found adrift in a small boat. The salvors shared a handsome reward for saving the ship and valuable cargo of rum, coffee and sugar. The *Caesar* was a large fishing lugger, possibly one of the few vessels that, with an expert crew, at the time was capable of handling such work. Newquay has a similar maritime history as St. Ives, with a substantial fishing fleet; exporting iron ore and china clay; and importing coal and timber. Fishing boats and gigs must have been used for pilotage work, but no early records have been traced. Further up the north coast of Cornwall, the only relatively safe harbour of refuge is Padstow. It is unlikely that sailing pilot boats were used here. High up on the awesome Stepper Point watchers might look out for approaching ships and signal to pilots further along the estuary shore, where there was a watch house and pilots' cottages at Hawker's cove. They would then go out in rowing gigs to guide their charges up the estuary over the infamous Doom Bar.

We now turn to the Falmouth pilot boats, which in their heyday were all rigged as cutters. The term 'cutter' was generally applied to certain small sailing craft with sails rigged in a particular way, although it could also be applied to other types of craft such as sloops and some naval rowing boats. The sailing cutter rig possibly evolved in Holland during the seventeenth century. Sails were mainly set fore and aft, along the axis of the vessel, rather than across it as with the case of square-rigged sails. There was a single mast, set about one third of the way back from the bows. The main driving power came from a big mainsail set on a gaff and boom. A fore, or staysail, was set on the mainmast stay at the bows. Several jibsails could be set on the long horizontal spar, know as the bowsprit, leading forward from the bow. The larger cutters, up to about 70 feet in

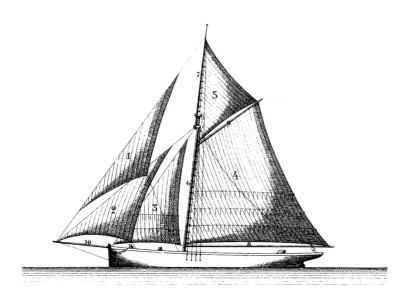

1	Jib-topsail.
2	Jib.
3	Fore-staysail.
4	Main-sail.
5	Gaff-topsail.
6	Mast.
7	Top-mast.
8	Boom; Main-boom.
9	Gaff.
10	Bowsprit,

Typical sail arrangement on a small nineteenth century cutter.

length, which evolved in English naval hands, also had a large powerful square sail forward of the mast. With this rig, set above a deep, broad hull, built for speed, they became a valuable asset to the Royal Navy as lightly armed dispatch and escort vessels. As Revenue cutters, they put fear into the hearts of the smuggling fraternity.

By the mid-nineteenth century, this type of naval cutter was being replaced by steam-powered vessels. However, the rig lived on, although usually without the square sail, in various types of small coastal merchantmen and fishing boats, particularly the East Coast fishing smacks. At the same time it was taken up by the Victorian yacht designers. On the smaller vessels a variety of versatile sails could be set on a comparatively simple rig, and therefore boats could be handled by a small crew. One of the 'by-products' of the development of the design was, of course, the pilot cutter. The rig may have reached its peak of excellence in the big, multi-crewed, and very expensive, Victorian racing yachts, but was no less eye-catching, and infinitely more practical, in the hands of the mid-nineteenth century pilot cutter builders, sail-makers and sailors of the West Country.

No eighteenth century Falmouth pilot boats have been traced. Before the escalation of maritime trade in the nineteenth century, and ships calling at Falmouth for orders, it may have been sufficient for pilots to use rowing boats to attend ships offshore, around the estuary and up the tidal rivers. Otherwise fishing boats may have been used, as was the case at Penzance and St. Ives. In 1839 the *Royal Cornwall Gazette* report of the Falmouth regatta pilot boat race made the comment that the race included boats of a very superior class to those of four or five years previously, when there was nothing of the kind in the port; the recent arrivals were now capable of going as far westward as Scilly. The first annual regatta of three years before had included a race for boats skippered by pilots: it included two small yawls, that is, with a main and a mizzen mast. These were probably open, undecked boats, similar to the later Falmouth quay punts. The few other boats listed were all under 40 feet in length. Any others that may have been used earlier in the century, apart from those in the present list, have left no record.

The 'very superior class' of 1839 still only included two locally built boats of over 40 feet in length; others were very much smaller, and built elsewhere, apart from two early St. Mawes boats. Some were probably little more than 'day' boats. By now most would have been rigged as cutters, and the larger ones decked in to provide accommodation below. During the 1840s and '50s local pilots ordered a number of larger cutters. At least ten were built at The Bar, in Falmouth, close to where the National Maritime Museum Cornwall now stands. (See *Falmouth Haven*). The work was undertaken at the shipyards of John Trethowan, James Mayn and Joseph Haly. Three St. Mawes pilots ordered boats from Plymouth and Polruan; four other boats were later built by Henry Trethowan at Little Falmouth.

By the 1850s the shipbuilders of The Bar seem to have developed a 'standard' hull shape which was acceptable to most of the pilots. It was the height of perfection as they knew it, being strong, stable, fast and 'sea kindly' for the conditions they were likely to face. All factors had to be balanced to reach the perfect compromise. The length times beam ratio is a major factor in the ultimate speed of a vessel. Basically, the narrower the hull, the faster it will travel through water. The pilot boat *Friendship* of 1818 had a ratio of only about 2.7 to 1, the dimensions of a fishing boat, whereas

Unplanked builder's
one-twelfth-scale half
model of an unidentified
(proposed?) 52 foot
Falmouth pilot cutter,
originally found at Peters'
boatyard, Freshwater,
St. Mawes. (Courtesy of
the National Maritime
Museum, Cornwall).

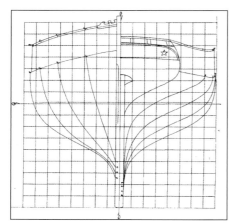

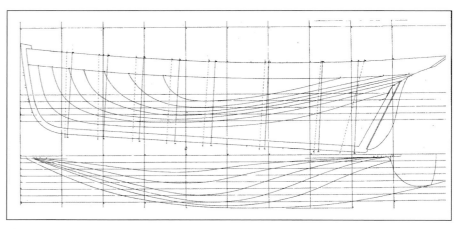

The lines of the
unidentified 52 foot
pilot cutter half-model
held at the National
Maritime Museum
Cornwall. (Drawn by
Luke Powell, 2011)

the later designers on The Bar aimed for a ratio of 4 to 1. The hulls had become so similar that in a newspaper report in 1862 of the building by Trethowan of *Arrow*, which had been designed by pilot William Old, the writer expressed some doubts as to her future: 'We hope that her sailing qualities will give satisfaction, as we hear that her lines differ very much from any of the other cutters'. Two years later the *Arrow* won the hotly contested regatta pilot boat race.

On 31 August 1878 the *Falmouth Packet* reported that 'On Thursday there was a very pretty little pilot cutter launched from the building yard of Mr. Henry S. Trethowan. She was named the 'Unexpected', and is built for the Bristol Channel. She is 40 tons B.M., and is likely to sail very fast'. This was the last of the full-size working pilot cutters to be built in Falmouth. She is recorded in the Mercantile Navy list at 34 tons, with dimensions of 40 feet in length, 14 in beam, and a depth of 9 feet. She was registered at Bristol as pilot boat number 21. The owner from 1879 to 1897 was George Dickens of Pill, the traditional base for Bristol pilots situated in a small muddy creek on the southern shore of the Bristol Avon. After 20 years service she was sold off and registered at Lowestoft, possibly still used as a pilot boat. However, by 1903 she had been converted to a yacht. She was given Hull registration although the owner, Lieutenant Francis Shipton, R.N., had a London address. She remained as such on Lloyds Yacht Register until 1927. One would like to speculate that the lines of this no doubt excellent example of a Trethowan-built cutter influenced the designers of some of the later famous, and sometimes surviving, Bristol Channel boats.

The fine underwater lines of the Falmouth pilot cutters are indicated in the photograph of the beached *Arrow*. Hulls were deep, for great stability, aided by a considerable amount of iron ballast. The near vertical stem led to a round forefoot. The hull was shaped with a fine entrance and run, towards the raked sternpost and rudder, shaped for minimum drag. Above water level the strakes had a greater sheer to the counter or lute stern; this was more pronounced in some vessels than others. The hull planks were usually of pitch pine, on oak frames; the keel was elm or oak. The whole was held together by treenails and iron spikes. The hull was caulked and pitched; the boat being periodically beached for re-caulking, cleaning and re-painting to a fine finish, the hull above and below the waterline being the regulation black.

Bulwarks, about one metre in height, gave some protection to the crew working around the extensive deck area. Running across the counter stern was an iron bar, the 'horse', on which the mainsheet block traveller slid as the boat was tacked. Forward of this the helmsman steered with a long tiller connected directly to the head of the rudder post. No compass binnacle can be seen on the photographs. Directly in front of the helmsman was the single companionway to the saloon below, protected by its wooden cover, the door of which could be closed in severe weather. Light and ventilation below may have been provided on all boats, by a box-like skylight hatch on the main deck just abaft of the mast (depicted on a photograph of *Richard Green*). Some boats are depicted sailing with a stove chimney fixed in the same area. This may have been removable, depending on weather conditions. The clinker-built boarding punt was kept on chocks on the port side of the main deck. On two cutters at least, a long cylindrical object can be seen laid on chocks on the deck by the starboard bulwark. This has been interpreted as the massive mainsail boom, fixed in its stored position when not in use. On a photograph of *Vincent*, an iron horse is fixed across the foredeck; this may have been for the traveller of the sheet of a small staysail. No mechanical winches can be observed around the mast base; all sail handling may have been accomplished with tackles on halyards and backstays, and sail sheets to cleats and belaying pins.

Advertisement for the sale of *Spy.* She was to have a new life in the Shetland Isles.

The single pole mast, of about 17 metres in length and probably made of pitch pine, was positioned about two fifths back from the bow, steadied by the usual forestay and shrouds. The topmast for working use was little more than a free-standing 5 or 6 metre pole to carry the large pilot flag; colours white over red. During summertime, and particularly for racing, this could be replaced by a more substantial stayed topmast 8 or 9 metres in length. This held a simple yard topsail, sheeted through a block on the end of the gaff. Forward of the mast, to balance the rig, a foresail was hanked to the mainstay, which ran from the bow to the masthead. A jibsail, which could be large or small, depending on conditions, was set flying on a traveller ring run out to the end of the long, heavy bowsprit. This spar, running between massive knightheads at the bow, could be run in and stowed inboard when the boat was beached for maintenance. An anchor windlass would also have been incorporated here, although none can be observed on the available photographs; however, anchors, chain and a winch are on *Arrow's* bill of sale.

The big gaff mainsail was attached to the mast with the usual wooden hoops. There now comes the difficulty of describing what would be a 'normal' Falmouth pilot cutter mainsail. In the book, *Falmouth Haven,* this writer was careful to state that 'according to available photographs' the Falmouth boats had loose-footed mainsails with no boom. Fortunately, a photograph and several paintings of cutters with booms have since been discovered: it now appears that the depicted boomless sails were known as trysails, that is, sails for winter or rough-weather use. When used on modern yachts, such sails are small, triangular, and set on the mast after the mainsail, its boom, and gaff, if so rigged, have been stowed down to the deck. On the Falmouth cutters the trysail was set up on the mainsail gaff yard, and was not substantially smaller than a conventional mainsail, especially when a bonnet, an extra strip of sailcloth, was laced to the foot of the sail. The gaff could then be raised further up the mast and the luff then tensioned with a powerful downhaul. The clew of the sail (the outer bottom corner) was hooked directly to the mainsheet, which went via a tackle to a block travelling on an iron horse fixed across the counter.

From the evidence of the photographs, this sail was used a great deal of the time; perhaps even throughout the year on some boats. It was powerful enough for all general use, especially in the late nineteenth and early twentieth century when there was little competition between boats and speed was of less importance. It could be easily reefed, the mainsheet hooked to a reef cringle further up the leach of the sail. The long mainsheet makes the sail look extremely unwieldy in the photographs, but in the right hands it was obviously efficient. Similar sails were used for generations on fishing boats such as the Thames bawleys. Although subject to flogging at some points of sailing, it could probably look after itself when hove to on station if properly balanced with the foresails.

The trysail could be said to be safer than a boomed sail: when tacking or gibing, a long heavy piece of timber, with flogging sail attached, flying across the deck, is a definite health hazard. The disadvantages of a boom were demonstrated by two separate instances, involving loss of a pilot and a crew member. In March 1860 a pilot boat was swamped by a heavy sea while off the Lizard: pilot Thomas Jenking was washed overboard and drowned. One of the contributory factors for his loss was that the boat became unmanageable after the rope holding the boom jaws to the mast was broken. In April 1871, James Barker, chief deck hand on the cutter *Vie*, was tying the reef pendants on the boom while reefing the mainsail, which can be a hazardous operation even on small yachts. In this case, the mainsheet came away from its cleat, causing the boom to fly out, taking Barker with it; he fell into the sea and was lost.

In spite of such tragedies, it appears that boomed mainsails, which were larger than the trysails, were used on some, if not all the boats, even during the winter. In February 1884 the boom on cutter *Richard Green* was carried away as she approached Falmouth in a gale, and she had to find refuge up

An oil painting by Henry Tozer, dated 1881, depicting the sea conditions sometimes faced by pilot boats. It possibly represents the *Telegraph*, although some features of the rig were not typical of Falmouth cutters. (Courtesy of Brian Kennell, also Mervyn Maggs for photography)

The yacht-like *Antelope* in Falmouth Bay, depicted with her big boomed mainsail, staysail and flying jib; but a working topmast to display the pilot flag. A fine oil painting by local artist Alexander Brander. (Tom Welch)

in the Truro River. Other clues to the use of the two types of rig are found in the notes of the Minutes of the F.D.P.B.A. In August 1887 the sailing captains of the cutters were instructed to have trysails ready for winter use. By 1890, emulating the pilots of the Bristol Channel, some Falmouth boats had converted their mainsails and booms to roller reefing. This involved the installation of mechanical gearing at the mast, which turned the boom, thereby rolling the sail around it. There is no record of how successful the system was when applied to a rig of such size and weight.

There seems to have been no hard and fast rule about the correct rig to use at any given time. An example of which is a photograph, in private hands, taken in about 1910, which depicts the *Richard Green* on the Percuil River, apparently on a summer's day, using a trysail, but also having a topsail set above it. On the other hand, in 1881 artist Henry Tozer made a dramatic oil painting of a Falmouth pilot cutter in extreme conditions, with mainsail reefed down to a long boom which extended past the counter stern. The boat was also equipped with shrouds to the topmast, and crosstrees. However, its authenticity is in doubt as the composition is remarkably similar to an oil painting by another artist a few years previously of Plymouth pilot cutters, and which may have been seen by Tozer. Another very recently (2010) discovered contemporary oil painting, by A.K. Brander, in private ownership, depicts *Antelope*, with pilot flag, no topsail, but with a boomed mainsail.

The author was also pleased to discover a unique photograph of *Antelope* in a museum collection. The print had fortunately been copied in the past from a very battered original. It must date to on or before 1884 when the pilots competed in their last Falmouth Regatta, for it depicts the beautiful vessel in full racing rig. She is running downwind, sporting a full mainsail, topsail, staysail, flying jib and jib topsail. A spare jib is set out to windward in 'goosewinged' fashion on a long boom from the mast base. One can at last see why the yacht-like Falmouth pilot cutters were so admired by the massed spectators on those far-off Victorian regatta days.

The Merchant Shipping Act of 1894, and presumably previous Acts, contains the following Regulations:

'611. All boats and ships regularly employed in the pilotage service of any district (in this Part of this Act referred to as pilot boats) shall be approved and licensed by the pilotage authority of the district, and that authority may, at their discretion, appoint and remove the masters of those pilot boats.

'612. – (1) Every pilot boat shall be distinguished by the following characteristics; namely, -

(a) On her stern the name of her owner and the port to which she belongs, painted in white letters at least one inch broad and three inches long, and on each bow the number of her licence.

(b) In all other parts a black colour painted or tarred outside, or such other colour or colours as the pilotage authority of the district, with the consent of the Board of Trade, direct.

(c) When afloat a flag (in this Act called a pilot flag) of large dimensions compared with the size of the pilot boat, and of two colours, the upper horizontal half white, and the lower horizontal half red, to be placed at the mast head, or on a sprit or staff, or in some equally conspicuous situation.

(2) It shall be the duty of the master of the pilot boat to see that the pilot boat possesses all the above characteristics, and that the pilot flag is kept clean and distinct, so as to be easily discerned at a reasonable distance and also that the names and numbers aforesaid are not at any time concealed; and if a master fails without reasonable cause to comply with the requirements of this section, he shall for each offence be liable to a fine not exceeding twenty pounds.

'613. – (1) When a qualified pilot is carried off in a vessel not in the pilotage service, he shall exhibit a pilot flag in order to show that the vessel has a qualified pilot on board; and if he fails, without reasonable cause, to do so, he shall for each offence be liable to a fine not exceeding fifty pounds.

(2) Where the master or mate of a ship holds a pilotage certificate, a pilot flag shall be displayed on board the ship while that master or mate is on board and the ship is within a pilotage district in which pilotage is compulsory, and if default is made in complying with the enactment, the master of the ship shall for each offence be liable to a fine not exceeding twenty pounds.

'615. – (1) Her Majesty may by Order in Council make rules as to the signals to be used or displayed where the services of a pilot are required on any vessel, and those signals are in this Act referred to as pilot signals.

(2) If a vessel requires the services of a pilot, the master of that vessel shall use or display the pilot signals.

(3) If a master of a vessel uses or displays, or causes or permits any person under his authority to use or display, any of the pilot signals for any other purpose than that of summoning a pilot, or uses or causes or permits any person under his authority to use any other signal for a pilot, he shall for each offence be liable to a fine not exceeding twenty pounds.

Unlike their more numerous cousins, the Bristol Channel pilot cutters, no Falmouth boats, nor those from other Cornish ports or the Isles of Scilly have survived. There are contemporary illustrations and models of Scilly boats in the museum on St. Mary's: it appears that generally the hulls and rigging of the Scilly boats were very similar to those at Falmouth, being designed to cope with the same sea conditions. There were a number of different styles of Bristol Channel boat; however, from those Bristol cutters, built around 1900, that are still sailing, it may be deduced that in their heyday the Falmouth boats were generally larger. The last of these were built between 1857 and 1874; the picture is somewhat confused by the fact that some hulls were lengthened during service to accommodate more pilots.

The photographs, a small restored model of an early Falmouth boat at St. Mary's Museum, and an existing builder's half model, may be sufficient for a full-size reconstruction to be made. Skilled shipwrights today are making new likenesses of Bristol Channel boats, so why not the same for a Falmouth boat? The project would just require an extremely wealthy entrepreneur, who is absolutely mad about wooden boats, and who would like to create a superb reproduction symbolising Falmouth's long history of shipbuilding, and its pilotage service, which is still respected throughout the maritime world.

6: Detail from a view of Falmouth waterfront, c.1876, depicting two moored pilot cutters: No. 11 *Nautilus* has her boomed mainstail and topsail set; to the left is Barker and Williams' *Vie*, with her low free-board and graceful curving hull profile. Her boom extends well beyond the counter; the crew's pride in her appearance is exemplified by the neatly stowed mainsail on the gaff. Both port and starboard removable sections of the bulwarks are open for access to the boarding punt; moored astern. (Copyright, The Francis Frith Collection)

The Pilot Cutters of the Port of Falmouth

Chronological list of the boats.
In the order of when built or first recorded in regatta reports etc.

Year	Name	Boat Number	Tonnage	Builder/Other report	Base
1811	Hiram		31	Roberts(?), St.Mawes	St.Mawes
1818	Friendship		28	Roberts, St.Mawes	St.Mawes
1820	Assistance			Incident Report	Falmouth
1834	Harriet (1)		24	Lelean, Mevagissey	St.Mawes
1834	Providence		16	Dunn, Mevagissey	St.Mawes
1836	Constantine		29	Regatta Report	Falmouth
1836	Industry			Regatta Report	Falmouth
1836	Triad			Regatta Report	St.Mawes
1836	Union		10	Regatta Report	Falmouth
1837	Dart		18	Lelean, Mevagissey	Falmouth
1837	Rob Roy		17	Regatta Report	St.Mawes
1837	Victoria (1)	7	22	Trethowan, Falmouth	Falmouth
1838	Spy	10	33	Lelean, Mevagissey	St.Mawes
1839	Betsey			Regatta Report	
1840	Eagle		15	Regatta Report	Falmouth
1840	Experiment		15	Regatta Report	
1840	Fal		10	Regatta Report	
1840	Pearl		35	Regatta Report	Falmouth
1841	New Providence	8	23	Trethowan, Falmouth	St.Mawes
1841	Perseverance	2	28	Lelean, Mevagissey	Falmouth
1841	Prince Albert		26	Trethowan, Falmouth	Falmouth
1843	Alarm (1)	5	29	Trethowan, Falmouth	Falmouth
1844	Harriet (2)	1	29	Trethowan, Falmouth	St.Mawes
1844	Water Nymph	6	26	Trethowan, Falmouth	Falmouth
1845	Gem	4	29	Mayn, Falmouth	Falmouth
1845	Vie	3	28	Built 1845, Falmouth	Falmouth
1847	Nicholas Jenking	12	23	Trethowan, Falmouth	St.Mawes
1848	Dash	9	31	Hocking, Plymouth	St.Mawes
1848	Wasp	13	28	Mayn, Falmouth	Falmouth
1850	Dan	11	26	Butson, Polruan	St.Mawes
1852	Harriet (3)	1	31	Haly, Falmouth	St.Mawes
1852	Victoria (2)	7	32	Trethowan, Falmouth	Falmouth
1852	Vincent	8	27	Hocking, Plymouth	St.Mawes
1857	Nautilus	11	29	Built 1842, Lymington	Falmouth
1857	Alarm (2)	5	31	Trethowan, Falmouth	Falmouth
1857	Andrews	2	33	Haly, Falmouth	St.Mawes
1857	Telegraph	4	30	Mayn, Falmouth	Falmouth
1862	Arrow	6	35	Trethowan, Falmouth	Falmouth
1866	Richard Green	10	28	Trethowan, Falmouth	St.Mawes
1870	Antelope	13	36	Trethowan, Falmouth	Falmouth
1874	Condor	12	32	Trethowan, Falmouth	St.Mawes
1878	Gwendolyn	1	38	Symons, Falmouth	Falmouth
1922	Arthur Rogers	1	22	-, Brixham	Falmouth

Note – The methods for calculating tonnage changed in the middle of the century; the later figures are considerably lower than the old. Therefore the tonnage for early boats such as Hiram, Friendship, Constantine, Spy and Pearl should possibly be reduced by roughly 25% to compare with the later ones. For instance, in 1842 the regatta report listed Spy at 33 tons, but the official figure in 1853 was 25 tons.

Opposite page:

1: Pilot cutter *Arrow*, sporting a trysail with deep laced-on bonnet, and a diminutive flying jib. (RCPS)

2: Harriet (3), heading out on a cold-looking day: note the stove chimney abaft the mast. The date must be pre-1897 when she was sold off. (National Maritime Museum, Greenwich)

3: Vincent, using *Harriet's* small trysail, requiring an extra-long mainsheet. The sail was probably transferred after the latter was decommissioned in 1897. Note the stove chimney, boarding punt, and extra bulwark cloths to protect the helmsman. (RCPS)

4: The St. Mawes' boat *Richard Green*. This view emphasises her blunt bow, sweeping hull lines and high bulwarks. (National Maritime Museum Greenwich).

5: Antelope, circa 1900, heading across Carrick Roads; setting a large flying jib, staysail, trysail and conspicuous pilot flag. There is a large complement of pilots and crew on board, reflecting the cut in available pilot boats to reduce overheads as pilotage revenue declined. (RCPS)

GAZETTEER OF THE FALMOUTH BOATS

A list of the boats, their builders and owners, 1818-1936, compiled from the Merchant Shipping Registers in the Cornwall Record Office (CRO/MSR/FAL); the Mercantile Navy Lists; the Bartlett Library database, National Maritime Museum Cornwall; and local directories and newspapers. (Abbreviations - F.D.P.B.A., Falmouth District Pilot Boat Association; M.N.L., Mercantile Navy List; M.S.R., Merchant Shipping Registers).

Vessels were owned under the share system, whereby perhaps several people, predominantly the pilots and close relatives, invested in shares towards the purchase of the boats and received a (hopefully) regular share of the working profits. Shares were bought or sold out of a total of 64 (e.g. thirty two 64ths = half ownership). Some shareholders from the MSR are included here, but not always the exact dates or the number of shares owned. Names changed over the years as shares were bought and sold, or transferred to widows, and so on. A 'Managing Owner', who had to be registered at the Custom House, was not necessarily the one with the most shares.

Dimensions of vessels are recorded in the register as, (in feet) length stem to sternpost x maximum width x depth in hold from tonnage deck to ceiling at midships. A surprising number of cutters were lengthened during their service: shipwrights usually did this by dismantling the middle of the boat and adding an extra central section. This incurred considerable expense and inconvenience, but was obviously thought necessary, the main reason being to create accommodation for extra pilots during the boom years.

ALARM 1   (MNL 17163, boat no. 5) 29 tons, 44.3' x 13.3' x 7'
Built in 1843 by John Trethowan at The Bar, Falmouth for James James of New Street, Falmouth. Other shareholders: Nicholas Lowry Andrew of Falmouth and Mark Tiddy of St. Mawes. Some shares later transferred to John Trethowan and ship owner John Phillips of Falmouth. James finished second in the 1843 regatta race. He was listed as 'gave up' in the 1853 race. In 1857 James replaced the boat with the second *Alarm*. The MNL of 1861 gives the port of registry as Lerwick.

ALARM 2   (MNL 20551, boat no. 5) 31.55 tons, 54.4' x 14' x 8'
Built in 1857 by John Trethowan at Little Falmouth for J. James & Co. First shareholders: John Trethowan 32, James James 16, Nicholas Lowry Andrew 16. Lengthened in 1872 to 67' x 14.6' x 8', 34 tons. Some shares later transferred to John Phillips, N. L. Andrew Jnr., and James Oakshott, the Falmouth Telegraph manager. Trethowan (Henry) shares to trustees and widow Mary, who sells to Andrew Snr. In 1886 he objects to proposed F.D.P.B.A. scheme; boat licence is withdrawn, for which he is paid £250 compensation, but retains the boat. He dies in December 1888, shares passing to his widow, Mary Ann. All shares sold to London merchant Hugh Matheson in 1889, who then sells to a Spanish subject. Managing owners and/or masters over the period: James, Phillips and Andrew.

ANDREWS   (MNL 19860, boat no. 2) 33 tons, 56' x 15.2' x 8.3'
Built in 1857 by Joseph Haly at The Bar, Falmouth for Messrs. Andrew of St. Mawes (*Falmouth Packet* report of launch 14.11.1857). First shareholders (and pilots) Richard senior, Richard junior, William, James, Frederick, John. Various family members were managing owners and Masters. All shares remained in the family until 1887, when boat was purchased by the F.D.P.B.A. for £450. Frederick Andrew then remained as managing owner. Michael Richards became Master in 1890. Boat remained in service to 1896, but possibly kept as a spare boat. Sold to John Chard in 1900. Broken up in 1910.

ANTELOPE   (MNL 62044, boat no. 13) 36 tons, 62.5' x 15.65' x 9.1'
Lengthened in 1872 to 69' x 15.65' x 9.1', 39.90 tons. Built in 1870 by Henry Trethowan, probably at Little Falmouth, for John Collins of Gylling Street, Falmouth. First shareholders: John Collins 24; Samuel Collins 16; Richard Lowry Rusden, apprentice pilot 16; William Lowry 8. John Collins competed in regattas 1870 - 74. He and his son John were drowned when the punt capsized in Falmouth Bay in December 1874. The cutter was taken over by John H. Collins, followed by Samuel Collins, who remained as managing owner under the F.D.P.B.A. from 1887. In 1879 the shareholders had been John and Samuel Collins, W. H. Jenking, Richard Bellman, H. F. Chard, and G. L. Collins. The boat was sunk in collision with a steamer off the Lizard on 24 April 1905.

ARROW   (MNL 43550, boat no. 6) 35 tons, length 67 feet
Built in 1862 by John Trethowan at The Bar, Falmouth. The newspaper report of her keel being laid down in February 1862 stated that she was designed by pilot William Old, with lines differing from the other cutters. She was launched in August. Shares towards purchase of the boat were £9 each. Henry Tonkin, W. J. Lowry, John Collins and M. Richards paid for a total of 43 shares; Mrs. Elizabeth Lowry 5; Philip Pope, the Falmouth accountant 16. The latter was the main shareholder until at least 1876. The itemized bill for construction and fitting out, drawn up by Pope, still exists. Tonkin and Lowry were named as Masters in regattas in the 1860s. Owned by the F.D.P.B.A. 1887 – 1914; by the time of the boat's purchase by the Association the Lowry family held 48 shares and the Popes 16. The boat was sold to Michael Richards in 1914, presumably for breaking up.

ARTHUR ROGERS (MNL 146376, boat no. 1) 22 tons
Built at Brixham in 1922 for the F.D.P.B.A. The last sailing cutter in service, with the motor launch, *A. R. Dawson.* The cutter was replaced in March 1936 by another launch, the *Harry Slater,* and auctioned off, being bought by Abraham Hipwell of Exeter. Later owners were, in 1940 Robert Byng of London, and from 1949 to 1955 Thomas Hepworth of Regents Park, London; by then she was listed as ketch-rigged. Argal and Bird (*Mariners Mirror*, Vol. 64, 1978) stated that she crossed the Atlantic and was later wrecked off the Bahamas.

ASSISTANCE   (MNL ? boat no.?)
Recorded in a *Royal Cornwall Gazette* report on 16 December 1820, following the capture of a six foot long sturgeon off Falmouth. 'The fish was taken by the Assistance pilot boat belonging to R (?) Chard.'

BETSEY   (MNL ? boat no.?)
Falmouth Packet report on 10 August 1839, recorded as competing in the regatta pilot boat race, skippered by Barker. No other details.

CONDOR   (MNL 72486, boat no. 12) 31.58 tons, 57.8' x 15' x 8.7'
Built in 1874 by Henry Trethowan at Little Falmouth. First shareholders Joseph Jane Vincent 20; Nicholas Jenking 16; Thomas Barret Collins 16; Hugh Andrew 12. In the 1880s and up to 1895 managed by J. J. Vincent, being sold to the F.D.P.B.A. in 1887 and in service until 1913. (*Condor's* logbook still exists, held at the Royal Cornwall Polytechnic Society archives.) In 1915 the owner was W. E. Morrison. In 1919 she was jointly owned by C. J. B. Cooke of St. Mawes and Doctor D. R. Harris of Falmouth. Reported wrecked and abandoned in 1942. Remnants of the boat are believed to still lie near Percuil.

CONSTANTINE   (MNL 17180?, boat no. 4?) 29 tons (regatta report, 'Old' tonnage)
Recorded in Falmouth regatta pilot boat races 1836, 1839-44, John Chard, master. (Comment in 1839 newspaper report – "*Constantine* … carried away her topsail sheet.") Chard replaced her with *Gem* in 1845. In 1859 it was reported that James Watts, owner of trawler *Constantine*, was drowned in the harbour. This is likely to have been the same boat.

DAN   (MNL 17169, boat no. 11) 26 tons, 46' x 13' x 8'
Built in 1850 by N. Butson at Polruan, for pilot Daniel Fittock; he held 43 shares and schoolmaster James Gant held 21. Transferred to Peter Fittock in 1854 on Daniel's retirement, aged 64. For an unknown reason, Peter soon gave up the boat and transferred to boat no. 1, *Harriet. Nautilus* was brought in as boat no. 11. The *Dan* was sold to F. Banfield on St. Mary's, Isles of Scilly, who held her to at least 1871. In 1874-5 held by John Ellis of Sennen, Cornwall. From 1876 to 1909 registered to several owners on the west coast of Southern Ireland.

DART   (MNL 17175, boat no. ?) Bartlett library database measurement, 18 tons, 38.2' x 10.9' x 6.6'
Built in 1837 by Nicholas Lelean at Mevagissey. MNL gives Phillip Pope of Falmouth as owner 1840 – c. 1872. J. Lowry raced her in regattas 1840 – 1843. A James Lowry ordered the pilot boat *Wasp* in 1848, therefore the Dart may have ceased as a pilot boat about that date. Possibly later owned by P. Pope & Co. She was broken up in 1872.

DASH   (MNL 17162, boat no. 9) 31 tons, 52.6' x 12.2' x 8.9'
Built in 1848 by Hocking and Sons at Stonehouse, Plymouth. First shareholders were James, John and William Dash of St. Mawes. They all raced and owned her until sold to the F.D.P.B.A. in 1887. Sold off, possibly to John Sprake of St. Mawes.

EAGLE   (MNL ?, boat no.?) 15 tons
Skippered by D. Fittock in the regatta pilot boat races (second class) in 1841 – 2. He may have replaced her with *Dan* in 1850.

EXPERIMENT   (MNL ?, boat no.?) 15 tons
Skippered by B. Chambers in pilot boat race (second class) in 1840, J. Chambers in 1841 and T. Chambers in 1842. Builder or subsequent history not known.

FAL   (MNL ?, boat no.?) 10 tons
Skippered by N. Jenking in pilot boat races (second class) 1840 – 1. Possibly replaced by *Nicholas Jenking* in 1847.

FRIENDSHIP   (MNL 9717, boat no.9?) 28 tons ('old' measurement?) 38.5' x 13.9' x 5.6'
Recorded in 1837 regatta report as 'undecked'.
Built in 1818 by Richard Roberts of St. Mawes for pilot J. Dash, who raced her in regattas from 1836 to 1846. She was replaced by *Dash* in 1848. In the 1850s, *Friendship* was registered in Jersey, with owners Gallie and Cooper.

GEM   (MNL 17168, boat no.4) 29 tons, 48.9' x 12.8' x 7'
Built in 1845 by James Mayn at The Bar, Falmouth. First shareholders were John Chard the younger 32; John Pearce, Falmouth merchant, 16; James Mayn 16. In 1847 Mayn sold his shares to Chard. Pilot William Lean Mark Tiddy bought 16 shares but sold to Chard in 1849. John Chard raced her in regattas 1846 – 53, replacing her with *Telegraph* in 1857. This may be the same *Gem* which, according to Jenkins, was registered at St. Agnes, Scilly in 1857, where owners were to be Banfield and Hicks. *Gem* was sold again and by 1864 registered at Yarmouth. Broken up or wrecked in 1874. In St. Mary's Museum on Scilly, there is a fine (although re-rigged) possibly contemporary model built by Peters of St. Mawes of a pilot cutter, *Gem*, which is probably this boat.

GWENDOLYN   (MNL 78188, boat no.1) 38 tons, 67.2' x 14.1' x 9.8'
Built in 1878 by George Symons at The Bar, Falmouth for tailor, Richard J. Toms of Falmouth. Used for plying for trade out to visiting ships. By 1883 ownership had passed to Falmouth banker W. M. Grylls who then sold to John Lewis of Dartmouth. The owner 1887 – 1905 was George Hutchings, also of Dartmouth. The boat was brought back to Falmouth by the F.D.P.B.A. for use as a pilot boat from 1906 – 18, then sold to France.

HARRIET 1   (MNL?, boat no. 1?) 24 tons
Built in 1834 by Nicholas Lelean of Mevagissey for pilot N. Vincent of St. Mawes. Raced in regattas 1836 – 43. Sold to pilot Nicholas Jenking in 1844 when Vincent replaced her with the second *Harriet*. Jenking was master on *Harriet 1* when she was run down and sunk by a Belgian brigantine outside Falmouth Harbour in late June 1846 (*Falmouth Packet* 4.7.1846).

HARRIET 2   (MNL 13996, boat no. 1) 29 tons, 46.2' x 13.3' x 7.8'
Built in 1844 by John Trethowan at The Bar, Falmouth for N. and W. Vincent. Nicholas Vincent raced her in regattas from 1846 to 1851. He replaced her with *Harriet 3* in 1852. *Harriet 2* was sold and later registered in Penzance and Plymouth. Wrecked in 1875.

HARRIET 3   (MNL 17173, boat no. 1) 31 tons, 54.7' x 13' x 8.3'
Built in 1852 by Joseph Haly at The Bar, Falmouth for N. Vincent & Co. First shareholders were Nicholas Vincent, Francis Lowry, James Oxenbury Tiddy. Raced in regattas 1853 – 79, skippered by Nicholas Vincent (possibly father and son). Managing owner 1880 – 83 was Frederick C. Watts. Master in 1884 was Charles Andrew. Owned by F.D.P.B.A. from 1887. Seven shareholders received payments. The new managing owner was Michael Richards. In 1892 three *Harriet* pilots, T. H. Coward, E. Lowry and William Andrew escaped drowning when their punt overturned off the

Lizard. In 1897 the boat was auctioned and sold for £75. Reported broken up in 1902.

HIRAM   (MNL?, boat no. ?) 31 tons ('old' measurement) 38.6' x 14.5' x 6.6'
Built in 1811 at St. Mawes (possibly by Roberts, who later built *Friendship*). Listed as a sloop, which probably indicated cutter rig. Owner in 1817 was Richard Andrew. Recorded in a *Falmouth Packet* report 6 July 1839:
'Mr. H. Andrew, pilot, was passing the Manacles … pointing out features to his son … when he overlooked the rock called the Pinman … the *Hiram* struck and immediately sank. Mr. Andrew and crew saved themselves in the punt … Captain Plumridge, Superintendant of the packets, offered to help salvage …' Sails etc. were later recovered. No other record.

INDUSTRY   (MNL ?, boat no. ?)
Sailed by pilot J. Chard in the 1836 regatta Subscription Cup Race 'for all sailing vessels belonging to the Port', in the under 29 foot class, and said to be yawl-rigged. During the race she 'unfortunately carried away her square sail yard'. (*Falmouth Packet*, 27.8.1836)

NAUTILUS   (MNL13301, boat no. 11) 27 tons, 52.5' x 14.6' x ?
Built in 1842 at Lymington. First registered in the Port of London. In 1857 bought by Henry Vincent of St. Mawes. He later sold 16 shares to Joseph Barker. In 1873 the boat was lengthened to 29 tons, 60.9' x 14.65' x 7.7'. Henry Vincent is reported skippering the boat in the regatta of 1879, but by this time had sold his shares to William John Lowry 32, and Philip Vercoe Vincent 16. Barker was then managing owner. The boat was sold to the F.D.P.B.A. in 1887 for £200. The Association disposed of her to the Bar ship builder Henry Trethowan for breaking up. In January the following year he advertised her timbers for sale, including oak, pitch pine, elm, and other woods, plus several masts and spars.

NEW PROVIDENCE   (MNL 13422, boat no. 8) 23 or 29 tons, length 37 feet.
Built in 1841 by John Trethowan at The Bar, Falmouth, for pilot Joseph Vincent, who raced her in regattas until 1851, replacing her with *Vincent* in 1852. *New Providence* was sold to R. Chambers and re-registered in St. Ives. She was later rebuilt as a 32 ton, 55 foot schooner, re-registered in Falmouth and owned by Nicholls of Gerrans. Later sold to the Beer family in Pembrokeshire who worked her as a coastal trading vessel until 1922.

NICHOLAS JENKING   (MNL 17164, boat no. 12) 23 tons, 44.2' x 12.8' x 7'
Built in 1847 by John Trethowan at The Bar, Falmouth, for pilot Nicholas Jenking of St. Mawes. Recorded in some regattas 1851 – 78, the last year skippered by N. Vincent. Presumably he had bought her as she had been offered for sale in 1875 (*Falmouth Packet*, 20.11.1875). She was advertised as 'recently a pilot cutter' but now suitable for trawling. By 1880 she was registered in Lerwick, being owned by Peter Tait of Scallaway, Shetland.

PEARL   (MNL?, boat no. 11?) 35 tons 'old' measurement; estimated 'new' measurement, 23 tons.
Recorded in regattas 1840 – 44. Masters were T. Barker and J. Barker. Replaced by *Vie* in 1845. (In April 1838 pilot Barker assisted in the salvage of a brig on the Manacles, on pilot boat no. 11, no name given). Boat possibly kept at Coverack.

PERSEVERANCE   (MNL17160, boat no. 2) 28 tons, 46' x 13.2' x 7.2'
Built in 1841 by Nicholas Lelean at Mevagissey for the Andrew family of St. Mawes: shareholders Richard snr., Richard jnr., William and James. They raced her in regattas 1842 – 53, replacing her with *Andrews* in 1857. Later owners of *Perseverance*, rebuilt as a 56 ton schooner, were B. H. Roberts of Mevagissey and G. Stewart of Peterhead. Last recorded in 1876.

PRINCE ALBERT   (MNL 17179, boat no. ?) 26 tons, 40' x 13' x 7'
Built in 1841 by John Trethowan at The Bar, Falmouth, for John and Elias Chard. The latter was Master in the 1842 regatta pilot boat race. She was not raced again, and may have proved unsuitable for pilotage duty; the following year the Chards were using boats *Constantine* and *Victoria*. However, they retained ownership until 1874. E. C. Pope was owner 1875 – 85, followed by the banker W. M. Grylls. Last record.

PROVIDENCE   (MNL 17184, boat no. ?) 16(?) tons, 30.6' x 11.8' x 8.6'
Built in 1834 by James Dunn at Mevagissey, for St. Mawes pilot J. Vincent, who competed in
regattas 1839 – 40, when the boat's tonnage was given as 23 tons. Vincent replaced her with *New
Providence* in 1841. 17184 *Providence* appears in the MNL for 1861 and 1866, registered at 26 tons,
owner John Triggs of Falmouth.

RICHARD GREEN   (MNL 50447, boat no. 10) 28 tons, length 58'
Built in 1866 by Henry Trethowan at Little Falmouth (*Falmouth Packet*, 23.6.1866) for Richard
Green & Co. Richard snr. died in October 1869, his 24 shares passing in his will to widow Olivia.
Richard jnr., who was an apprentice on board when his father died, received his licence in 1871
and later joined the boat as a pilot second class. Also an apprentice was William Henry Green,
who later joined *Dash*. The managing owner and Master from 1870 – 87 was Nicholas William
Bickford. He had the boat lengthened in 1875, to 32 tons, 65.7' x 14.65' x 8.3'. In 1875 Ann
Nancarrow sold her 8 shares to William Green. By 1887 shares were held by Olivia Green, William
Green, and Bickford. With the establishment of the F.D.P.B.A., the three received payments of
£150, £100, £100 respectively. The boat continued in service under various masters, until broken
up in 1918.

ROB ROY   (MNL ?, boat no. ?) 17 tons, length 33.5'
Recorded in regatta pilot boat races (second class) 1837 – 44, Master W. Vincent. The 1855
Plymouth Ships Register lists a *Rob Roy* as being built in that town in 1835. She was a 12 ton
cutter with dimensions of 31.7' x 10.4' x 6'. Registered in Falmouth 1841-45, sold in 1847.
Probably the same boat.

SPY   (MNL 17166, boat no. 10) 25 tons 45.8' x 13' x 6'
Built in 1838 by Nicholas Lelean at Mevagissey. George Bickford raced her in regattas 1839 – 42,
tragically drowning in the Harbour (with William Richards) on the 1842 regatta night, leaving
a widow and 5 children. In 1846 Matilda Bickford, two accountants, and two pilots held shares.
In 1851 Matilda held onto her 12 shares, but the others sold to the Master, Richard Green 18;
pilot Henry Chard 17; and Samuel Williams mariner 17. In June 1854 Richard Green sought
permission to lengthen *Spy* and by 1857 her measurements were 36 tons, 54.2' x 14.3' x 6.7'.
Some shares were transferred in the 1860s, leaving shareholders Richard Green, Ebet (?) Williams
and Matilda Bickford. In 1865 they sold the boat to A. J. Hay and others of Lerwick, Shetland;
she remained on the MNL until 1905. *Spy* had been replaced as 'no. 10' in 1866 by the newly
built *Richard Green*.

TELEGRAPH   (MNL 19859, boat no. 4) 30 tons, 56.5' x 14.6' x 8.1'
Built in 1857 by James Mayn at The Bar, Falmouth. Lengthened prior to 1866 to 63.3', 33 tons.
Owned by the Chard family of Falmouth throughout its service. Masters in regattas were J., H.,
or C. Chard. In 1887 purchased by the F.D.P.B.A. for £300, but then broken up.

TRIAD   (MNL ?, boat no.?)
Recorded in the *Falmouth Packet* regatta report in August 1836: Subscription Cup race 'for all
sailing vessels belonging to the Port'. She was yawl-rigged and in the under 29 foot class, Master
J. Fittock.

UNION   (MNL ?, boat no,?)
Recorded in Falmouth Regattas 1840 – 42 pilot boat races (second class) 10 tons. Master J. James.
This may be the *Union* (length 34', 17 tons) which Jenkins states was built on St. Mary's, having
various owners, and decked in 1827 – Scilly registration was cancelled in 1840. Re-registered
there in 1845.

VICTORIA 1   (MNL ?, boat no. 7) 22 tons, 44.4' x 12.7' x 7'
Built in 1837 by John Trethowan at The Bar, Falmouth. Shareholders, J. and E. Chard. Lengthened
by September 1842, to 49.2' x 12.7' x 6.8'. Recorded in regattas 1837 – 51, Masters J. or E. Chard.
Wrecked on the Manacles 25 November 1851: reported to the Custom House by Elias Chard in a
letter on 9 December.

VICTORIA 2   (MNL 17171, boat no. 7) 32 tons, 52.8' x 13' x 8.5'
Built in 1852 by John Trethowan at The Bar, Falmouth, to replace the lost boat. Elias Chard held all 64 shares, racing in regattas 1853 – 80, followed by William David Chard as managing owner. The boat was lengthened in 1876 to 61.8' x 14.2' x 8.2', 32.18 tons, following a request for permission by the pilots. In 1880 an acting Master was appointed; Elias was then aged about 72, and he may have retired or died.   William Chard was owner and master in 1884. In 1887 the boat was purchased by the F.D.P.B.A. for £375, the main beneficiary being Hester Chard, presumably the widow of William. The F.D.P.B.A. then sold the boat to John Buckingham, a Falmouth fish merchant. On his death it was bought by John Chard of Market Street, Falmouth (not a pilot). It was broken up in 1904.

VIE   (MNL17165, boat no. 3) 28 tons. In MNL as Gweek registered, but Falmouth in the Merchant Shipping Register.
Built in 1845 at Falmouth. The Barker and Williams families were the principle shareholders. In 1871 their addresses were given as Coverack and St. Keverne on the Lizard, but later at Falmouth. In the *John* shipwreck enquiry of 1855 pilot John Barker stated that a pilot cutter was based at Coverack: this was probably *Vie*. Managing owners and Masters included John, Joseph and George Barker and William Williams. Some crew lists exist at the County Record Office (MSR 317). Two of the Barker family, Francis and James in 1856 and 1871 respectively, fell overboard and drowned while working as deckhands. In June 1882, *Vie* was run down and sunk by a steamer off Falmouth. Fortunately all five crew were saved.

VINCENT   (MNL 17161, boat no. 8) 27 tons, 54.9' x 11.8' x 8.4'
Built in 1852 by Richard and Hugh Hocking at Stonehouse, Plymouth for the Vincent family of St. Mawes. (A Richard Hocking built a sloop barge at St. Mawes in 1798 before moving to Stonehouse in 1813, therefore there may have been family connections with the Vincents.) Shares were held by William, John and Joseph Vincent. The latter seems to have died in 1858 for his shares passed to his widow Maria. William and John later mortgaged some of their shares but by 1878 had reclaimed them. In 1887 the boat was sold to the F.D.P.B.A. for £450; eight persons, including Vincents, pilots and others, received payment for their shares. Joseph was the Master in the 1850s, followed by William. He had the boat lengthened in 1877 to 68' x 15' x 8.4', 33.71 tons. The F.D.P.B.A. continued using the cutter until 1922 when she was advertised for sale (*Western Morning News* in June, *Cornish Echo* in August). *Vincent* was probably the most long-lived cutter (70 years) being replaced by the *Arthur Rogers*, the last sailing cutter. Part of Vincent's mast, the beaching legs, and the main hatchcover were incorporated into a cottage built near St. Mawes in about 1930.

WASP   (MNL 17159, boat no. 13) 28 tons, 51' x 12.5' x 7'
Built in 1848 by James Mayn at The Bar, Falmouth for James Lowry of Falmouth. Ownership was transferred to Isaac Lower of St. Mawes in 1851. James Lowry was still recorded as Master in regatta reports until 1864, James Junior having replaced his father in 1860. Pilot Isaac Lower was the owner in 1869 when for an unknown reason the boat licence was returned to Trinity House. *Wasp* was replaced as no. 13 the following year by *Antelope*; Lower moved onto the new boat as a pilot. Wasp was sold to Pembrokeshire: owners 1874 H. Edmonds, 1875 H. Williams 1876 – 87, David Mathias, 1888 – 96 Robert Ellis.

WATER NYMPH   (MNL 17167, boat no. 6) 26 tons, 46.2' x 13.3' x 7'
Built in 1844 by John Trethowan at The Bar, Falmouth. First shareholders, the accountant Philip Pope the younger 32; Bennet Lowry 11, Henry Tonkin 11, James Lowry 10, all of Falmouth. Recorded in regattas with Masters – 1844 E. Lowry; 1846–51 Bennet Lowry; 1852 Henry Tonkin. In 1858 some shares had been passed to Elizabeth Lowry, widow, and to William James Lowry, second class pilot, presumably the son of James. Also in 1858, the boat was lengthened to 54.6' x 14.2' x 7.4', 38.71 tons. She was replaced as pilot boat no. 6 in 1862 by *Arrow*. Shares in *Water Nymph* were later sold to Edward Colin Pope, so that by 1884 he and Philip Pope had 32 shares each. It is not known to what use the boat had been put. In 1885 it passed to the banker W. M. Grylls, and lastly in 1887, to shipbuilder W. H. Lean, presumably for breaking up.

APPENDIX 1

The cost of building and fitting out a pilot boat, from the original statement written by accountant Philip Pope. (RCPS document). Note that some items were purchased from the owners of Arrow's predecessor.

Particulars of the Cost of the "Arrow" Pilot Cutter and Materials

		£	s	d	£	s	d
J Trethowan	For hull, mast & spars per contract	£ 440	0	0			
J. Trethowan	For extra work	14	10	0	454	10	0
Abbey Iron	For 36 tons iron ballast at 55						
Company	shillings and insurance	£ 99	13	6			
	Freight of (the above) per sloop Active (barge)	11	14	0			
John Jackett	For 10c (hundredweight) iron Ballast	1	10	0			
		112	17	6			
	Less received for 1 ton sold (to) sloop Dart	3	3	0	109	14	6
E.C. Pope & Co	Sailmakers and for blocks				93	0	0
Wm. Carne	Ropemaker				26	6	2
Jn. Stephens & Son	For wire forestay				2	9	0
J. H. Pope & Co.	Blacksmiths and Chandlers				62	0	0
Robert Snow	Cooper				1	6	6
	Painter				4	18	0
	For rigging leather				1	17	0
Haly	For painting punt etc.					18	6
Taylor	For making cabin table etc. per agreement				1	2	0
Water Nymph	For punt oars & paddles, winch,						
	2 spyglasses, binoculars etc.				20	0	0
Customs	For Register 1 shilling, Pilot				1	16	0
	Cutters licence, £1.15.0						
For mooring chain				3	5	0	
Philip Pope	For two mooring anchors				3	0	0
John Brewer	For mooring boat				4	0	0
Philip Jeffery	Foreman for his services				2	0	0
Riggers and labourers about ballast					7	15	0
Scraping vessel 30 shillings, paid for grease 10s2d					2	0	2
Mr. Kellaway for allowances					8	9	0
					£810	6	10
Received of Henry Tonkin, W. J. Lowry, John Collins, M. Richards 43/64ths at £9		£ 387	0	0			
Mrs Elizabeth Lowry 5/64ths at £9		45	0	0			
Philip Pope 16/64ths at £9		144	0	0			
Sloop Arrow earnings		234	6	10	810	6	10
					£ -	-	-
Falmouth 31st December 1863. Philip Pope.							

Author's Note: This statement was issued 16 months after the launch of *Arrow*, therefore the figure of £234.6.10 may represent her earnings over that period

APPENDIX 2

<u>Sub Commissioners Minutes, Tuesday 1st May 1888</u>

Present The Collector and Capt. Burrows.

The minutes of the previous meeting were read and confirmed.

The Secretary reported the receipt of a letter dated 24 Apr. from the Trinity House, London, enclosing in accordance with the request of the Pilot Boat Association forwarded by the Sub Commrs. on 17 Apr. a statement of the earnings of the Pilots at Falmouth for each year from 1860 to 1887 inclusive, and that he had sent a copy of the statement to the Association on the 25th ult. Ordered that the statement in question be copied in the Minutes as a local record. (Plus later figures for 1888-1900 added by author).

Statement showing the amount of Pilotage earned by the Pilots at Falmouth in the undermentioned years:

	£	s	d		£	s	d
1860	10604	4	1	1881	10023	1	11
1861	12952	2	3	1882	12565	1	5
1882	13548	8	5	1883	10850	10	8
1863	11904	1	10	1884	9887	1	1
1864	10563	5	-	1885	9758	9	10
1865	10132	3	-	1886	7989	16	5
1866	11133	10	7	1887	6834	1	5
1867	11621	6	7	1888	7461	15	7
1868	12809	19	1	1889	7470	5	7
1869	14022	13	-	1890	7770	9	1
1870	12787	15	5	1891	8249	11	7
1871	14341	17	3	1892	8187	12	8
1872	15271	14	2	1893	6128	12	4
1873	14492	17	9	1894	6826	12	5
1874	13705	7	2	1895	6400	1	5
1875	13285	0	8	1896	5476	18	5
1876	14363	8	10	1897	4569	18	8
1877	14859	9	3	1898	5005	2	-
1878	13093	16	-	1899	4348	10	-
1879	10925	2	10	1900	4793	17	-
1880	10736	18	8				

PORT OF FALMOUTH.

Falmouth being a harbour that vessels can enter and depart from at any time of tide, or any weather, no tug boats are kept.

Pilotage, per Act 6 *Geo. IV. c.* 125.

From sea to Carrick Roads, Falmouth, and St. Mawes' Harbours, or St. Just's Pool, and *vice versa :—*

	£	s.		£	s.
Vessels drawing 8 feet water,	1	4	Vessels drawing 16 feet water,	3	0
„ 10 „	1	10	„ 17 „	3	7
„ 11 „	1	15	„ 18 „	3	15
„ 12 „	2	2	„ 19 „	4	4
„ 13 „	2	6	„ 20 „	4	14
„ 14 „	2	10	„ 21 „	5	5
„ 15 „	2	15	, 22 „	6	0

From sea to Helford Harbour, and *vice versa :—*

	£	s.		£	s.
Vessels drawing 8 feet water,	1	1	Vessels drawing 14 feet water,	1	18
„ 10 „	1	4	„ 15 „	2	2
„ 11 „	1	7	„ 16 „	2	7
„ 12 „	1	10	„ 17 „	2	12
„ 13 „	1	14	„ 18 „	3	0

From Carrick Roads to Falmouth, St. Mawes' Harbours, or St. Just's Pool, and *vice versa,* 1s. 6d. per foot.

Masters of vessels taking a pilot at sea are to pay :—For putting a pilot on board without a line drawn from the Manacles to the Dodman, £2 2s. For putting a pilot on board without a line drawn from the entrance of Helford Harbour to the Gull Rock, £1 1s. For putting a pilot on board without a line drawn a mile without the Shag Rock, or Pendinnis Point, 10s. 6d. For putting a pilot on board without a line drawn off the Lizard, or in the parallel of the Lizard, or meeting a vessel there, and running before her, not being able to put a pilot on board, provided the master of the vessel consents to receive a pilot at that distance, £3 3s.

All vessels belonging to the port of Truro, bound to or from foreign parts, are to pay no more than one-half of the above rates of pilotage, when navigating within the limits of this port, on their passage to or from Truro; otherwise to pay the usual rates.

Harbour Dues.—All vessels from or to abroad, 2s. 6d. each; coasters, 2s. either wind-bound or entering to load or discharge cargoes, by prescription.

Pier Dues.—All vessels loading or discharging cargoes, 1s. per mast per month.

Ballast is put on board any vessel, from alongside the Quay, at 9d. per ton, and in the harbour, afloat, at 1s. per ton. These charges are not regulated by any authority whatever.

Depth of Water at Falmouth Pier.—Springs, 18 feet ; Neaps, 10 feet. In Carrick Roads, or the outer harbour, from 5 to 13 fathoms ; 5 on the banks, and 13 in the channel. In inner harbour, 4 fathoms at high water.

Falmouth Pilotage rates and Harbour dues, published in the Ship Owners and Ship Masters Directory, 1846.

APPENDIX 4

THE HISTORIC SHIPYARDS OF THE FAL

The approximate dates of occupation of ship and boat building firms and a fear of the types of vessels produced. The major source is the database of Cornish-built vessels in the Bartlett Library, National Maritime Museum Cornwall, plus local newspapers and residents of Falmouth

Truro

1800 – 1805	(Including Newham). Brigs built for merchants Ralph Daniell and John Vivien. Builders not known.		
1823	Thomas Treloar	-	Schooner
1837	John Gatley	-	Schooner
1847	Thomas Beer	-	Schooner

Calenick Creek

1892 – 1905	Stephen Brabyn	-	Oyster dredging boats

Sunny Corner

1854 – 1866	W. Withiel	-	Fal Barges, schooner
1866 – 1885	Charles Dyer	-	Brigantine, schooners, ketches, barges

Tresillian

1835	John Gatley	-	Sloop

Malpas

1850 – 1866	Thomas Coad	-	Schooner, barges
1866 – 1920	William Scoble & John Davis	-	Brigantine, schooners, ketches, yachts

Cowlands Creek

1872	J H Wellington	-	Schooner
1874 – 1876	William Burley	-	Fal barge, schooner

Roundwood

1846	John Harris	-	Schooner
1874 – 1876	Henry Stevens Trethowan	-	Barge, schooner

Pill Creek

1806 –	Peter Ferris (1)	-	Fal Barges
1861 –	Peter Ferris (2)	-	Schooner, smacks
1863 – 1865	W Hodge	-	Schooners
1875 – 1879	Frank Hitchens (and Ford)	-	Schooners
1886 – 1903	William Ferris	-	Oyster dredging boats, yachts

Devoran

1869 – 1878	H E Stephens	-	Schooners, barges
1879 – 1881	Richard Gilbert	-	Barge, ketch
1986 – 2007	Ralph Bird	-	Pilot Gigs

Yard Point/ Carnon Yard

1806	Peter Ferris	-	Barges
1836 – 1858	Thomas Ferris	-	Schooners, barges
1859 – 1880	John Stephens (William "Foreman" Ferris)	-	Schooners
1880 – 1895	William Ferris	-	Oyster dredging boats
1870 – 1900	Frank Hitchens	-	Oyster dredging boats

Mylor Creek

1855	William Withey	-	Smack
1878	Emanuel Martin	-	Ketches
1879	Thomas Gray	-	Ketch
1960 –2009	Terry & Martin Heard (Tregatreath Boatyard)	-	Oyster dredging boats, yachts

St Mawes

1804	Lane, Hawkins, Roberts, Jennings		
1790 – 1903	Peters Family	-	Smack, pilot gigs, small craft

Penryn

1804	Richard Dingle		
1862 – 1881	Sara & Burgess	-	Wood & iron steam-powered vessels
1873	John T Rapson		

1894 – 1900	Thomas Rapson	-	Ketch, smack, cutter

Ponsharden

1867 – 1878	Francis John Holm	-	Ship repairs
1879 – 1891	Emanuel Martin	-	Ketches (North Sea fishing smacks), steam trawler
1919 – 1939	Exe Transport Co (WJ Burt, EJ Burt, managers)	-	Ship repairs, breaking
1940 – 1958	Falmouth Boat Construction Co	-	Fitting out & repairing Admiralty vessels, ship repairs
1960 – 1980	Penryn Boat Building Co Ltd	-	Wood and GRP yachts
1968 – 1970	Falcraft Ltd	-	Yachts
1970 – 1977	Dredge & Marine Company	-	Steel barges, ferry, dredgers
1979	Williams Boatyard Ltd	-	Yachts
1980 – 1989	Riverside Fabrications Co	-	Steel barges, tugs, fishing boats
2002 –2010	Cockwells Modern & Classic Boatbuilding Ltd (moved to Mylor Creek 2010)	-	Wooden passenger ferry, pilot cutter, motor launches

Turnpike Creek

1926 – 1972	WE Thomas Yacht Yard (Bert & Cyril Thomas, Collins & Williams as managers/owners)	-	Yachts

Victoria Yard, High Street, Falmouth

1862	Thomas Henry Truscott	-	Boats
1873	Edward Truscott		
1876	HS Trethowan		
1880	Thomas Gray		
1888	Betts & Williams	-	Yachts
1893 – 1912	Thomas Jackett	-	Yachts, quay punts
1933 – 1980	EJ Burt & Co Ltd (Falmouth Yacht & Boat Building Co)	-	Yachts, dinghies, Admiralty whalers in World War Two

No.39, High Street, Falmouth

1939 – 1972	Falmouth Boat Construction Ltd	-	World War Two Admiralty Fairmile "D" launches, later yachts, motor cruisers

Little Falmouth, Flushing

1760 – 1793	Peter Symons (Father & son)	-	Falmouth packet
1793 – 1837	Richard Symons	-	Falmouth packets, Royal Navy brigs
1837 – 1851	Thomas Symons		
1851 – 1876	John Trethowan/ Henry Trethowan	-	Barques, brigantines, schooners cutters, tugs
1893 –	Robert Lee/Charles Lee		ketches, yachts
1928 – 1935	RS Burt (Little Falmouth Yacht Yard)		
1935 –	Falmouth Boat Construction Co	-	Repairing naval craft in World War Two. Various firms later operating under the same name, building and repairing pleasure craft, refitting RNLI Lifeboats

Falmouth Docks

1878 – 1930	Cox & Co	-	Iron & steel pleasure launches, tugs, passenger steamers, naval craft, trawlers
1890 – 1896	Pool, Skinner &Williams (Dockhead Ironworks)	-	Steel tugs, launches, 132 ton schooner
1988 –	Pendennis Shipyard Ltd	-	Building & refitting steel & aluminium sailing & motor yachts

THE BAR

The area encompassing Bar Road and the National Maritime Museum Cornwall. Possibly the site of the building in 1668 of the "Falmouth Frigatt", the first large vessel ("of 80 or 90 tuns") to be built in Falmouth.

Outer Bar Yards (Maritime Museum Area)

Symon's Shipyard

1794 – 1821	John & Robert Symons	-	Merchant ships, sailing barges, Falmouth packets

1822- 1860	Francis Symons	-	Falmouth packet, barques, brigs, schooner, barges, cutter, steam tugs
1860 – 1889	George Symons	-	Cutters, tugs

Burt's Shipyard

1900 – 1926	Richard Stevens Burt	-	Quay punts, Yachts

Lean's Shipyard

1880 – 1912	William Henry Lean	-	Schooners (wood & steel), Steam tugs, 550 ton iron merchant steamer

Inner Bar yards. Museum car park to the western end of Bar Road

Trethowan's Yard

1832 – 1864	John Trethowan	-	Schooners, barges, pilot cutters, quay punts
1864 – 1889	Henry Stevens Trethowan	-	Schooners, smack, cutter

Thomas's Yard (South side of Bar Road)

1870 – 1900	William Edward Thomas	-	Quay punts, salvage steamer

Manor Yard area

1783 – 1802	Richard Bluett	-	Schooner, Falmouth packet, merchant ship
1830 – 1856	James Mayn	-	Schooners, pilot cutters
1852 – 1861	John & Joseph Haley	-	Pilot cutters
1878 – 1900	Charles Burt	-	Schooners, ketches, cutters, steam tugs
1902 – 1926	William Edward Thomas	-	Quay punts, yachts, motor cruisers
1862 – 1922	William Henry Lean (Including Outer Bar)	-	Wood & steel schooners, ketches, cutters, quay punts Steam tugs, passenger launches

BIBLIOGRAPHY

Acton, Viv, and Carter, Derek. *Operation Cornwall, 1940-1944*. Landfall Publications (1994).

Armstrong, Richard. *Powered Ships*. Ernest Benn Ltd. (1974).

Barnicoat, David. *Dodman to Black Head*. Packet Publishing (1998).

Beck, John. *A History of the Falmouth Packet Service, 1689-1850*. Maritime Monograph No.5, South West Maritime Hist. Soc. (2009).

Bird, Sheila. *Mayday! Preserving Life from Shipwreck off Cornwall*. Ex Libris Press (1991).

Brett, R.L., ed. *Barclay Fox's Journal*. Bell & Hyman, London (1979).

Bristow, Colin M. *Cornwall's Geology and Scenery*. Cornish Hillside Pub. (1996).

Burney, Dr. William. *Falconer's Marine Dictionary*. (1830).

Carter, Clive. *The Blizzard of '91*. David & Charles (1971).

Clancey, Roger. *Ships, Ports, and Pilots*. McFarland & Co. (1984).

Cornwall Archaeological Unit. *Fal Estuary Historic Audit*. Cornwall County Council (1997).

Davies, Alun. *History of the Falmouth Working Boats*. Davies (1989).

Douglas and Green. *The Law of Harbours and Pilotage*. Lloyds of London Press (1993).

Dudszus and Henriot. *Dictionary of Ship Types*. Conway Maritime Press (1986).

Dunstan, Bob. *The Book of Falmouth and Penryn*. Barracuda Books (1989).

Fisher, H.E.S., ed. *Ports and Shipping in the South West*. Exeter Papers in Economic History, University of Exeter. (1971)

Gardiner, Robert, ed. *Sails Last Century – The Merchant Ships 1830-1930*. Conway Maritime Press (2001).

Gardiner, Dorothy M, ed. *A Calender of Early Chancery Proceedings relating to West Country Shipping*. Devon and Cornwall Record Society, new series, vol.21 (1976).

Gay, Susan, E. *Old Falmouth*. Headley Press (1903).

Gilbert, C.S. *A Historical Survey of the County of Cornwall*. London (1817).

Gilbert, C.S. *The Parochial History of Cornwall*. London (1838).

Gilson, Peter. *Falmouth in Old Photographs*. Alan Sutton (1990).

Gilson, Peter. *The Lower Fal*. Alan Sutton (1993).

Gilson, Peter. *The Upper Fal*. Alan Sutton (1994).

Ginsberg, B.W. *Hints on the Legal Duties of Shipmasters*. Charles Griffin & Co. (1903).

Gregg, Pauline. *The Social and Economic History of Britain 1760-1965*. George Harrap & Co. (1950).

Guthrie, A. *Cornwall in the Age of Steam*. Tabb House (1994).

Halliday, F.E. *A History of Cornwall*. Gerald Duckworth & Co. (1959).

Harris, Keith. *Azook, The Story of Pilot Gigs of Cornwall and Scilly*. Dyllansow Truran (1994).

Hignett, Harry. *The History of the United Kingdom Pilots' Association*. UKPA (1984).

Jeffery, H.M., FRS. *The Early Topography of Falmouth*. Journal of the Royal Institution of Cornwall, (1886) pp.147-159.

Jenkins, Alf. *Gigs and Cutters of the Isles of Scilly*. Scilly (1975).

Jenkins, Alf. *The Scillonian and His Boat*. Scilly (1982).

Kirkham, Graeme, MA. *Cornwall and Scilly Urban Survey (Falmouth)*. Historical Environment Service, Cornwall County Council (2005).

Kittridge, Alan. *Passenger Steamers of the River Fal*. Twelveheads Press (1988).

Langley, M, and Small, E. *Lost Ships of the West Country*. Stanford Maritime (1988).

Larne, Richard and Bridget. *Shipwreck Index of the British Isles*. Lloyd's Register of Shipping (1997).

Leifschild, J.R. *Cornwall, Its Mines and Miners*. (1855).

Lysons, D. and S. *Magna Brittania,*vol. 3 (Cornwall). (1814).

Maber and Tregonning, ed. *Kilvert's Cornish Diary*. Alison Hodge (1989).

McMullen, R.T. *Down Channel*. Grafton Books (1986).

McNair and Honour. *Temperley's Merchant Shipping Acts, 5th ed.* Stevens & Sons (1954).

Mead, Commander Hilary P. *Trinity House*. Sampson Low, Marston & Co. Ltd.

Mudd, David. *Cornish Sea Lights*. Bossiney Books. (1978)

Newton, Jill. *The Lizard*. Bossiney Books (1978).

Noall, C, and Farr, G. *Wreck and Rescue Round the Cornish Coast*. D. Bradford Barton (1965).

Noall, Cyril. *Smuggling in Cornwall*. D. Bradford Barton (1971).

Oliver, S. Pasfield, *Pendennis and St. Mawes, A Historical Sketch of Two Cornish Castles*. W. Lake. (1875).

Paasch, Captain H. *Illustrated Marine Encyclopedia*. (1890).

Pawlyn, Tony. *The Falmouth Packets*. Truran. (2003).

Penaluna, William. *The Circle, or Historical Survey of 60 Parishes and Towns of Cornwall*. (1819).

Pollard, Chris. *The Book of St. Mawes*. Halsgrove (2007).

Pollock, John. *Falmouth for Instructions*. Pollock (c.2005).

Radford, J. *Pilot Stations of the British Isles*. Brown , Son and Ferguson Ltd. (1939).

Rich, John. *The Bristol Pilots*. Rich (1996).

Rowe, John. *Cornwall in the Age of the Industrial Revolution*. Cornish Hillside Press. (1993).

Shipowners and Shipmasters Directory to the Port Charges of Great Britain and Ireland. London (1846).

Smart, Dave. *The Cornish Fishing Industry*. Tormark Press (1992).

Starkey, David J. *British Privateering in the Eighteenth Century*. University of Exeter Press. (1990).

Stern, Walter M. *Britain Yesterday and Today, An Outline of Economic History*. Longmans. (1962).

Stuckey, Peter J. *Sailing Pilots of the Bristol Channel*. David & Charles (1977).

Swansea Museum. *The Rise and Fall of the Copper Industry, Lower Swansea Valley*. Factsheet 7. Swansea Museum. (1989).

Thomas, Charles. *Exploration of a Drowned Landscape*. Batsford (1985).

Thomas, Richard. *A History of the Town and Harbour of Falmouth*. (1827).

Warne's *Directory and Guide to Falmouth*. (1864).

Warner, Rev. Richard. *A Tour through Cornwall*. (1808).

West of England Steamship Owners Protection and Indemnity Association Ltd. *Handy Book for Shipowners and Masters*. (1921).

Whetter, Dr. James. *The History of Falmouth*. Dyllansow Truran (1981).

Wilson, D.G. *Falmouth Haven*. Tempus Publishing (2007).

Worth, R.N. *Guide to the Harbour, Town and Neighbourhood of Falmouth*. (1877).

INDEX